REVERSALS OF
FORTUNE

REVERSALS OF
FORTUNE

Contents

Foreword   *xi*
Acknowledgments   *xiii*
About the Team   *xv*
Abbreviations   *xix*

Overview   1

Poverty reduction was slowing before the crisis   2

Shared prosperity was positive for the period 2012–17, but gains were
uneven and slowing   4

COVID-19, conflict, and climate change have reversed the gains in poverty
eradication for the first time in a generation   5

COVID-19, conflict, and climate impacts will change the profile of
the global poor   8

Conclusion: Tackling the crisis while looking to the long term   15

Notes   18

References   19

Introduction: Global Goals, Shared Challenges   21

1 Monitoring Global Poverty   27

Introduction   27

Monitoring global poverty: Tracking progress toward the 2030 goals   31

Beyond extreme poverty: The US$3.20-a-day and US$5.50-a-day poverty lines   39

A relative poverty measure: The societal poverty line   41

Beyond monetary poverty: The multidimensional poverty measure   43

A focus on extreme poverty in Sub-Saharan Africa   46

Annex 1A   PovcalNet data and methodology for measuring extreme poverty   50

Annex 1B   Higher poverty lines: US$3.20 and US$5.50 a day   63

Annex 1C   Societal poverty line   65

Annex 1D   Multidimensional poverty   68

Notes   71

References   77

2 Shared Prosperity: Monitoring Inclusive Growth   81

Introduction: Shared prosperity—Focusing on the bottom 40   81

The most recent estimates of shared prosperity and the shared
prosperity premium   82

Outlook: COVID-19 and prospects for shared prosperity   90

Shared prosperity and its connection to other welfare indicators   95

Who is in the bottom 40?   100

Annex 2A   Shared prosperity estimates, by economy   102

Annex 2B   Data for shared prosperity over different periods   106

Annex 2C   Comparison of two shared prosperity rounds   111

Notes   115

References   116

3 Key Socioeconomic Characteristics of the Global Poor: Vulnerability to Conflict, Climate Risks, and COVID-19   121

Introduction   121

Key socioeconomic characteristics of the global poor   122

Poverty and conflict: A global and subnational perspective   129

Poverty and climate risks   138

Vulnerability and multiple risks: Poverty in the face of COVID-19, conflict, and climate risks   142

Annex 3A   New vintage of the Global Monitoring Database   150

Annex 3B   Robustness of poverty profiles: Adding and subtracting countries   151

Annex 3C   Construction of the Global Subnational Atlas of Poverty, Second edition   154

Notes   155

References   156

4 Navigating Tough Terrain: Sound Principles, Good Maps, and Adaptive Learning   159

Introduction   160

The poorest suffer most from COVID-19, conflict, and climate change   161

Familiar development challenges persist   163

Responding to COVID-19 presents unique challenges   164

How might strategies to reverse reversals be strengthened and sustained?   166

Conclusion   172

Notes   172

References   174

Boxes

1.1 Different Measures for Understanding Poverty   29

1.2 Measuring Poverty in India without Recent Data   30

1.3 How Is Climate Change Affecting Poverty? Nowcasts and Forecasts   37

2.1 Data Challenges: Shared Prosperity Cannot Be Measured in Some of the Most Deprived Economies   84

2.2 Early Evidence of the Impact of COVID-19: The High-Frequency Surveys   92

2.3 The Importance of Equity for Poverty Reduction   97

3.1 The Rural and Urban Poor   123

3.2 Data Limitations to Profiling the Global Poor   128

3.3 Poverty and Conflict: A Vicious Circle?   130

3.4 Estimating the Number of Poor Affected by Flood Risk on a Global Scale   139

Figures

O.1 Global Poverty Rate and Number of Poor at the US$1.90-a-Day Poverty Line, 1990–2017   2

O.2 Trends in Poverty Rates at the US$1.90-a-Day Poverty Line, by Region, 1990–2018   3

O.3 Nowcast of the Global Poverty Rate at the US$1.90-a-Day Poverty Line, 2015–21   5

O.4 Additional Poor at the US$1.90-a-Day Poverty Line in 2020, per the COVID-19-Baseline and COVID-19-Downside Scenarios   6

O.5 Four Profiles of the Global Poor, by Region, Gender, Age, and Educational Attainment, circa 2018   9

O.6 Share of the Global Poor and of the Global Population, by FCS 2020 Typology   12

O.7 Number of Poor Living at the Three Poverty Lines Who Are Also Exposed to Catastrophic Floods   13

1.1 Global Poverty Rate and Number of Poor at the US$1.90-a-Day Poverty Line, 1990–2017   32

1.2 Number of Poor at the US$1.90-a-Day Poverty Line, by Region, 1990–2017   32

1.3 Trends in Poverty Rates at the US$1.90-a-Day Poverty Line, by Region, 1990–2018   33

1.4 Nowcasts of the Global Poverty Rate and Number of Poor at the US$1.90-a-Day Poverty Line, 2015–21   34

1.5 Additional Poor at the US$1.90-a-Day Poverty Line in 2020, per the COVID-19-Baseline, and COVID-19-Downside Scenarios   35

1.6 Projection of Global Poverty at the US$1.90-a-Day Poverty Line, to 2030   36

1.7 Global Poverty Rate and Number of Poor, US$3.20-a-Day and US$5.50-a-Day Poverty Lines, 1990–2017   39

1.8 Poverty Rates at the US$3.20-a-Day and US$5.50-a-Day Poverty Lines, by Region, 1990–2018   40

1.9 Poverty Rates and Number of Poor, US$3.20-a-Day and US$5.50-a-Day Poverty Lines, Sub-Saharan Africa, 1990–2018   41

1.10 Global Societal Poverty Rate and Number of Poor, Compared with International Poverty Line Estimates, 1990–2017   42

1.11 Societal Poverty Rates, by Region, 1990–2018   43

1.12 Correlation between Monetary and Multidimensional Poverty Headcount, circa 2017   43

1.13 Deprivation in Multiple Dimensions, circa 2017   45

1.14 Variation in Poverty Rates, East Asia and Pacific versus Sub-Saharan Africa, 1990–2018   47

1.15 Distribution of Extreme Poor, by Economy, Sub-Saharan Africa, 2018   49

1A.1 Global Distribution at the US$1.90-a-Day Poverty Line, by Region and Economy, 2017   56

1A.2 Projection of Global Poverty at the US$1.90-a-Day Poverty Line, 1990–2030   61

1A.3 Projection of Global Poverty at the US$1.90-a-Day Poverty Line to 2030 with Changes in the Gini Index   62

2.1 Shared Prosperity and the Shared Prosperity Premium, by Economy, circa 2012–17   83

2.2 Correlation between Shared Prosperity and Growth in Mean Incomes, 91 Economies, circa 2012–17   87

2.3 Positive and Negative Values for Shared Prosperity and the Shared Prosperity Premium   88

2.4 Shared Prosperity and the Shared Prosperity Premium across Rounds   89

2.5 Projected Growth in Mean Incomes, 2019–21, and Past Shared Prosperity, circa 2012–17   90

B2.2.1 Share of Survey Respondents Who Stopped Working or Experienced Job Losses 93

2.6 Shared Prosperity and Growth of the Median 95

2.7 Share of Income, by Decile 96

2.8 Correlation of Shared Prosperity and the Shared Prosperity Premium with Poverty and Inequality 97

B2.3.1 Growth's Impact on Poverty Reduction Depends on the Mean and Distribution of Income 98

2.9 Changes in the Gini Coefficient 100

2.10 Representation of Different Groups in the Bottom 40, by Economy 101

2B.1 Varying Periods of Measurement for Shared Prosperity, Global Database of Shared Prosperity, Seventh Edition 106

2B.2 Data Coverage for Shared Prosperity and Poverty Indicators 109

2B.3 Shared Prosperity Indicator, Population Coverage 110

3.1 Share of Rural Poor and Rural Population, by Region 122

3.2 Educational Attainment among the Poor, by Region (age 15 and older) 124

3.3 Educational Attainment of the Population, by Region (age 15 and older) 124

3.4 Changes in the Share of Global Poor and of the Global Population, by Educational Attainment, 2015–18 125

3.5 Age Profile of the Global Poor in 2018, by Region 126

3.6 Age Profile of the Population in 2018, by Region 126

3.7 Ratio of Poor Women to Women in the Overall Population, by Region 127

3.8 Comparing Changes in the Share of Poor and Global Population Share, by Age Group, 2015 and 2018 127

3.9 Share of the Global Poor and of the Global Population, by FCS 2020 Typology 129

3.10 Educational Attainment, by FCS Grouping 130

B3.3.1 Relationship between Contemporaneous and Past Cumulative Conflict and Poverty 131

B3.3.2 Simulating Poverty Dynamics with a Single Conflict Episode and Recurrent Conflict 132

B3.3.3 Subnational Poverty Rates and Cumulative Number of Past Conflict Years 133

3.11 Share of Global Population, by Age Group 134

3.12 Share of Global Poor, by Age Group 134

3.13 Share of Poor Residing in Areas with at Least Some Conflict History 136

3.14 Distribution of the Poor and of the Population, by Conflict Type, Globally and in Sub-Saharan Africa 137

3.15 Share of Population and of the Poor with High Flood Exposure, by Region 140

3.16 Joint Exposure to Conflict and Floods and Share of the Total Population below the International Poverty Line 143

3.17 Share of Rural Population among US$3.20-a-Day Poor and in the Overall Population 144

3.18 Profile of US$3.20-a-Day Poor, by Educational Attainment (age 15 and older) 144

3.19 Age Distribution among the US$3.20-a-Day Poor, by Region 145

3.20 Ratio of Poor Women (Living on US$3.20 a Day) to Women in the Overall Population, by Region 145

3.21 Share of Population Living on US$1.90-a-Day to US$3.20-a-Day and of the Total Population, by Country Conflict Category 146

3.22 Number of Poor Living at the Three Poverty Lines Who Are Also Exposed to Catastrophic Floods 146

3.23 Comparative Regional Profile of US$1.90-a-Day and US$3.20-a-Day Poverty Lines, without India 147

Maps

O.1 Joint Distribution of Poverty and Flood Risk in Sub-Saharan Africa   14

1.1 Poverty Rate at the US$1.90-a-Day Poverty Line, by Economy, 2017   46

1.2 Poverty Rate at the US$1.90-a-Day Poverty Line at the Subnational Level, Lined-Up Estimates, Sub-Saharan Africa, 2018   48

2B.1 Shared Prosperity Indicator, Economy Coverage   108

3.1 Joint Distribution of Subnational Poverty (at the US$1.90-a-Day Poverty Line) and Conflict in Sub-Saharan Africa   135

3.2 Share of Global Population with High Flood Exposure   140

3.3 Share of Population That Lives below the US$1.90-a-Day Poverty Line and Has High Flood Exposure   141

3.4 Joint Distribution of Poverty and Flood Risk in Sub-Saharan Africa   142

Tables

1.1 Monetary and Multidimensional Poverty Headcount, by Region and the World, circa 2017   44

1.2 Share of Population Deprived in Each Indicator, 114 Economies, circa 2017   44

1A.1 Data Coverage, by Region and Income Group, 2013 and 2017   50

1A.2 Global and Regional Extreme Poverty   55

1A.3 Poverty Rate at the US$1.90-a-Day Poverty Line, by Economy, Most Recent Survey Year   56

1B.1 Global and Regional Poverty at the US$3.20-a-Day Poverty Line   63

1B.2 Global and Regional Poverty at the US$5.50-a-Day Poverty Line   64

1C.1 Global and Regional Societal Poverty   65

1D.1 Multidimensional Poverty Measure Indicators and Weights   69

1D.2 Individuals in Households Deprived in Each Indicator, 114 Economies, circa 2017   69

B2.1.1 Data Coverage Summary, Global Database of Shared Prosperity, Seventh Edition   84

2.1 Shared Prosperity and Shared Prosperity Premium: Summary   86

2A.1 Data on Shared Prosperity, by Economy   103

2B.1 Number of Economies in the Global Database of Shared Prosperity, by Edition   107

2B.2 Changing Economy Coverage in the Global Database of Shared Prosperity, Sixth and Seventh Editions   107

2C.1 Comparing the Changes in Shared Prosperity across Two Editions of the Global Database of Shared Prosperity   112

2C.2 Comparing the Changes in the Shared Prosperity Premium across Two Editions of the Global Database of Shared Prosperity   112

2C.3 Comparing the Changes in the Fifth and Seventh Editions of the Global Database of Shared Prosperity, 68 Economies   113

3A.1 New Surveys in the Global Monitoring Database, April 2020 Vintage   150

3B.1 Coverage of Population and of the Global Poor, by Region, without India   152

3B.2 Implications of Removing India from the Global Profile of the Poor   152

3B.3 Comparing the 2018 Poverty Profile (Full Set of Economies) with Those Economies also Present in the 2015 Poverty Profile   153

Foreword

The mission of the World Bank Group is to work with countries toward alleviating extreme poverty and boosting shared prosperity through inclusive, sustainable growth. Today, with COVID-19 sweeping across the globe, a historic global recession, and the world's poorest bearing the brunt of the crisis, good development outcomes are both more difficult and more essential.

As countries work to address these converging shocks, the World Bank Group's new report, *Poverty and Shared Prosperity 2020: Reversals of Fortune*, presents new data, original economic simulations and forecasts, and analysis that provide insight into the roots of the current reversal of economic fortune, what it means for the world's poorest, how countries are taking action to address this crisis, and how to put poverty reduction and development back on track.

The human cost of COVID-19 is immense, with hundreds of millions of people in the developing world reversing back into poverty. The report's projections suggest that, in 2020, between 88 million and 115 million people could fall back into extreme poverty as a result of the pandemic, with an additional increase of between 23 million and 35 million in 2021, potentially bringing the total number of new people living in extreme poverty to between 110 million and 150 million. Early evidence also suggests that the crisis is poised to increase inequality in much of the world. The crisis risks large human capital losses among people who are already disadvantaged, making it harder for countries to return to inclusive growth even after acute shocks recede.

Our *Poverty and Shared Prosperity 2020* report jointly analyzes three converging forces that are driving this increase in global poverty and that threaten to extend its effects far into the future: COVID-19, armed conflict, and climate change. Climate change may drive about 100 million additional people into poverty by 2030, many of whom reside in countries affected by institutional fragility and armed conflict, and where global extreme poverty is increasingly concentrated. Facing these multiple shocks, nations will need to work on many fronts to save lives and livelihoods, provide for their most vulnerable citizens, and restart inclusive growth.

This report provides new evidence on emerging "hot spots," where multiple threats to poor people's lives and livelihoods converge. Many of these hot spots are in Sub-Saharan Africa, a region now expected to be home to about a third of the people who are newly impoverished by COVID-19. The World Bank Group has stepped up its support for regions in which extreme poverty is increasingly concentrated, armed conflict is disproportionately prevalent, and large populations face severe risks linked to climate change, from flooding to locust swarms. We are working on a multitude of urgent issues, including food support, digital connectivity, and equitable access to COVID-19 diagnostics, therapeutics, and vaccines.

As we look beyond immediate responses to the pandemic, policy makers should remain attentive to broader development challenges. Even before the pandemic, development for many people in the world's poorest countries was too slow to raise their incomes, enhance living standards, or narrow inequality. During the recovery period, nations must look to reengage with a longer-term development agenda that includes promoting sustainable and inclusive growth, investing in human capital, and improving the quality of public administration and services while upholding political legitimacy, and ensuring that debt levels remain both manageable and transparent.

Well-tailored strategies can incorporate approaches that countries have advanced successfully in recent years, while drawing on the research and insights that the development community has accumulated over time. Every nation must look to achieve a strong recovery and come out better prepared for future threats, and the World Bank Group is prepared to help.

I am encouraged by countries that are already taking bold action, learning fast, and sharing their experiences and results for the benefit of others. We must communicate clearly and work together to undo COVID-19's reversal of fortune and build a better world after this crisis has passed.

David Malpass
President
World Bank Group

Acknowledgments

This report was prepared by a team co-led by Samuel Freije-Rodríguez and Michael Woolcock. The core team included R. Andrés Castañeda, Alexandru Cojocaru, Elizabeth Howton, Christoph Lakner, Minh Cong Nguyen, Marta Schoch, Judy Yang, and Nishant Yonzan. The extended team—who worked on background papers, on the preparation of case study material, or as consultants or advisors to chapter authors—included Marje Aksli, Samuel Kofi Tetteh Baah, Katy Bergstrom, Ifeanyi Nzegwu Edochie, Alejandro De la Fuente, Stéphane Hallegatte, Bramka Jafino, Dean Jolliffe, Daniel Gerszon Mahler, Laura L. Moreno Herrera, Hannes Mueller, David Newhouse, Philomena Panagoulias, Katie Parry, Jun Rentschler, Melda Salhab, Sutirtha Sinha Roy, Chanon Techasunthornwat, Brian James Walsh, and Nobuo Yoshida.

The authors are especially grateful to the PovcalNet team, comprising Tony Fujs, David Leonardo Vargas Mogollon, and Martha C. Viveros Mendoza, who have worked tirelessly and professionally to ensure that the global poverty numbers and projections are reported in a clear, consistent, and careful manner. This is important at the best of times, of course, but the challenges of doing these calculations under the evolving pressures of COVID-19 (coronavirus) have been considerable. Thanks as well to the D4G (Data for Goals) team and the regional statistical teams for their contribution to global poverty monitoring and the preparation of the Global Monitoring Database.

The report was prepared under the general direction of Francisco Ferreira, Aart Kraay, and Carolina Sánchez-Páramo, with specific inputs provided by Benu Bidani, Haishan Fu, and Ambar Narayan. The team is also grateful for the overall guidance received from Ceyla Pazarbasioglu, Pinelopi Goldberg, and Carmen Reinhart.

There would be no *Poverty and Shared Prosperity 2020* report without the efforts of the editorial, production, and communications teams, including Mark Felsenthal, Melina Fleury, Chisako Fukuda, Paul Gallagher, Amy Lynn Grossman, Elizabeth Howton, Alexander Irwin, Patricia Katayama, Ravi Kumar, Paul McClure, and Mikael Reventar.

More than 190 colleagues attended the decision meeting on the report in late July, with many contributing to a fruitful discussion on how to convey constructive policy messages to a world suffering a historic reversal in poverty trends as a result of a pandemic (and an associated global economic recession), climate change, and, in certain places, armed conflict. Peer review comments were provided by Verena Fritz, Maria Ana Lugo, Hannes Mueller, and Rinku Murgai; helpful feedback and suggestions were received from the Offices of the Chief Economist of the following Regions: East Asia and Pacific, Europe and Central Asia, Latin America and the Caribbean, and Sub-Saharan Africa. Staff from the South Asia Region and its Office of the Chief Economist also provided helpful input and advice. At the earlier concept note stage, external comments were received from Yuen Yuen Ang (University of Michigan).

Much of the report was written as the full empirical and practical implications of COVID-19 became apparent, which has meant (among other things) working from home while also managing domestic commitments; the team thus wishes to thank the significant others in their lives who have had to accommodate these additional and unexpected challenges.

The report is a joint project of the Development Data and Research Groups in the Development Economics Vice Presidency, and the Poverty and Equity Global Practice in the Equitable Growth, Finance and Institutions Vice Presidency of the World Bank. Financing from the government of the United Kingdom helped support analytical work on the global poverty counts and the COVID-19 simulations through the Data and Evidence for Tackling Extreme Poverty Research Programme.

About the Team

Co-Leads of the Report

Samuel Freije-Rodríguez is a lead economist in the Poverty and Equity Global Practice at the World Bank. He joined the World Bank in 2008, and his main areas of work include labor economics and the welfare impacts of public policy. He has participated in World Bank studies on labor markets, poverty, equality of opportunities, and the distributive impact of tax policy for several Latin American countries, China, Mongolia, and the Russian Federation. He is a member of the team that produced *World Development Report 2013: Jobs*. Before joining the World Bank, Samuel was an associate professor at Universidad de las Americas in Puebla, Mexico, and at Instituto de Estudios Superiores de Administración in Caracas, República Bolivariana de Venezuela. He was associate editor of *Economía, Journal of the Latin American and Caribbean Economic Association*. Samuel holds a PhD in labor economics from Cornell University.

Michael Woolcock is the lead social scientist in the Development Research Group at the World Bank, where he has worked since 1998. For 14 of these years, he has also taught (part-time) at Harvard Kennedy School, with periods of leave spent at the University of Cambridge (2002, as the Von Hügel Visiting Fellow) and the University of Manchester (2007–09, as the founding research director of the Brooks World Poverty Institute). His current research focuses on strategies for enhancing the effectiveness of policy implementation, extending work addressed in his recent book, *Building State Capability: Evidence, Analysis, Action* (with Matt Andrews and Lant Pritchett; Oxford University Press, 2017). Michael is a co-recipient of the American Sociological Association's awards for best book (2012) and best article (2014) on economic development. He holds undergraduate degrees from the University of Queensland (Australia) and a PhD in comparative-historical sociology from Brown University.

Core Team

R. Andrés Castañeda is an economist and data scientist in the Development Data Group at the World Bank. During the past 10 years, he has worked on socioeconomic analysis in topics related to poverty, welfare distribution, inequality of opportunities, development economics, and conflict economics. In particular, he is interested in the analysis of data for policy dialogue, statistical and methodological research, and the development of computational tools in Stata and R to make socioeconomic analysis intuitive, easier, and faster. Andrés has an MSc in economics from Universidad el Rosario and an MA in apologetics and philosophy from Biola University.

Alexandru Cojocaru is a senior economist with the Global Unit of the World Bank's Poverty and Equity Global Practice, where he co-leads the Systematic Country Diagnostic central support team. His research focuses primarily on issues related to poverty, inequality, and subjective well-being. Previously, he led the World Bank's engagement on poverty and equity in a number of countries in the Europe and Central Asia Region, including Belarus, Bosnia and Herzegovina, Kosovo, Moldova, and Ukraine. Alexandru is a co-author of *Fair Progress: Economic Mobility across Generations around the World* (World Bank, 2018). His research has also been published in academic journals including the *Journal of Comparative Economics* and the *European Journal of Political Economy*. Alexandru holds a master's degree from Georgetown University and a PhD from the University of Maryland.

Elizabeth Howton is the senior external affairs officer for the Poverty and Equity Global Practice. Previously, she worked with the infoDev program, which helps start-up entrepreneurs in developing countries grow their businesses. Before that, she was the World Bank Group's Global Web editor. She joined the World Bank in 2012 as an online communications officer for the South Asia Region. Before joining the World Bank, she was an editor at the *San Jose Mercury News* in California's Silicon Valley for 10 years. She was a Knight Science Journalism Fellow at the Massachusetts Institute of Technology and earned a bachelor's degree from Stanford University and a master's degree from George Washington University.

Christoph Lakner is a senior economist in the Development Data Group at the World Bank. His research interests include inequality, poverty, and labor markets in developing countries. In particular, he has been working on global inequality, the relationship between inequality of opportunity and growth, the implications of regional price differences for inequality, and the income composition of top incomes. He is also involved in the World Bank's global poverty monitoring. He leads the PovcalNet team, the home of the World Bank's global poverty numbers. He holds a DPhil, MPhil, and BA in economics from the University of Oxford.

Minh Cong Nguyen is a senior data scientist in the Poverty and Equity Global Practice of the World Bank. His research interests include poverty, inequality, welfare measurement, small area estimations and imputation methods, and data systems. He currently leads the Middle East and North Africa Team for Statistical Development and also co-leads the Data for Goals Team. Previously, he worked for the Europe and Central Asia Team for Statistical Development, the Sub-Saharan Africa Region, the South Asia Region, the Human Development Network, and the Private Sector Development Network. Minh holds a PhD in economics (applied microeconometrics) from American University.

Marta Schoch is a consultant in the Development Data Group. Her research interests include inequality, poverty, political economy, and migration, with a focus on the relationship between economic inequality and political preferences. Marta worked for the Imperial College Business School, for the Migrating Out of Poverty research consortium, and for the University of Sussex collaborating on several research projects on poverty and migration and impact evaluations on development and gender-related policies. Marta holds a PhD in economics from the University of Sussex.

Judy Yang is a senior economist in the Poverty and Equity Global Practice, where she has worked on multiple countries in the East Asia and Pacific and the Europe and Central Asia Regions. Previously, she worked for teams in the Middle East and North Africa Office of the Chief Economist, in private sector development in the Sub-Saharan Africa Region, and in the Enterprise Surveys group. Before joining the World Bank, she worked at the US Department of Labor. Her research interests include migration, the business environment, household welfare, and inequality. Judy holds a PhD in economics from Georgetown University.

Nishant Yonzan is a consultant to the Poverty and Inequality Data team in the Development Data Group at the World Bank, contributing to the group's global agenda on measuring poverty and inequality. His research focuses on the causes, consequences, and measurement of poverty and inequality. Nishant is a doctoral candidate at the Graduate Center of the City University of New York.

Abbreviations

COVID-19	Coronavirus Disease 2019
CPI	consumer price index
D4G	Data for Goals
FCS	fragile and conflict-affected situations
FCV	fragility, conflict, and violence
G2Px	Government-to-Person Initiative
GDP	gross domestic product
GDSP	Global Database of Shared Prosperity
GEP	Global Economic Prospects
GMD	Global Monitoring Database
GSAP	Global Subnational Atlas of Poverty
H1N1	influenza A virus subtype H1N1
HFCE	household final consumption expenditure
ICP	International Comparison Program
IDA	International Development Association
IPL	international poverty line
IOTWMS	Indian Ocean Tsunami Warning and Mitigation System
JET	Jobs and Economic Transformation
LIS	Luxembourg Income Study
LMIC	lower-middle-income country
MERS	Middle East Respiratory Syndrome
MPM	multidimensional poverty measure
PPP	purchasing power parity
SARS	severe acute respiratory syndrome
SCDs	Systematic Country Diagnoses
SP	shared prosperity
SPL	societal poverty line
SPP	shared prosperity premium
UMIC	upper-middle-income country

For a list of the 3-letter country codes used by the World Bank, please go to: https://datahelpdesk
.worldbank.org/knowledgebase/articles/906519-world-bank-country-and-lending-groups.

Overview

Poverty reduction has suffered its worst setback in decades, after nearly a quarter century of steady global declines in extreme poverty. *Poverty and Shared Prosperity 2020: Reversals of Fortune* provides new data on and analysis of the causes and consequences of this reversal and identifies policy principles that countries can use to counter it. The report presents new estimates of the impacts of COVID-19 (coronavirus) on global poverty and shared prosperity. Harnessing fresh data from frontline surveys and economic simulations, it shows that pandemic-related job losses and deprivation worldwide are hitting already-poor and vulnerable people hard, while also partly changing the profile of global poverty by creating millions of "new poor." Original analysis included in the report shows that the new poor are more urban, better educated, and less likely to work in agriculture than those living in extreme poverty before COVID-19. These results are important for targeting policies to safeguard lives and livelihoods. The report discusses early evidence that the pandemic is deepening income inequality, threatening inclusive economic recovery and future growth. It shows how some countries are deploying agile, adaptive policies to reverse the crisis, protect the most vulnerable, and promote a resilient recovery.

The 2020 *Poverty and Shared Prosperity* report breaks new ground by jointly analyzing three factors whose convergence is driving the current crisis and will extend its impact into the future: a pandemic (COVID-19 and the associated global economic recession, which are reversing poverty abatement trends rapidly), armed conflict (whose effects have been steadily building in recent years), and climate change (a slowly accelerating risk that will potentially drive millions into poverty). According to updated estimates included in the report, COVID-19 is expected to push some 100 million people into extreme poverty during 2020 alone. Armed conflict is also driving increases in poverty in some countries and regions. In the Middle East and North Africa, for example, extreme poverty rates nearly doubled between 2015 and 2018, from 3.8 percent to 7.2 percent, spurred by the conflicts in the Syrian Arab Republic and the Republic of Yemen. This report presents new research that helps explain the prolonged impoverishing impact of conflict and suggests priorities for prevention and mitigation. New estimates commissioned for this report indicate that up to 132 million people may fall into poverty by 2030 due to the manifold effects of climate change. Although the worst economic and welfare effects lie further in the future, in some settings, poverty is already intertwined with vulnerability to climate-related threats such as flooding and vector-borne diseases. New analysis featured in the report focuses on the convergence of poverty and flood risks, especially in Sub-Saharan Africa.

Along with its direct cost in human lives, COVID-19 has unleashed a worldwide economic disaster whose shock waves continue to spread, putting still more lives at risk. Without an adequate global response, the cumulative effects of the pandemic and its economic fallout, armed conflict, and climate change will exact high human and economic costs well into the future. Poverty nowcasts commissioned for this report suggest that the effects of the current crisis will almost certainly be felt in most countries through 2030. Under these conditions, the goal of bringing the global absolute poverty rate to less than 3 percent by 2030, which was already at risk before the crisis, is now harder than ever to reach. Advancing shared prosperity—by boosting the incomes of the poorest 40 percent of people in every country—will also be much more difficult now. Current projections indicate that shared prosperity will drop sharply in nearly all economies in 2020–21, as the pandemic's economic burden is felt across the entire income distribution, and will drop even more if impacts are disproportionately felt by people whose incomes were already relatively low. This uneven impact means the crisis is likely to increase inequality within countries in the longer term, which, without preemptive action, may trigger large human capital losses among disadvantaged groups and make it more difficult for countries to generate inclusive growth in the future.

This report appears at a moment of critical choices in most of the world. The powerful reversal of fortune now striking the poorest people needs an even more powerful response from countries and the global community. *the 2018 Poverty and Shared Prosperity* report documents how some countries are taking bold action, learning as they go, and sharing results as they emerge. Acting urgently, in concert, and at the scale of the crisis itself, we can halt the pandemic and counter its economic damage, which will save lives and livelihoods today; create conditions for a resilient, equitable recovery; and help draw lessons to better manage future emergencies.

Poverty reduction was slowing before the crisis

The world has made unprecedented progress in reducing poverty over the past quarter century, showing what collective global efforts can achieve (panel a of figure O.1). Major threats to poverty eradication goals emerged well before COVID-19, however. This report presents new global poverty data showing that the sustained decline in extreme poverty that began in the 1990s continued through 2017, but that progress was stalling. Between 2015 and 2017, the number of people worldwide living below the international poverty line fell from 741 million to 689 million (panel b of figure O.1). Yet the 2017 figures confirm the deceleration in the rate of poverty reduction that was reported in the 2018 *Poverty and Shared Prosperity* report. Globally, extreme poverty dropped by an average of about 1 percentage point per year over the quarter century from 1990 to 2015, but the rate of decline slowed from 2013 to 2015 to just 0.6 percentage point per year (World Bank 2018a). Between 2015 and 2017, the rate slowed further, to half a percentage

FIGURE O.1 Global Poverty Rate and Number of Poor at the US$1.90-a-Day Poverty Line, 1990–2017

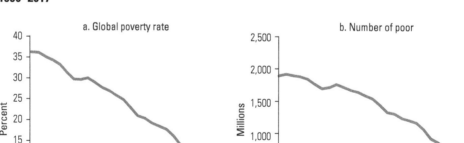

Source: PovcalNet (online analysis tool), World Bank, Washington, DC, http://iresearch.worldbank.org/PovcalNet/.
Note: The global coverage rule is applied (see annex 1A in chapter 1 in this report).

point per year. Given this decelerating trend, the goal of bringing global extreme poverty to less than 3 percent by 2030 was already at risk.

In 2018, the World Bank introduced four additional poverty metrics to capture the changing nature of global poverty. Higher poverty lines at US$3.20 and US$5.50 a day reflect *national poverty lines* in lower-middle-income and upper-middle-income economies respectively. The *societal poverty line*, which adjusts to each country's income, captures the increase in basic needs that a person requires to conduct a dignified life as a country becomes richer. The *multidimensional poverty measure* incorporates deprivations in three indicators of well-being (monetary poverty, access to education, and basic infrastructure), thus giving further insight into the complex nature of poverty.

This report presents new data on and analysis of poverty at these lines from 2015 to 2017. The findings may help explain some of the impoverishing impacts of the current crisis and reveal entry points for policy. In South Asia and Sub-Saharan Africa, poverty reduction against the US$3.20 and US$5.50 lines has been slower than against the extreme poverty line, suggesting that many millions of people in these regions had only narrowly escaped extreme poverty before COVID-19. Those who have just escaped extreme poverty can easily fall back; they are thus especially vulnerable to the impoverishing effects of the pandemic, conflict, and climate change. Job creation through inclusive growth and social protection measures targeting this population may yield strong benefits in reversing poverty increases spurred by the current crisis and preventing other vulnerable people from falling into extreme poverty.

What caused the slowdown in global poverty reduction, which was happening even before the pandemic hit? One explanation is the increasing concentration of extreme poverty in Sub-Saharan Africa, which is experiencing a slower reduction in poverty than are other regions. Figure O.2 shows the proportion of the extreme poor in each region for the period 1990–2018. It underscores the concerns for Sub-Saharan Africa, but also shows problems elsewhere. The Middle East and North Africa has recently seen its extreme poverty rate rise,

FIGURE O.2 Trends in Poverty Rates at the US$1.90-a-Day Poverty Line, by Region, 1990–2018

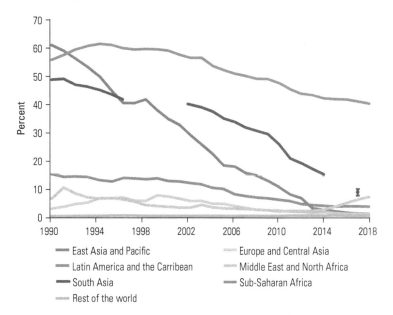

Source: PovcalNet (online analysis tool), World Bank, Washington, DC, http://iresearch.worldbank.org/PovcalNet/.
Note: Lined-up poverty estimates for South Asia are not reported for 1997–2001 and after 2014 because of a lack of population coverage (see box 1.2 on India and annex 1A in chapter 1 of this report). For South Asia in 2017, a range [7.7; 10.0] is reported, as described in box 1.2 in chapter 1 of this report.

from 2.3 percent in 2013 to 3.8 percent in 2015; it then almost doubled to 7.2 percent in 2018, with conflicts in Syria and the Republic of Yemen driving the increase (Corral et al. 2020).

The ability to monitor global poverty depends on the availability of household survey data collected by national authorities. The number of recent household surveys has improved somewhat since the first edition of this report (World Bank 2016). In particular, the number of surveys and population coverage have improved in Sub-Saharan Africa, driven largely by a new survey that recently became available for Nigeria. But the lack of recent data for India severely hinders the ability to monitor global poverty (see box 1.2 in chapter 1 of this report). Hence, the last year for which global poverty was reported is 2017, and the series published for South Asia was interrupted in 2014, whereas for all other regions it extends to 2018. Data on countries experiencing fragility or conflict also remain severely limited, particularly affecting the estimates for the Middle East and North Africa. For poverty to be measured effectively, it is crucial that the current crisis not prompt governments to reduce their investment in surveys and other forms of data collection. Under crisis conditions, reliable poverty data are even more important for guiding response and recovery policies that will not leave vulnerable groups behind.

Shared prosperity was positive for the period 2012–17, but gains were uneven and slowing

One of the World Bank's two main goals is to ensure that relatively poor people in all societies are participating in and benefiting from economic gains. This analysis uses shared prosperity as the measure of progress in this area. Shared prosperity focuses on the poorest 40 percent of a population (the bottom 40) and is defined as the annualized growth rate of their mean household per capita income or consumption. The shared prosperity premium, which is the difference in growth rates between the bottom 40 and the overall mean, is also measured. A high level of shared prosperity is an important indicator of inclusion and well-being in any country.

This report presents new data on shared prosperity and the shared prosperity premium for 91 economies between 2012 and 2017. Growth was inclusive for most of these 91 economies: 74 had positive shared prosperity, and 53 had positive shared prosperity premiums, indicating a reduction in inequality in the majority of economies. Some regions showed especially encouraging results. In East Asia and Pacific and in South Asia, shared prosperity was positive for all economies where it could be measured. This encouraging result suggests that poorer members of societies in these regions were largely being included in countries' economic progress. Evidence from the current sample of 91 economies shows that positive shared prosperity is correlated with poverty reduction, and that a positive shared prosperity premium is associated with a reduction in inequality.

Gains in shared prosperity, however, were unevenly distributed across country income categories and regions. In global terms, the average shared prosperity index was 2.3 percent for 2012–17, but this figure masks wide heterogeneity. Upper-middle-income economies experienced an average shared prosperity of 2.9 percent, followed by high-income economies with 2.7 percent, lower-middle-income economies with 1.8 percent, and low-income economies with 0.2 percent. Countries affected by fragility, conflict, and violence (FCV) fared worse. For the few FCV economies where shared prosperity could be measured, the average result was a decline of 0.8 percent in the income (or consumption) of households in the bottom 40. Across regions, average shared prosperity ranged from 4.9 percent and 3.5 percent in East Asia and Pacific and in Europe and Central Asia, respectively, to 0.7 percent in Sub-Saharan Africa and 0.5 percent in the Middle East and North Africa.

The shared prosperity premium exhibits considerable heterogeneity. A simple average of the premium across 91 economies for the period is 0.3 percentage point, meaning that consumption or income among the bottom 40 percent of the population was growing, on average, 0.3 percentage point faster than at the mean. But the regional averages ranged from 1.0 percentage point in East Asia and Pacific and in Latin America and the Caribbean to negative values in three other regions: the Middle East and North Africa (−0.4), South Asia (−0.5), and Sub-Saharan Africa (−0.6). Two out of the three FCV economies in the sample had both negative shared prosperity and a negative shared prosperity premium. More than half of the economies receiving support from the World Bank's International Development Association also had negative shared prosperity premiums.

Even before COVID-19 and the ensuing economic crisis, time trends in shared prosperity were mixed across economies and regions. A new analysis developed for this report compares the 2012–17 shared prosperity measures for 68 economies with a previous period (2010–15). Comparing across the two rounds, about half of the economies had higher shared prosperity, and the other half had lower. Although the average change in shared prosperity is positive, there are large differences across regions. On average, shared prosperity was higher in the more recent period (2.3 percent) than in the previous period (1.8 percent), but this increase is concentrated in only three regions: East Asia and Pacific, Europe and Central Asia, and the rest of the world (mostly high-income economies outside the World Bank's six developing regions). Higher shared prosperity on average persists over time: most economies with positive shared prosperity in the previous period also had it in the most recent period.

The ability to measure shared prosperity has improved, but substantial gaps in data coverage remain. The 91 economies for which the analysis was able to calculate shared prosperity between 2012 and 2017 represent just 59.9 percent of the world's population. This number still marks a meaningful advance over initial efforts to measure this indicator, in 2014, when adequate data were available for only 65 economies. However, with limited data, shared prosperity is hardest to measure in the very settings where tracking it is most important, often in poorer, fragile, and small countries. Shared prosperity can be measured for only about a quarter of all low-income economies, covering 37.7 percent of the population in this income group.

COVID-19, conflict, and climate change have reversed the gains in poverty eradication for the first time in a generation

COVID-19 and its associated economic crisis, compounded by the effects of armed conflict and climate change, are reversing hard-won gains in poverty reduction and shared prosperity. New findings in this report clarify the short-term impacts and show that negative effects on poverty and inequality may extend and intensify in the medium term.

Today, COVID-19 and the economic crisis are already reversing hard-won gains against global poverty, ending more than two decades of continuous progress. New analysis for this report estimates the magnitude and potential duration of these effects. Poverty as measured by the international poverty line is expected to rise in 2020 for the first time since 1998. Economic forecasts indicate that the pandemic will cause a contraction in global per capita gross domestic product (GDP) growth of between 5 percent (in a baseline scenario) and 8 percent (in a downside scenario) during

FIGURE O.3 Nowcast of the Global Poverty Rate at the US$1.90-a-Day Poverty Line, 2015–21

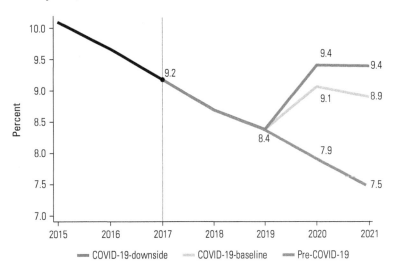

Source: Updated estimates based on Lakner et al. (2020), PovcalNet (online analysis tool), World Bank, Washington, DC, http://iresearch.worldbank.org/PovcalNet/, and Global Economic Prospects.
Note: Three growth scenarios are considered: (1) pre-COVID-19 uses the January 2020 Global Economic Prospects growth rate projections, predating the COVID-19 crisis; (2) COVID-19-downside and (3) COVID-19-baseline use the June 2020 Global Economic Prospects growth rates projecting a contraction in global growth for 2020 of 8 percent and 5 percent, respectively.

2020. Nowcasts of poverty commissioned for the report suggest that, in the baseline scenario, poverty would increase by 1.2 percentage points in 2020 and 1.4 percentage points in 2021, while in the downside scenario, the increase would reach 1.5 percentage points in 2020 and 1.9 percentage points in 2021 (figure O.3). The scenarios translate into a global poverty rate of between 9.1 percent and 9.4 percent in 2020 and between 8.9 percent and 9.4 percent in 2021. These new results suggest that, in 2020, an estimated 88 million people worldwide will be pushed into poverty under the baseline COVID-19 scenario and as many as 115 million people under the downside scenario. The projected poverty rates in 2020 are similar to those in 2017; hence, the impacts of COVID-19 are expected to set back progress toward ending extreme poverty by at least three years.

These estimates suggest that South Asia will be the region hardest hit, with 49 million (almost 57 million under the downside scenario) additional people pushed into extreme poverty. Sub-Saharan Africa would be the next most affected region, with between 26 million and 40 million additional people predicted to be pushed into extreme poverty. Overall, some 72 million of the projected new poor in the baseline scenario will be in middle-income countries—more than four-fifths of the total new poor. When applying the higher regional poverty thresholds appropriate for lower-middle-income countries (US$3.20 a day) and upper-middle-income countries (US$5.50 a day), the poverty impact of COVID-19 will be much greater (figure O.4).

Forecasts projecting the economic impacts of COVID-19 and its aftermath allow us to estimate the pandemic's effects on poverty rates through 2030, the target year for the World Bank's twin goals and the Sustainable Development Goals. Even under the optimistic assumption that, after 2021, growth returns to its historical rates—that is, a per capita annualized growth rate for each country from 2021 to 2030 that matches its average rate between 2008 and 2018—the pandemic's impoverishing effects will be vast. Under the COVID-19-baseline scenario, 6.7 percent of the global population will live under the international poverty line in 2030, compared with the target level of 3 percent. Starting instead from the downside scenario results in an extreme poverty headcount rate of 7 percent in 2030.

Based on these new forecasts, the report confirms that the 2030 target will likely not be reached under either of these two COVID-19 scenarios. Achieving the target would require that all economies grow at 8.0 percent (baseline) or 8.5 percent (downside) per capita per year, which would be equivalent to about five times the historical growth rates for Sub Saharan Africa. These scenarios describing COVID-19's future effects carry high degrees of uncertainty, given that the pandemic is still evolving, but they underline the difficulty of eradicating extreme poverty by 2030. Achieving the goal of ending extreme poverty by 2030 will require significant, swift, and sustained action to ignite inclusive growth in countries where extreme poverty persists.

Frontline surveys confirm swift, large losses in jobs and income from COVID-19

High-frequency telephone surveys conducted by the World Bank in a range of countries provide a real-time, ground-level picture of what has been happening in these settings as the COVID-19 pandemic unfolds.

FIGURE O.4 Additional Poor at the US$1.90-a-Day Poverty Line in 2020, per the COVID-19-Baseline and COVID-19-Downside Scenarios

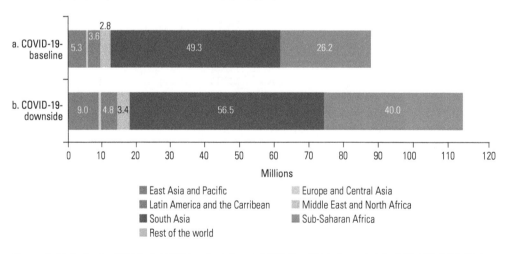

Sources: Updated estimates of Mahler et al. 2020, based on Lakner et al. 2020; PovcalNet (online analysis tool), World Bank, Washington, DC, http://iresearch.worldbank.org/PovcalNet/; World Bank 2020a, 2020b.

Early data indicate sweeping income and employment losses in many countries, at least in the short term. Most countries have experienced drops in labor incomes of a magnitude rarely seen on the national scale (Hill and Narayan 2020). For example, 42 percent of respondents in Nigeria who were working before the outbreak reported being out of work because of COVID-19 in May 2020, and nearly 80 percent of respondents reported income reductions since mid-March (Siwatu et al. 2020). In Ethiopia, 13 percent of respondents surveyed between April 2 and May 13 reported losing their jobs (including 19 percent in urban areas), and 55 percent reported reduced household income (Wieser et al. 2020). Income reductions have quickly translated into reduced consumption. In seven countries in Latin America and the Caribbean, 40 percent or more of people surveyed reported running out of food during lockdowns (Hill and Narayan 2020). Some countries have rolled out ambitious policies in response. Peru initially approved S/. 3 billion (0.5 percent of GDP) to tackle the health emergency and approximately S/. 7 billion (1.1 percent of GDP) in direct transfers to support vulnerable households during the national lockdown period. In late July 2020, the government announced an additional cash transfer to vulnerable households of approximately S/. 6.4 billion (0.9 percent of GDP).[1]

People who are already poor and vulnerable are bearing the brunt of the crisis

People in virtually all countries and at all levels of income are affected by the health and economic consequences of COVID-19. However, emerging evidence shows that people who are currently poor or vulnerable are being hit especially hard. These people include those with lower levels of education and assets, those in insecure employment, and those in lower-skilled occupations, among others.

Why do the poor face greater risks? One reason is that their jobs may be more easily disrupted or eliminated under recession conditions. For example, poorer people and those with lower levels of education and fewer skills are less likely to be able to work remotely. Businesses such as restaurants, hotels, and bars, along with the wholesale and retail trade, which typically employ less-educated workers, are rarely able to accommodate working from home. In Ethiopia, these sectors accounted for the highest share of job losses by mid-May 2020 (Wieser et al. 2020). Poorer workers are also more likely to work in occupations and sectors that are less compatible with social distancing (for example, construction, labor-intensive manufacturing, and small retail), thus increasing their risk of personal exposure to COVID-19, with its health and income consequences. The poorest may also be hit harder because they have fewer coping mechanisms, such as savings that can cover basic needs during periods of unemployment. In developing countries, inadequate social security systems may fail to compensate for this differential impact of the pandemic.

Disproportionate vulnerability in poor and marginalized communities makes containing the virus there especially critical. Effective approaches have tapped the skills and dedication of community members. In Mumbai, India, city officials were able to stem the rapid spread of the coronavirus in Dharavi, one of the city's largest urban settlements, by mobilizing community members and staff from private medical clinics for a strategy based on mass screening for fever and oxygen levels. In the space of three months, by July 2020, reported cases in the area had been cut to 20 percent of their peak in May. To help poor families during the lockdown, foundations, nongovernmental organizations, and volunteers provided thousands of households with ration kits. Dharavi's success stemmed from a combination of "customized solutions, community involvement, and perseverance" (Masih 2020).

Women in some countries may be suffering greater exposure to the coronavirus because of their overrepresentation in frontline health sector professions and their care responsibilities in many households. Women face other specific health risks in the context of the pandemic, because stringent lockdown measures may lead to heightened levels of domestic violence against women and children (Galea, Merchant, and Lurie 2020; UN Women 2020).

In some settings, women's higher burden of care responsibilities may force them to reduce paid working time or to leave the labor market altogether (Hill and Narayan 2020).

Without strong action, COVID-19 will reduce inclusive growth and deepen inequality

Forecasts conducted for this report suggest that, as a result of the global recession, inclusive growth will decline in the coming years in all but 13 of 91 economies with data. By reducing growth in average incomes, the pandemic has already sharply diminished shared prosperity. Forecasts for 2019–21 indicate that most economies will continue to see substantially lower shared prosperity across this period. Average shared prosperity was 2.3 percent in 2012–17; the average for 2019–21 would be 0 percent if shared prosperity is equal to growth in the mean (that is, assuming a zero shared prosperity premium in all economies), and even less if the impact of the crisis affects poorer segments of the population more than proportionately. Hitting the poorest people hardest, the economic crisis caused by COVID-19 will also drive negative shared prosperity premiums. Revised forecasts of the shared prosperity premium are not yet available, but historical data on recent major epidemics (from severe acute respiratory syndrome in 2003 to Zika in 2016) suggest that these events raise income inequality and significantly diminish employment prospects among people with basic education. Increases in inequality will also have medium-term impacts. The report projects that, if an annual increase of 1 percent in the Gini coefficient were to occur, the global poverty rate would rise to 8.6 percent in 2030.

Although short-term patterns may vary, the negative longer-term consequences of COVID-19 for income inequality are clear. Without strong interventions, the crisis may trigger cycles of higher income inequality, lower social mobility among the vulnerable, and lower resilience to future shocks (Hill and Narayan 2020). Rising inequality may be fueled by factors such as the destruction of many micro and small enterprises, the potentially durable effects of unemployment on the careers and earning potential of younger and lower-skilled workers, and severe human capital losses among disadvantaged households,

partly due to the coping strategies they have to adopt. One of the first and potentially most destructive of these coping strategies is reducing food consumption. Emerging data from COVID-19 phone surveys suggest that this strategy is being widely used. In Nigeria, for example, more than half of households reported reducing their food consumption (Siwatu et al. 2020). Depending on duration and severity, the impact of reduced food intake on children's health, cognitive development, and future human capital accumulation, as well as on current adult health and productivity, may be substantial.

Early evidence from frontline phone surveys also suggests that human capital losses due to school closures are likely to affect poor and rural children disproportionately, notably because they are often unable to engage in distance learning. In Nigeria, the richest 20 percent of households were much more likely than the rest of the population to report that their children were pursuing learning activities, including remote learning, following school closures (Siwatu et al. 2020). As part of its response to COVID-19, however, Niger has announced the Learning Improvement for Results in Education (LIRE) project, which seeks to reach children unable to attend school and develop an online platform to enhance teacher training. In a country where, before COVID-19, half of children between ages 7 and 12 were not in school at all, or completed primary schooling but with few basic skills, the LIRE project has the potential to help families manage the COVID-19 crisis while also modernizing Niger's education system. Such findings and innovative responses contain lessons for countries' recovery strategies, which need to incorporate an equity lens and targeting methods that can protect human capital among vulnerable groups (Hill and Narayan 2020).

COVID-19, conflict, and climate impacts will change the profile of the global poor

This *Poverty and Shared Prosperity* report updates the demographic profile of the global poor by age, gender, schooling, and location; and it also expands the profile across several dimensions, including the extent to which, within countries, the poor may be concentrated in areas that are more exposed to conflict or climate risks. In addition, the report analyzes data from the Global Monitoring Database to show how COVID-19 may now be changing the profile of people living in poverty.

The new profile of the poor population

The poor remain predominantly rural, young, and undereducated (figure O.5). Four of every five individuals living below the international poverty line reside in rural areas, circa 2018, although the rural population accounts for only 48 percent of the global population (figure O.5, panel a). In fact, poverty became more rural between 2015 and 2018. The share of the rural poor in the total population of poor people increased by more than 2 percentage points during that period.

The profile of the global poor is also very young. In 2018, half of the poor were children younger than age 15, even though this age group accounted for only a quarter of the world's population. Children and youth (ages 15–24) together account for two-thirds of the global poor, much higher than the cumulative population share of the 0–24 age group globally (40 percent of the total). The high share of children and youth among the global poor is most prominent in Sub-Saharan Africa, but it can be observed across most regions. A different profile is seen only in high-income economies, where the poor are skewed toward the elderly.

Women are overrepresented among the poor globally and also across most regions of the world. While Europe and Central Asia, Latin America and the Caribbean, and other high-income economies have low female poverty, East Asia and Pacific, South Asia, and Sub-Saharan Africa have high female poverty; the widest gaps are among children. Girls are more likely than boys to be overrepresented among the poor, as are women in their main reproductive years (ages 25–34) across most world regions (Muñoz-Boudet et al. 2020; World Bank 2018a).

Worldwide, 35 percent of poor adults in the 15-and-older age group in 2018 had no schooling (compared with only 9 percent of the nonpoor), and a further 35 percent of global poor adults had only some education (including those who completed primary education). Lower levels of educational attainment are more common among both poor and nonpoor individuals in rural areas

FIGURE O.5 Four Profiles of the Global Poor, by Region, Gender, Age, and Educational Attainment, circa 2018

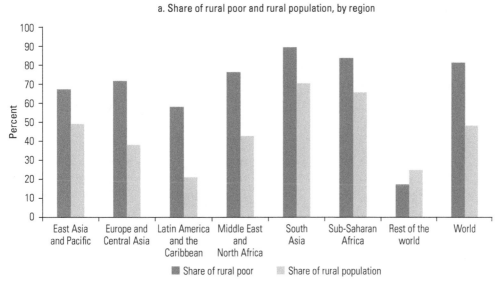

a. Share of rural poor and rural population, by region

■ Share of rural poor   ■ Share of rural population

(continued)

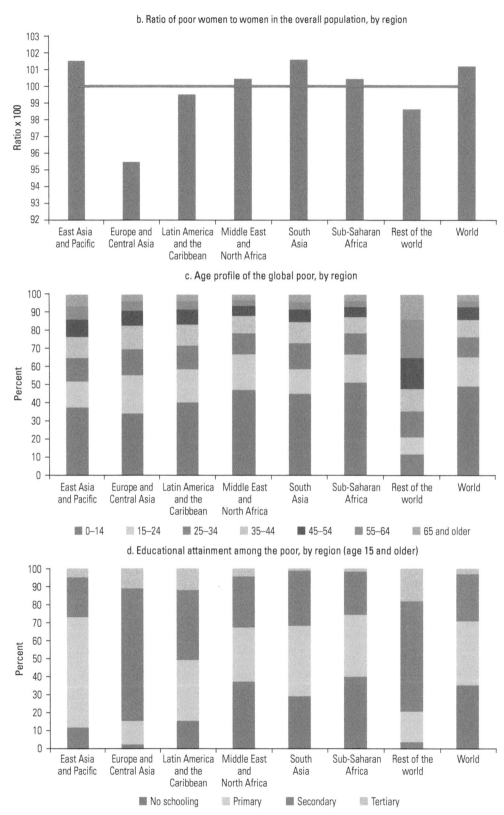

b. Ratio of poor women to women in the overall population, by region

c. Age profile of the global poor, by region

d. Educational attainment among the poor, by region (age 15 and older)

Source: World Bank estimates based on Global Monitoring Database data.

as compared with urban areas. It is the quality of schooling, however, that is key to poverty reduction, and this is a concern for both non-poor and (especially) poor students, in rural and urban areas alike (World Bank 2020d). This disparity highlights the multidimensional character of rural poverty: among poor adults residing in rural areas, 39 percent report having no education, more than double the share of poor adults in urban areas having no education.

The pandemic is set to increase poverty among groups that had been less affected

The COVID-19 pandemic may push more than 100 million people into extreme poverty in 2020. Although existing data do not yet permit a detailed description of this population to be formulated, evidence is emerging based on simulations of COVID-19 impacts and newly collected data from high-frequency surveys. A new analysis of these findings in this report suggests that the new poor may differ from those who were poor before the onset of the pandemic in ways that are important for policy.

Although a large share of the new poor will be concentrated in countries that are already struggling with high poverty rates, middle-income countries will also be significantly affected. Overall, some 72 million of the projected new poor in the baseline scenario (and 94 million in the downside scenario) will be in middle-income countries—more than three-quarters of the total.

People forced into poverty by COVID-19 may also differ from the current global poor in other ways. Within countries, a large share of the extreme poor are rural, whereas many of the new poor are likely to live in congested urban settings, which can serve as a conduit for infection. Many of the new poor are likely to be engaged in informal services, construction, and manufacturing—the sectors in which economic activity is most affected by lockdowns and other mobility restrictions as well as mandatory social distancing. The recent simulations of profiles of the new poor based on population-weighted estimates from a sample of 110 economies show that the new poor are projected to be more likely to live in urban areas, live in dwellings with better access to infrastructure, and own

slightly more basic assets than those who are poor in both 2019 and 2020. The new poor who are 15 and older are also more likely to be paid employees and work more in nonagriculture (manufacturing, services, and commerce sectors) than the chronic poor. The new poor tend to be more educated than the chronic poor, and significantly less educated than the nonpoor (of those age 15 and older).[2] These early estimates assume that the relationship between GDP growth and the change in poverty is distribution neutral in all countries, which implies that a loss in GDP affects all parts of the distribution proportionally. If that were not the case (that is, if the crisis affects some groups more than others), the profile and composition of the poor may be more or less heterogeneous.

The emerging global profile of the new poor is supported by simulations developed for specific countries, including Bangladesh, Brazil, Nigeria, and South Africa. This work confirms that a large share of the new poor will be urban. It also shows that the new poor are likely to be disproportionately employed outside agriculture (for example, in manufacturing, construction, and wholesale and retail trade in South Africa; and in services in Nigeria and Indonesia) (Sánchez-Páramo 2020). These patterns are borne out by emerging data from high-frequency monitoring surveys of COVID-19 impacts on households. A survey in Mongolia, for example, found that 14 percent of urban respondents report having lost employment compared with only 9 percent in rural households (World Bank 2020a). In Uzbekistan, the figures were 46 percent for urban versus 37 percent for rural (World Bank 2020b).

Conflict and climate change may force rising numbers of people into poverty in the medium term

Along with COVID-19 and the economic crisis, armed conflict and climate change are already driving poverty increases in parts of the world. Their impoverishing effects are likely to intensify.

The association with fragility and conflict is an increasingly salient feature of global poverty. Corral et al. (2020) indicate that the 43 economies with the highest poverty rates are all either located in Sub-Saharan Africa or included in the World Bank's list of fragile and conflict-affected situations (FCS). In 2020, the 37 economies formally classified as affected by fragility, conflict, and violence are home to only about 10 percent of the world's population, but they account for more than 40 percent of the global poor (figure O.6). Before COVID-19, Corral et al. (2020) projected that fragile and conflict-affected economies would represent a majority of the extreme poor by 2030, with Sub-Saharan Africa contributing a large share of the total. In the most recent COVID-19 projections, FCS economies represent only 20 percent of the new poor, which hints at a smaller share of FCS poor among the global poor in coming years.[3]

Armed conflict can exert swift and powerful effects on economic growth and poverty. But evidence increasingly suggests that its impacts on poverty and human capital accumulation can persist for decades, even for generations (Corral et al. 2020). New research commissioned for this report shows how conflict weakens poverty reduction long term by creating a "conflict debt" that a country can only resolve by maintaining peaceful conditions for a sustained period once violent conflict ends. The concept of conflict debt underscores that a cumulative history of past conflict, not just contemporaneous conflict, impedes a country's ability to address poverty or inclusive growth (Mueller and Techasunthornwat 2020).

Human capital is a key transmission channel for these effects. Gaps in human capital, manifested in poor educational and health outcomes, affect the future productivity of workers and the future competitiveness of economies (World Bank 2018b, World Bank 2020d). Conflict contributes directly to these gaps by affecting long-term workforce productivity through less access to education, increases in deaths and injuries, more stunting, and worsened mental health. Expectations of further outbreaks of violence also inhibit capital inflows and further reduce productivity, while fear of the spread of violence can amplify its impact beyond the individuals, firms, and regions that are directly affected. And although conflict is a symptom of weak state capacity, it also perpetuates weak capacity, with repercussions for the state's ability to pursue effective poverty alleviation strategies and policy interventions.

Climate change also poses both acute and medium-term threats to poverty reduction, particularly in Sub-Saharan Africa and South Asia—the regions where most of the global poor are concentrated. The World Bank's *Shock Waves* report estimated that, if unaddressed, climate change has the potential to push more than 100 million people into poverty by 2030 (Hallegatte et al. 2016). An update of these analyses commissioned for this report estimates the number of people who would become impoverished at between 68 million and 132 million, depending on the scope and severity of climate-change impacts during the period.

Ample evidence indicates that those living in poverty or near the poverty line are particularly vulnerable to shocks such as natural disasters; greater vulnerability means that they lose more when such shocks occur. This exposure reflects many factors, including lower-quality assets, such as housing stock; greater dependence on livelihoods derived from agriculture and ecosystems that are vulnerable to natural disasters; greater vulnerability to rising food prices during disaster-related supply shocks; and greater susceptibility to climate-related diseases such as diarrhea and malaria (Hallegate et al. 2016).

FIGURE O.6 Share of the Global Poor and of the Global Population, by FCS 2020 Typology

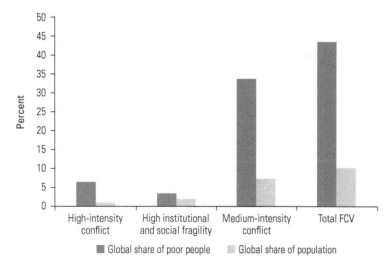

Source: World Bank estimates based on Global Monitoring Database data.
Note: FCS = fragile and conflict-affected situations; FCV = fragility, conflict, and violence.

The deleterious effects of conflict and of climate change on poverty are also likely to be concentrated among those whose incomes are not far above the poverty threshold. A profile of the population below the US$3.20-a-day threshold provides a better sense of the global poverty profile for households that may fall below the international poverty line because of the COVID-19 pandemic or other negative income shocks. This profile, interestingly, shows that the population living below the US$3.20-a-day threshold is also predominantly rural, underaged, and underschooled, and has higher exposure to armed conflict. As indicated in previous paragraphs, new evidence shows that the "new poor" are different, but the total profile of global poverty will still contain a large share of rural groups, children, and underschooled adults, underscoring the double challenge of implementing new and specific policy responses for the "new poor" without diminishing support to the regularly vulnerable.

This report also includes an estimate of the number of people in poverty who are exposed to intense flood risk, one of the potential impacts of climate change. For each country and each subnational administrative unit, a single flood hazard layer is created by combining different flood types. Globally, some 1.47 billion people are estimated to be living in areas with high flood risk, including about 132 million poor people, as defined by the international poverty line of US$1.90 a day. If using higher poverty lines (for instance, the US$5.50 line), about half the population exposed to catastrophic floods is poor (figure O.7).

The impoverishing impacts of COVID-19, conflict, and climate change converge in Sub-Saharan Africa

The forces propelling the upsurge in global poverty affect every part of the world, but they are hitting Sub-Saharan Africa especially hard. Extreme poverty was already becoming increasingly concentrated there even before the crisis: among the world's economies for which poverty can be measured, 18 of the 20 poorest are in Sub-Saharan Africa. Some 40 percent of the region's population still lived on less than US$1.90 a day in 2018, and almost 70 percent lived on less than $3.20 a day, the poverty line typical of lower-middle-income economies. Perhaps even more alarming is the stagnation of poverty rates at high levels over the past three decades. The 2018 *Poverty and Shared Prosperity* report (World Bank

FIGURE O.7 Number of Poor Living at the Three Poverty Lines Who Are Also Exposed to Catastrophic Floods

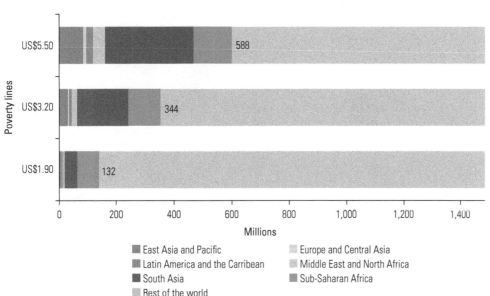

Source: Rentschler and Salhab 2020.

2018a) analyzes this pattern and identifies key drivers in some African countries, including weak initial conditions, low per capita growth, high reliance on extractive industries, limited institutional stability and policy effectiveness, and vulnerability to natural disasters such as droughts.

Some of the most destructive impacts of climate change are also expected to affect Sub-Saharan Africa disproportionately. Original analysis included in the report looks at the incidence of poverty and exposure to catastrophic floods due to climate change. Here, too, Sub-Saharan Africa stands out for the joint occurrence of poverty and flood exposure. Whereas the region accounts for slightly more than 10 percent of the global population with high flood risks, it is home to more than half of the global poor facing high flood risks (map O.1).

Poverty is not uniform across Sub-Saharan Africa. Some countries have recently made impressive strides in reducing poverty, but this progress is now threatened by COVID-19. Ethiopia saw a decrease of 7 percentage points in the extreme poverty rate between 2004/05 and 2015/16, confirming a virtuous trend since the early 2000s. In Kenya, the share of population living below the international poverty line decreased from 44 percent to 37 percent between 2005 and 2015; in Namibia, it dropped from 23 percent to 13 percent between 2009 and 2015. The economic crisis unleashed by COVID-19 could reverse such hard-won gains. Although the decline in economic growth is projected to be more modest in Sub-Saharan Africa than in advanced economies, it will likely spur one of the largest increases in extreme poverty, reflecting the large number of people

MAP O.1 Joint Distribution of Poverty and Flood Risk in Sub-Saharan Africa

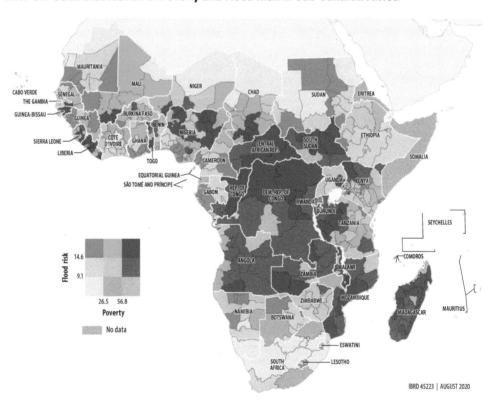

Sources: World Bank estimates based on data from the Global Subnational Atlas of Poverty, Global Monitoring Database, and Rentschler and Salhab 2020.
Note: Scale thresholds for poverty and climate risk are based on terciles. Both axes represent the percentage of the population. Those who live with a flood risk face inundation depths of over 0.15 meters in the event of a 1-to-100-year flood. Those in poverty live below the US$1.90-a-day poverty line.

in the region living on the edge of poverty. The nowcasts in this report of the pandemic's global poverty impacts through 2021 suggest that Sub-Saharan Africa will be the second most severely affected region (after South Asia), with 26 million to 40 million more of its people falling into extreme poverty.

Conclusion: Tackling the crisis while looking to the long term

As this report was written, a slowing of inclusive growth and global poverty reduction became a historic reversal, with the potential to erase years of hard-won poverty eradication and development gains. COVID-19 triggered this reversal, but its effects are intensified by armed conflict in some economies and the growing impact of climate change worldwide. Global economic growth is predicted to fall by 5.2 percent in 2020, the largest drop in eight decades. The shock may leave lasting scars on investment levels, remittances flows, the skills and health of the millions now unemployed, learning outcomes (through school closures), and supply chains (World Bank 2020c).

This report presents new evidence that the crisis is sharply reducing incomes and welfare among people who were already poor, while impoverishing tens of millions more who may differ from the existing poor in ways important for the policy response. The new poor tend to be more urban than the chronically poor and to work outside of agriculture, in sectors including informal services, construction, and manufacturing. New analysis included in the report shows that the crisis has rapidly reduced shared prosperity and threatens to durably widen income inequalities in many settings, leading to lower social mobility in the longer term and making it harder for economies to return to inclusive growth.

These findings call for urgent action. If the global response fails the world's poor and vulnerable people now, the losses they have experienced to date may be dwarfed by what lies ahead. We must not fail. "Not failing" obviously means stopping COVID-19, but

success over the long term will require much more. As efforts to curb the disease and its economic fallout intensify, the interrupted development agenda in low- and middle-income countries must be put back on track. Reversing today's reversals of fortune requires tackling the economic crisis unleashed by COVID-19 with means proportional to the crisis itself. In doing so, countries can also plant the seeds for dealing with the long-term development challenges of promoting inclusive growth, capital accumulation, and risk prevention, particularly the risks of conflict and climate change.

Policy responses need to reflect the changing profile of the poor

Findings about the new poor have important policy implications, in particular for the design of safety nets and for measures to rebuild jobs and strengthen human capital in the recovery phase. Currently, even though many countries face challenges with the targeting and coverage of existing safety nets, support to poor households already covered by such programs can be mobilized relatively quickly. By contrast, those in the urban informal sector who are affected by job and income losses, along with groups such as seasonal migrants and refugees, may not be covered by the emergency response measures being deployed.

Protecting households from the impacts of COVID-19 will require policies and programs that reach both the existing and the new poor. Safety net programs will need to adopt innovative targeting and delivery mechanisms, in particular to reach people in the informal sector in both rural and urban areas (Sánchez-Páramo 2020, Bowen et al. 2020). Countries are taking action to meet the challenge. Kenya, for example, has reallocated all domestic and international travel budgets from government agencies to combat COVID-19 and committed up to KSh 2 billion (US$20 million) recovered from corruption proceeds to support vulnerable groups, especially the urban poor.[4] Afghanistan has rolled out a relief package designed for both the rural and urban poor. The package amounts to 1.6 percent of GDP and will provide support to households with incomes of US$2 a day or less (twice the national poverty line). It will cover about 90 percent of all Afghan households. Households in rural areas will receive the equivalent of US$50 in essential food staples and hygiene products, while those in urban areas will receive a combination of cash and in-kind support equivalent to US$100, in two tranches.[5]

As the recovery gathers momentum, countries will also need to consider the changing profile of poverty and vulnerability as they invest in jobs. Policy options may include providing grants and wage subsidies to firms to minimize layoffs, supporting micro and small enterprises through measures such as tax exemptions and grants, and active labor market programs to facilitate transitions among workers who have lost jobs (Hill and Narayan 2020). Bangladesh's 2.5 million small and medium enterprises contribute some 20 percent of the country's GDP. The stimulus package announced by the government of Bangladesh in April 2020 earmarked US$2.3 billion as working capital for small and medium enterprises at government-subsidized interest rates. The government's relief effort has also included a low-rate loan package to pay workers' wages in the country's hard-hit readymade garment industry.[6]

Poverty action needs to address hot spots of conflict, climate change, and COVID-19

In the years ahead, the persistent effects of the pandemic, new conflicts and old "conflict debt," and climate change will continue to affect the geographic distribution of populations living in or near absolute poverty. Policies to eradicate poverty and mitigate its effects will increasingly need to target areas marked by the convergence of two, or in some cases all three, of these factors.

Today, countries in which a large share of the poor reside in areas affected by recent or past conflicts and high flood risk include Cameroon, the Republic of Congo, Liberia, Nepal, and South Sudan. Postcrisis recovery and future poverty reduction in these complex settings will require

tailored policy approaches, and the optimal solution in each case will need to be found. To identify them, targeted research needs to clarify interactions among poverty, conflict, flood risks, and other phenomena associated with climate change—including extreme temperature events, the prevalence of vector-borne and other diseases, and food security, among others.

Countries are taking action, innovating, and learning as they go

Countries around the world have undertaken bold initiatives in response to the COVID-19 pandemic, including approaches that encompass responses to other ongoing development challenges. Although it is too soon to rigorously assess the effectiveness of such initiatives, their early results can inform future efforts. Current policies need to engage multiple sectors, in keeping with the pandemic's pervasive effects.

For instance, Indonesia has taken assertive steps to curb the human and economic costs of COVID-19, initiating four fiscal policy packages since March 2020, with the early-June 2020 package amounting to 4.2 percent of GDP. These efforts have focused on expanding the COVID-19 response capability in the health sector; strengthening social protection programs and expanding unemployment benefits, including to workers in the informal sector; reducing taxes for individuals and in the tourism sector; and permanently reducing the corporate income tax, from 25 percent to 22 percent in 2020–21 and to 20 percent in 2022. Capital has also been provided to shore up state-owned industries, to support credit guarantees, and to lend restructuring funds to micro, small, and medium enterprises.

Because crises can create opportunities, some countries are harnessing the recovery to catalyze regulatory reforms and expand investments in digital technology. In Ecuador, the Philippines, and Uganda, for example, reforms in these areas have facilitated access to finance, enabled greater logistical support to small and medium enterprises, and expanded workers' awareness of employment opportunities.

Some countries have had to confront COVID-19 and large-scale natural disasters such as cyclones simultaneously. In countries including India and Vanuatu, disaster risk management laws and governance structures have supported the ability of officials to undertake emergency measures and manage the response not only to tropical storms but also to the nonpharmacological aspects of COVID-19 (Kishore 2020).

A practical challenge for many governments is providing monetary assistance to those most in need, for example, social protection payments to those who have recently become unemployed. Direct payments or transfers from governments to people are faster, more accurate, and less expensive if they can be made electronically. COVID-19 has already prompted Chile, Peru, Thailand, and more than 50 other countries to expand their government-to-people cash transfer systems (Rutkowski et al. 2020).

Emergency action and long-term development can share lessons

Responses to the triple challenges of COVID-19, conflict, and climate change need to reflect past experience and lessons from recent assessments of complex development interventions. Four areas of intersection and shared learning may be especially important for coordinating action on current and ongoing development challenges.

1. *Closing the gap between policy aspiration and attainment.* Recent development research has shined fresh light on a persistent problem that also concerns the COVID-19 response: to tackle tough challenges, sound policies are crucial but not sufficient. Especially as the challenges intensify in reaching and responding to the poorest communities, success requires leadership that is fully committed to securing political accountability and financial support, building robust implementation systems (Page and Pande 2018), and providing complementary support factors (for example, hungry children will struggle to learn even in well-equipped schools,

so they may need food support). Recent research suggests that implementation capability in most low-income economies has been stagnant or declining in recent years (Andrews, Pritchett, and Woolcock 2017; Pritchett 2020). Much more attention needs to be given not just to "getting policies right" but to building the capability of the administrative systems that are tasked with implementing them.

2. *Enhancing learning and improving data.* Faced with the unprecedented scientific, organizational, and societal uncertainty provoked by COVID-19, governments and their partners need to learn—very quickly— how to identify, enact, and scale up effective, context-specific responses. Development experience itself can supply evidence on promising approaches and common pitfalls, so it is important to remain open to innovative responses, no matter where they come from, and to share them. Indeed, the diverse response and recovery strategies now unfolding around the world will generate vast quantities of data and opportunities for learning. In general, data limitations create doubts among the general public, obstruct scientific progress, and hinder the implementation of sound, evidence-based development policies. If captured and curated, data from the crisis response can guide rapid course corrections in COVID-19 policy and inform future action on core development problems. Accessible, high-quality data are a public good whose importance increases during crises.

3. *Investing in preparedness and prevention.* COVID-19, armed conflict, and climate change underscore the need to invest in comprehensive preparedness and prevention within countries and across borders. Multilateral agencies, including the Global Facility for Disaster Reduction and Recovery, are already active in this area. An example of successful international cooperation in disaster preparedness is the Indian Ocean Tsunami Warning and Mitigation System (IOTWMS). Following the 2004 earthquake and tsunami in the region, Australia, India, Indonesia, Malaysia, and Thailand moved to set up their own warning

centers but initially struggled to coordinate their work. After years of political negotiation, technical challenges, and persistent shared efforts, IOTWMS became fully operational in 2013. Since the 2004 Indian Ocean tsunami, regional warning systems have also been created in the Mediterranean and the Caribbean. Cooperation and coordination are also crucial tasks for regional agencies, such as the Regional Disease Surveillance Systems Enhancement Program (in West and Central Africa) and the East Africa Public Health Laboratory Networking Project (Wetzel 2020)—all the more so if the effects of COVID-19 linger or periodic outbreaks eventuate.

4. *Expanding cooperation and coordination.* Cooperation and coordination are vital, not only to improve the empirical foundations of policy making, but also to nurture social solidarity in affected countries and communities and ensure that governments' decisions are both trusted and trustworthy. Strikingly different levels of cooperation and coordination are evident in the ways in which countries and local jurisdictions have responded to COVID-19 to date—some with decisive collective action from the outset, others hesitating or denying the threat until the pandemic was far advanced. Vietnam stands out as a country that, despite this inherent uncertainty, provided clear and regular public information from the outset, thereby crowding out space for "fake news," conspiracy theories, and misinformation (Ravallion 2020). Even where scientific expertise and political leadership unite behind a credible COVID-19 strategy, success depends on communities following the rules and being prepared to make sacrifices. Although the pandemic has different impacts on different social groups, the fact that *all* are affected is an opportunity for leaders to promote a sense of social inclusion and collective resolve, the benefits of which could extend beyond the crisis.

No country acting alone can adequately control, much less prevent, the type of emergency the world is now experiencing. Future preparedness, prevention, and crisis responses must be global and collaborative. Reversing even a massive reversal of fortune, such as we are seeing with COVID-19, is possible. It has been done many times in the past, in the face of what were regarded at the time as insurmountable challenges—for example, eradicating smallpox, ending World War II, creating national parks, closing the ozone hole—and it will be done again in the future. This global crisis is also a defining historical moment. To address development challenges, whether large or small, the world needs to commit to cooperation and coordination both within and between countries. We must commit to working together, and to working better, for the long term.

Notes

1. "Policy Responses to COVID-19, Policy Tracker: Peru," International Monetary Fund, Washington, DC, https://www.imf.org/en/Topics/imf-and-covid19/Policy-Responses-to-COVID-19#P.

2. Estimates as of August 6, 2020. "Profiles of the New Poor due to the COVID-19 Pandemic," Brief, August 6, World Bank, Washington, DC, https://www.worldbank.org/en/topic/poverty/brief/Profiles-of-the-new-poor-due-to-the-COVID-19-pandemic.

3. This estimate is preliminary and only indicative because the methods adopted in Corral et al. (2020) aim to overcome data limitations in FCS economies and are not strictly comparable with the COVID-19 impact projection methods adopted in this report. Further research is needed to recalibrate projections of the share of the FCS poor in the world in the decade after COVID-19.

4. "Country Policy Responses," International Labour Organization, Geneva, https://www.ilo.org/global/topics/coronavirus/country-responses/lang--en/index.htm#KE.

5. "Policy Responses to COVID-19," International Monetary Fund, Washington, DC, https://www.imf.org/en/Topics/imf-and-covid19/Policy-Responses-to-COVID-19.

6. "Country Policy Responses," International Labour Organization, Geneva, https://www.ilo.org/global/topics/coronavirus/country-responses/lang--en/index.htm#BD; "EU to provide €113m as wages for 1m RMG workers in Bangladesh," Dhaka Tribune, June 2, 2020, https://www.dhakatribune.com/business/2020/06/02/eu-to-provide-97m-for-1m-rmg-workers-wages-for-3-months.

References

Andrews, Matt, Lant Pritchett, and Michael Woolcock. 2017. *Building State Capability: Evidence, Analysis, Action*. New York: Oxford University Press.

Bowen, Thomas, Carlo Del Ninno, Colin Andrews, Sarah Coll-Black, Ugo Gentilini, Kelly Johnson, Yasuhiro Kawasoe, Adea Kryeziu, Barry Maher, and Asha Williams. 2020. "Adaptive Social Protection: Building Resilience to Shocks." Washington, DC: World Bank.

Corral, Paul, Alexander Irwin, Nandini Krishnan, Daniel Gerszon Mahler, and Tara Vishwanath. 2020. *Fragility and Violence: On the Front Lines of the Fight against Poverty*. Washington, DC: World Bank.

Galea, Sandro, Raina M. Merchant, and Nicole Lurie. 2020. "The Mental Health Consequences of COVID-19 and Physical Distancing: The Need for Prevention and Early Intervention." *Journal of the American Medical Association (JAMA): Internal Medicine* 180 (6): 817–18.

Hallegatte, Stéphane, Mook Bangalore, Laura Bonzanigo, Marianne Fay, Tamaro Kane, Ulf Narloch, Julie Rozenberg, David Treguer, and Adrien Vogt-Schilb. 2016. *Shock Waves: Managing the Impacts of Climate Change on Poverty*. Climate Change and Development Series. Washington, DC: World Bank.

Hill, Ruth Vargas, and Ambar Narayan. 2020. "How is COVID-19 Likely to Affect Inequality? A Discussion Note." Unpublished report, World Bank, Washington, DC.

Kishore, Kamal. 2020. "Managing Tropical Storms during COVID-19: Early Lessons Learned and Reflections from India." *World Bank Blogs: Development and a Changing Climate*, July 27. https://blogs.worldbank.org/climatechange/managing-tropical-storms-during-covid-19-early-lessons-learned-and-reflections-india.

Lakner, Christoph, Daniel Gerszon Mahler, Mario Negre, and Espen Beer Prydz. 2020. "How Much Does Reducing Inequality Matter for Global Poverty?" Global Poverty Monitoring Technical Note 13 (June), World Bank, Washington, DC.

Masih, Niha. 2020. "How a Packed Slum in Mumbai Beat Back the Coronavirus, as India's Cases Continue to Soar." *Washington Post*, July 31, 2020.

Mueller, Hannes, and Chanon Techasunthornwat. 2020. "Conflict and Poverty." Background paper for this report, World Bank, Washington, DC.

Muñoz-Boudet, Ana María, Antra Bhatt, Ginette Azcona, Jayne Jungsun Yoo, and Kathleen Beegle. 2020. "A Global View of Poverty, Gender, and Household Composition." World Bank, Washington, DC.

Page, Lucy, and Rohini Pande. 2018. "Ending Global Poverty: Why Money Isn't Enough." *Journal of Economic Perspectives* 32 (4): 173–200.

Pritchett, Lant. 2020. "Trends in State Capability, 1996–2018: An Update of National Indicators." Background paper for this report, World Bank, Washington, DC.

Ravallion, Martin. 2020. "Pandemic Policies in Poor Places." CGD Note (April 24), Center for Global Development, Washington, DC.

Rentschler, Jun Erik Maruyama, and Melda Salhab. 2020. "People's Exposure to Flooding and Poverty." Background paper for this report, World Bank, Washington, DC.

Rutkowski, Michal, Alfonso Garcia Mora, Greta L. Bull, Boutheina Guermazi, and Caren Grown. 2020. "Responding to Crisis with Digital Payments for Social Protection: Short-Term Measures with Long-Term Benefits." *World Bank Blogs: Voices*, March 31. https://blogs.worldbank.org/voices/responding-crisis-digital-payments-social-protection-short-term-measures-long-term-benefits.

Sánchez-Páramo, Carolina. 2020. "The New Poor Are Different: Who They Are and Why It Matters." *World Bank Blogs: Let's Talk Development*, August 13. https://blogs.worldbank.org/developmenttalk/new-poor-are-different-who-they-are-and-why-it-matters.

Siwatu, Gbemisola Oseni, Amparo Palacios-Lopez, Kevin Robert Mcgee, Akuffo Amankwah, Tara Vishwanath, and M. Abdul Kalam Azad. 2020. "Impact of COVID-19 on Nigerian Households: Baseline Results." World Bank, Washington, DC.

UN Women. 2020. "COVID-19 and Ending Violence against Women and Girls." UN Women, New York.

Wetzel, Deborah. 2020. "Pandemics Know No Borders: In Africa, Regional Cooperation is Key to Fighting COVID-19." https://blogs.worldbank.org/africacan/pandemics-know-no-borders-africa-regional-collaboration-key-fighting-covid-19.

Wieser, Christina, Alemayehu Ambel, Tom Bundervoet, and Asmelash Haile. 2020.

"Monitoring COVID-19 Impacts on Households in Ethiopia: Results from a High-Frequency Phone Survey of Households." World Bank, Washington, DC.

World Bank. 2016. *Poverty and Shared Prosperity 2016: Taking on Inequality*. Washington, DC: World Bank.

World Bank. 2018a. *Poverty and Shared Prosperity 2018: Piecing Together the Poverty Puzzle*. Washington, DC: World Bank.

World Bank. 2018b. "The Human Capital Project." World Bank, Washington, DC.

World Bank. 2020a. "Results of Mongolia COVID-19 Household Response Survey." World Bank, Washington, DC.

World Bank. 2020b. "Economic and Social Impacts of COVID-19: June 2020 Update from Listening to the Citizens of Uzbekistan." World Bank, Washington, DC.

World Bank. 2020c. *Global Economic Prospects, June 2020*. Washington, DC: World Bank.

World Bank. 2020d. "Human Capital in the Time of COVID-19: The Human Capital Index 2020 Update." Washington, DC: World Bank.

Introduction: Global Goals, Shared Challenges

The clear message from previous *Poverty and Shared Prosperity* reports (in 2016 and 2018) was that, although important gains in reducing global poverty have been made steadily since 1998, the pace of this reduction had slowed considerably in recent years. It was becoming increasingly unrealistic to expect that the goal of reducing extreme poverty to less than 3 percent would be attained at the global level by 2030 unless widespread and sustained improvement in inclusive economic growth could be attained. The effects of this slowdown have been apparent for some time, and increasingly have been exacerbated by the impacts of armed conflict and climate change, but these factors have now been overwhelmed by COVID-19 (coronavirus) and its associated global economic crisis. Current projections suggest that the COVID-19 pandemic will not merely slow global poverty reduction further but will reverse the trend in much of the world: the number of people living in extreme poverty will increase this year by as much as 115 million. In the coming decade, the accumulating effects of climate change may impoverish between 68 million and 132 million people. By 2030, it is expected that most of the world's poorest people will live in situations characterized by fragility, conflict, and violence.

This report examines how the COVID-19 crisis, compounding the risks posed by armed conflict and climate change, is affecting poverty trends, inclusive growth, and the characteristics of the poor around the world. It seeks to identify ways in which the sudden shift in poverty reduction and the anticipated impact on shared prosperity might themselves be reversed.

COVID-19 and its associated economic crisis are already the most powerful driver of the reversal in global poverty. Current projections suggest that, in 2020, between 88 million and 115 million people could fall back into extreme poverty as a result of the pandemic—returning global poverty rates to 2017 levels—with even larger numbers (up to 150 million) in 2021. Though humanity has experienced major pandemics across the centuries, COVID-19 is unprecedented because it is being experienced globally and simultaneously, disrupting everything from daily work schedules and social activities to education and international trade. Thus far it has infected more than 33 million people across every country in the world and led to more than one million deaths, with many more expected to come. And, as the world is steadily realizing, it is the poorest people, in rich and poor countries alike, who are suffering most: from lost jobs, vulnerability to contagion because they live and work in high-risk settings, and lack of access to health care and social protection. In all countries, the poorest are most likely to endure the highest incidence of the disease and suffer the highest death rates.

Responding effectively to COVID-19, however, presents unique challenges across three domains: science, states, and society. Because it is so new, the science of the coronavirus remains only partially understood, with much still unknown about even its core characteristics. Hence, advice in the crucial early stages from medical experts and public health officials—on how governments, firms, and citizens should respond, individually and collectively—has evolved rapidly, even as trusting professional expertise has never been more important. Responding to rapidly evolving, and sometimes conflicting, messages requires that the public be able to trust in leaders and their advisors, given that halting the spread of COVID-19 requires all citizens to abide by onerous restrictions for extended periods, with the burden of these restrictions (staying home, social distancing) falling most heavily on the poor. States and societies vary considerably in the extent to which they can devise, implement, and sustain their commitment to such complex and contested tasks.

The wide variations in responses to COVID-19 around the world highlight key factors that are also central to more familiar development challenges. As with COVID-19, an inclusive and sustainable development process must accommodate knowledge of different kinds, some of it technical and well understood, but much of it nontechnical, idiosyncratic, inherently uncertain, and evolving—and all subject to constant public criticism and necessary debate. Responding effectively to complex development issues requires deep understanding of context-specific conditions because the political and implementation challenges related to them, if carefully addressed, can often make a decisive difference. Such challenges are always present, but COVID-19 amplifies the combined importance of skillful public leadership and robust delivery systems, as well as active citizen support, for finding and implementing solutions. Likewise, a credible development strategy requires that states be willing and able to plan, implement, and assess an array of complex tasks, at scale, under pressure. And they must do so to the benefit of all, not just a select few, including when governments' actions may require certain groups (for example, business owners) to comply with directives they might otherwise prefer to avoid (taxes, regulations). For such tasks to be accomplished, and because the poor are often a weak political constituency, an effective development process also needs to be informed by and accountable to broad cross-sections of society.

Conflict, especially violent conflict, is another factor driving the reversal in global poverty reduction. As previous World Bank reports have shown, more than 40 percent of the world's poor now live in conflict-affected countries, a number expected to rise further in the coming decade. The poorest people suffer most from violent conflict: it destroys their assets and livelihoods while discouraging further investment, and subjects them to a range of debilitating risks. Large-scale conflicts can have regional consequences, destabilizing otherwise peaceful places if key trade routes are blocked or destroyed, or if refugees arrive en masse. Along with the grief of losing friends and relatives to violence is the likely loss of crucial social support networks. The effects of these material, social, and psychological deprivations can endure long after episodes of violence have ended. For many survivors of long-term conflict, the last remaining option may be to migrate. But that, in turn, creates new forms of difficulty, as strangers in a strange land, whose mere presence may trigger hostility. Though violent conflict happens not only in low- but also in middle-income countries, it is still often the poorest citizens who suffer most.

Even in more peaceful circumstances, however, development itself promotes social change, which can contribute to conflict by destabilizing established ways of conducting everyday activities. Household life may become strained if children are educated but their parents and elders are not, or if gender norms and roles begin to shift; new methods of farming or land titling may render more traditional approaches and occupations obsolete; demands for more accountability and transparency in decision-making may challenge the interests of influential groups. More broadly, realizing the rule of law at the national level necessarily entails forging coherence from local rules systems that may be otherwise quite distinct, even contradictory. Credible and legitimate mechanisms for anticipating, mediating, and redressing conflict, at all levels and between countries, are thus central to the development process more generally. These mechanisms must be included in efforts to promote inclusive growth and poverty reduction.

Climate change is the third main driver of the reversal in global poverty reduction: its effects are already evident but will intensify in the years to come. Under baseline scenarios, the combined effects of climate change could push between 68 million and 132 million more people into poverty by 2030. A changing climate affects the availability of clean water and the salination of soil, and increases sea levels and average temperatures, all of which are steadily and inexorably making life more difficult for the poorest. With their livelihoods predominantly based on agriculture and fishing, the poorest are least able to adapt or move elsewhere—even though they have contributed least to this problem in the first place. The impacts of climate change can also raise food prices, worsen people's health, and increase exposure to disasters. Although the poor are not always the most exposed, they are certainly more vulnerable and less resilient to the impacts of climate change. The richest and most energy intensive countries have contributed the most to this problem, but they can assist the poorest countries by upholding sustained commitments to reducing their carbon emissions, investing in new energy technologies, and allowing higher levels of migration. But, as noted in the World Bank's *Shock Waves* report, even the boldest actions for reducing global poverty are most likely to help after, rather than before, the 2030 goal. In the short term, however, global cooperation to facilitate poor communities' more effective adaptation and resilience to the effects of climate change is both a moral imperative and a strategic necessity.

COVID-19 and its associated economic crisis, armed conflict, and climate change are three very different global challenges, each unfolding over different time trajectories and requiring distinct global responses and policy solutions. However, there is ample space for countries to find and deploy their own responses, from which others can learn. Moreover, the challenges that most poor people face most of the time are those they have always faced: insufficiently inclusive economic growth, including the employment and entrepreneurial opportunities associated with it; limited accumulation of productive assets (health, education, housing) to take advantage of growth; and heightened exposure and vulnerability to risks (illness, unemployment, disasters, and crime) that may erode or destroy these assets. These structural factors are often compounded by problems such as geographic isolation, social exclusion, injustice, discrimination, insecurity, and lack of rights and opportunity.

Even in the absence of pandemics, wars, and natural disasters, the poorest people endure severe challenges across the life cycle. Before they are born, their mothers are less likely to receive adequate nutrition and antenatal care; at birth, their very existence is often not officially registered; and as children and adults they are more likely to be missed in official censuses and surveys. If they are illiterate, have limited schooling, or speak a minority language, their community may struggle to complete basic administrative forms; to understand laws, policies, and safety recommendations; and to learn in government schools. Many poor people live in countries or communities with weak mechanisms of political accountability and implementation capacity. This makes them likely to suffer most from policies skewed to serve the interests of more influential groups (with few realistic avenues for complaint or redress) and to endure low-quality delivery of basic public services (education, health, water, sanitation, credit, transport). And, even if the poorest do manage to escape extreme poverty, their challenges continue: those living on slightly higher daily incomes routinely suffer many of the same indignities and deprivations and are at constant risk of falling back into deeper poverty. These factors combine to render the poorest people the hardest to reach, the most vulnerable to shocks, and the least likely to participate in their communities, the political process, and broader economic life. For all these reasons, reaching those still living in extreme poverty becomes more difficult even as their numbers shrink.

For now, however, the highest priority must be halting the spread of COVID-19 and responding effectively to the global economic crisis it has precipitated. The longer such responses are delayed, the more intense and consequential these effects will be, especially for the poorest and most vulnerable.

Poverty and Shared Prosperity 2020: Reversals of Fortune is presented in four chapters. The first three document trends in global poverty, shared prosperity, and the global profile of the poor. The fourth outlines some of the ways in which countries are responding to the COVID-19 crisis, and also explores broader implications emerging from research on implementing interventions to address complex development issues.

Chapter 1 reports that, consistent with the 2018 *Poverty and Shared Prosperity* report, global poverty reduction had recently slowed compared with previous decades, making it increasingly difficult to reach the global goal of reducing extreme poverty to 3 percent by 2030. The COVID-19 pandemic, however, now is expected to push about 100 million more people into extreme poverty during 2020. Other factors have also contributed to this reversal. In the Middle East and North Africa, for example, extreme poverty has risen in recent years as a result of sustained violent conflict. In Sub-Saharan Africa, some economies have made progress, but high rates of extreme poverty remain stubbornly persistent, with high levels of multidimensional poverty and considerable overlaps across the different dimensions, suggesting that nonmonetary deprivations are compounding monetary poverty.

Poverty reduction has also slowed when assessed at the US$3.20-a-day and US$5.50-a-day lines, but at rates lower in Sub-Saharan Africa and South Asia than at the extreme poverty line (US$1.90), implying that many people have barely escaped extreme poverty and are at risk of falling back. Encouragingly, the gains across most of East Asia and Pacific have been steady at all three poverty lines. When poverty is considered at the societal level—using a poverty line that rises as economies themselves become more prosperous—some 2 billion people remain in poverty, that is, living below the standards their own societies have set for a dignified life, although this was 15 million fewer people than in 2015. Ethiopia, Kenya, and Namibia stand out for impressive reductions in poverty rates between 2005 and 2015, yet rapid population growth counters these gains in Ethiopia and Kenya, resulting in higher absolute numbers of poor people. However, now all countries that have made hard-fought progress against poverty are seeing these improvements threatened by the COVID-19 crisis.

Chapter 2 explores trends in shared prosperity, defined as the annualized growth rate of mean household per capita income (or consumption) of the bottom 40 percent of the income distribution. The shared prosperity premium is the difference in growth rates between the bottom 40 and the overall mean. The chapter explores changes in these two dimensions in the recent past, as well as the expectation of less inclusive growth and growing inequality in the year ahead caused by the pandemic. Between 2012 and 2017, growth had been inclusive in most of the 91 countries the report measures: 74 had positive shared prosperity (associated with a decline in poverty), and 53 had positive shared prosperity premiums (associated with a decline in inequality). But the gains are uneven: both shared prosperity and shared prosperity premiums are lower on average in fragile and low-income economies, but higher in middle- and high-income economies. When these results are compared with measures for 68 economies from a previous period (2008–13), however, we find that the shared prosperity trend is mixed, with only half the economies having higher shared prosperity in the most recent round, though there are sustained gains in two developing regions—East Asia and Pacific and Europe and Central Asia—and in high-income economies. Data limitations mean that comprehensive projections about future trends are inherently uncertain, but in the coming year, based on conservative assumptions (for example, that inequality will remain the same), the global pandemic is likely to reduce shared prosperity in all but 13 of the 91 economies for which data are available.

Chapter 3 considers the key characteristics of the poor: who they are, where they live, and how they are affected by the global challenges of conflict and climate change. The latest survey data show that the poor remain overwhelmingly rural: 80 percent of individuals below the international poverty line reside in rural areas, even though the rural population accounts for less than half of the global population. In fact, poverty has become more rural over time—between 2015 and 2018, the share of rural poor in the total population of poor people increased by more than 2 percentage points. The poor are also disproportionately young: children account for half of the world's poor even though they are just a quarter of the total population. Among the poor age 15 and older, 35 percent have no schooling (compared with only 9 percent of the nonpoor); a further 35 percent have only some education. Globally, women are also overrepresented among the poor in almost every region. And, for a variety of reasons, significant segments of the poor remain uncounted in official surveys.

Today's major global challenges overlap, exposing many of the poor to multiple risks. About 132 million poor people live in areas with high flood risk, for example, and in a number of countries a large share of the poor lives in areas that are both affected by conflict and facing high exposure to floods. Globally, the association of poverty with fragility and conflict is increasing. As recent World Bank reports have shown, the 43 economies with the highest poverty rates are all either located in Sub-Saharan Africa or included in the World Bank's list of fragile and conflict-affected situations. In 2020, the 37 countries formally classified as affected by fragility, conflict, and violence are home to only about 10 percent of the world's population, yet they account for more than 40 percent of the global poor. The share of the global poor in fragile and conflict-affected countries is expected to rise by 2030, with Sub-Saharan Africa contributing a large share of the total. And with the pandemic, the newly poor are more likely to live in congested urban settings and to work in the sectors most affected by lockdowns and mobility restrictions; many are engaged in informal services and not reached by existing social safety nets.

Together, these three chapters describe how, after more than two decades of steady decline, extreme poverty is now likely to rise considerably. There has been a decisive reversal of fortune, the result of an urgent global threat (COVID-19 and the economic crisis it has spawned), destructive events building in recent years in many places (armed conflict), and slow-moving processes whose effects will only intensify in coming years (climate change). The report offers no simple answers to these major challenges currently confronting the world, because there are not any; the impacts of COVID-19 remain especially fluid and may intensify. The report can, however, identify ways in which COVID-19 is distinctive in the effects it is likely to have on poor people (for example, urban residents who work in the informal sector). It can also provide constructive examples of promising responses that are already underway (such as communities in rural India that have successfully faced down both COVID-19 and cyclones). And it can draw upon lessons from recent assessments of complex development interventions to offer broader recommendations.

Chapter 4 addresses these issues. For poor people to be able to improve their lives, stopping COVID-19 is not sufficient. Underlying long-term development challenges must also be addressed. Thus, reversing today's reversals of fortune requires a two-track approach: responding effectively to COVID-19 and conflict in the short term while continuing to focus on long-term development problems, including climate change. These are complementary rather than competing challenges, and the lessons emerging from each can fruitfully inform the other. These connections will be especially important in four areas.

First, the gap between policy aspiration and attainment must be closed. Beyond sound policies, effective action requires forging administrative systems that are capable of implementing them—at scale, under pressure, for all. Second, learning must be enhanced and data must be improved. Precisely because the current challenges are novel, everyone needs to learn quickly and intentionally how to respond effectively. Reliable, comprehensive, readily available data are needed to inform difficult decisions and monitor progress. Third, investments must be made in preparedness and prevention. If the current crisis has made one thing clear, it is that no country acting alone can adequately prepare for and manage, much less preempt, the type of emergency the world is now experiencing. Future preparedness and prevention efforts will be global and collaborative, or they will be illusory. And, fourth, cooperation and coordination must be expanded, not just to improve the empirical foundations of policy making but also to nurture social solidarity in affected countries and communities, to help ensure that governments' decisions can be trusted, and to share effective responses no matter where they originate.

This is a moment of historic importance. Unprecedented levels of global prosperity are threatened by three global forces that are intertwined, aggregating, and reinforcing one another: a pandemic (linked to an economic crisis), armed conflict, and climate change. The world can rise to the occasion—or succumb: neither outcome is foreordained. But, as many leaders across the world have demonstrated over the centuries, if the true measure of collective worth is the level of welfare experienced by the least privileged, then it behooves everyone, especially the beneficiaries of today's prosperity, to help forge a world that is equitable and peaceful as well as materially prosperous. Learning what needs to be done in response to COVID-19 is the first urgent step. Following close behind is the need to determine how it will be done, by whom, for whom, and at what cost, borne by whom. Here there are risks associated with long-standing human forces—a reluctance to work together even when the gains are clear, a propensity to be consumed by differences, and a desire to exploit power that may override the common good. However, history's finest moments show that these forces can be overcome. Now is our opportunity to come together and commit to ensuring that progress against poverty will resume.

Monitoring Global Poverty

Through 2017, the last year for which global data are available, extreme poverty reduction slowed compared with previous decades, continuing the trend reported in *Poverty and Shared Prosperity 2018: Piecing Together the Poverty Puzzle* (World Bank 2018). This deceleration alone would have made it hard to reach the 2030 target of 3 percent global poverty. Now, the COVID-19 (coronavirus) pandemic has reversed the gains in global poverty for the first time in a generation. This report estimates that this reversal of fortune is expected to push between 88 million and 115 million more people into extreme poverty in 2020. But COVID-19 is not the only reversal that threatens the poverty goals: confronting conflict and climate change will also be critical to putting poverty eradication back on track. Current estimates show that poverty rates are rising in the Middle East and North Africa, driven largely by economies affected by conflict. Moreover, recent estimates indicate that between 68 million and 132 million people could be pushed into poverty by 2030 because of the multiple impacts of climate change.

In 2018, the World Bank presented poverty lines at US$3.20 a day and US$5.50 a day to reflect national poverty lines in lower-middle-income and upper-middle-income countries, respectively, which underscore that poverty eradication is far from attained once the extreme poverty threshold of US$1.90 a day has been reached. In South Asia and Sub-Saharan Africa, poverty reduction against these lines has been slower than at the extreme poverty line, suggesting that many people have barely escaped extreme poverty. The societal poverty line (SPL), which increases with a country's level of income, leads to similar conclusions: 2 billion people are still poor by this definition.

Poverty reduction has been too slow in Sub-Saharan Africa for global poverty to reach the 2030 goal. Some economies in the region have made gains, but high poverty rates persist in too many. Sub-Saharan Africa faces high levels of multidimensional poverty with high overlaps across the different dimensions, suggesting that nonmonetary deprivations are compounding monetary poverty. Extreme poverty is predicted to become increasingly concentrated in the region.

Introduction

This report paints a sobering picture of the prospect of eliminating extreme poverty by 2030. The global poverty estimates show that poverty reduction continues to slow, confirming previous predictions that the world will not reach the goal of lowering global extreme poverty to 3 percent by 2030 unless swift, significant, and sustained action is taken. The predicted effects of the COVID-19 pandemic reinforce this unwelcome outlook. The still-evolving pandemic threatens to reverse the trend in global extreme poverty reduction for the first time in 20 years, putting millions at risk of extreme poverty and pushing the attainment of the 3 percent goal even further away.

This chapter reports new global poverty estimates for 2017.[1] An estimated 9.2 percent of the global population still lives below the international poverty line (IPL) of US$1.90 a day, which represents the typical poverty line of some of the poorest economies in the world. This percentage amounts to 689 million extreme poor, 52 million fewer than in 2015. Even though these numbers are already unacceptably high, the nowcasts of global poverty in 2020 and forecasts to 2030 raise additional concerns.[2] These estimates, largely based on Lakner et al. (2020) and Mahler et al. (2020), incorporate the effect of the COVID-19 pandemic on global poverty in both the short and long term. The results of the nowcasts show that between 88 million and 115 million people will be pushed into extreme poverty in 2020 because of the global contraction in growth caused by COVID-19. These numbers translate to a poverty rate of between 9.1 percent and 9.4 percent in 2020, offsetting past progress in poverty reduction by three years.[3] Turning to the long-term forecasts, the 2030 goal of 3 percent extreme poverty was difficult to reach under business-as-usual scenarios, as noted in the previous two editions of this report. The COVID-19 pandemic is expected to set back achievement of this goal even more unless unprecedented efforts are successful in promoting faster inclusive growth in the future.

COVID-19 is not the only driver of a reversal of fortune in progress on poverty. Regional trends in extreme poverty continue to show the enduring negative effect of conflict and fragility on poverty (Corral et al. 2020). Estimates of extreme poverty in the Middle East and North Africa show an increase between 2015 and 2018, largely driven by countries affected by conflict, although it is important to note that data gaps are particularly severe in these countries. The extreme poverty rate in Sub-Saharan Africa, although falling slightly between 2015 and 2018 (by less than 2 percentage points), remains as high as 40 percent. Because of rapid population growth, the number of Africans living below the IPL actually increased from 416 million in 2015 to 433 million in 2018.

Although this chapter focuses on tracking progress in reducing extreme poverty, as measured according to the IPL of US$1.90 per person per day, it also reports several additional poverty measures that broaden the understanding of poverty (see box 1.1 for an overview of the additional measures). The effects of the COVID-19 pandemic, as well as conflict, climate change, and the scant success in extreme poverty reduction in Sub-Saharan Africa, highlight the need for a continued focus on extreme poverty. At the same time, it is important to stress that poverty does not end when a person crosses the monetary threshold of US$1.90 a day.

Whereas extreme poverty is steadily concentrated in Sub-Saharan Africa, this geographic pattern is less pronounced when using the higher poverty lines of US$3.20 and US$5.50, which are typical of lower-middle- and upper-middle-income countries. More than 50 percent of the population in South Asia was living below the US$3.20 poverty line in 2014. In contrast, the success in reducing poverty in East Asia goes well beyond extreme poverty because 7.2 percent of the population in the region was living below the US$3.20 line and 25 percent was living below the US$5.50 poverty line in 2018. Almost 70 percent of Sub-Saharan Africa's population lives on less than US$3.20 per day; however, about half of the region's population lives in economies that are lower-middle income or richer, making the US$3.20 line a poverty measure that is also pertinent to Africa.

The SPL adapts to the income level of each country and is thus relevant even in high-income economies, where poverty rates at the absolute lines considered here are close to zero. Two billion people in the world are living in societal poverty—that is, they lack the resources necessary to lead a dignified life, taking into account that this threshold increases as countries become richer. The regional trends are similar to the other poverty measures: East Asia and Pacific shows the largest progress in reducing societal poverty, even as it is on the rise in the Middle East and North Africa and largely stagnating in Latin America and the Caribbean. Societal poverty also sheds light on the relationship between poverty, shared prosperity, and inequality, which is explored in greater detail in chapter 2.

BOX 1.1 Different Measures for Understanding Poverty

This box provides a brief overview of the additional poverty measures that were explained in depth in the previous edition of this report (World Bank 2018). Two of the measures were introduced at the recommendation of the Atkinson Commission on Global Poverty (World Bank 2017a).

Higher absolute poverty lines: US$3.20 and US$5.50 per person per day

The international poverty line (IPL) was constructed using the national poverty lines for some of the poorest economies in the world (Ferreira et al. 2016; Ravallion, Chen, and Sangraula 2009). When it was set up, 60 percent of the global population lived in low-income countries, making the IPL a meaningful measure for a large share of the world's population (World Bank 2018). As of 2017, only about 9 percent of the world's population lived in low-income countries, while 41 percent of people lived in lower-middle-income countries (LMICs) and 35 percent in upper-middle-income countries (UMICs). Based on this shift in the global distribution of income, the World Bank introduced two additional poverty lines to reflect poverty lines typically found in LMICs (US$3.20 a day) and UMICs (US$5.50 a day) (World Bank 2018). These additional poverty lines represent the median value of national poverty lines in LMICs and UMICs as of 2011 (Jolliffe and Prydz 2016). Similar to the IPL, these higher poverty lines remain fixed over time and across countries.

Societal poverty

Following the recommendations of the Atkinson Commission on Global Poverty (World Bank 2017a), the World Bank introduced the societal poverty measure, which is also a way to measure poverty as countries grow. Unlike the US$3.20-a-day and US$5.50-a-day poverty lines, which remain fixed over time, the societal poverty line (SPL) varies across countries and within countries over time. Formally, it is defined as $SPL = \max$ (US$1.90, US$1.00 $+ 0.5 \times$ median), where median is the daily median level of income or consumption per capita in the household survey. The SPL combines elements of absolute poverty with elements of relative poverty.[a] It incorporates a floor at the IPL to emphasize that the focus of the World Bank remains on extreme poverty and that the value of the SPL will never be lower than the IPL.[b] At the same time, the SPL rises with higher levels of the median (above the floor set at the IPL); that is, it is relative to median consumption across countries (Jolliffe and Prydz 2017) to capture the increasing basic needs that a person faces to conduct a dignified life as a country becomes richer. Although the SPL varies across countries and within countries over time, it still allows for meaningful global comparisons because it is defined the same way for all countries.

Multidimensional poverty measure

Also in response to the Atkinson Commission on Global Poverty (World Bank 2017a), the World Bank developed a multidimensional poverty measure (MPM) in 2018 (World Bank 2018). Six indicators (consumption or income, educational attainment, educational enrollment, drinking water, sanitation, and electricity) are selected and mapped into three dimensions of well-being (monetary standard of living, education, and basic infrastructure services) to construct the MPM. Annex 1D, table 1D.1, provides an overview of the dimensions that are included and their weight in the index, and it explains how the estimation of the index has been updated. See chapter 4 in the previous edition of this report (World Bank 2018) for a review of the relevant literature, data, and methodology for calculating the World Bank's MPM.

a. Measures of absolute poverty are based on a parameter that remains fixed over time, for example, the IPL and the US$3.20 and the US$5.50 poverty lines, and they help track poverty changes over time by keeping the benchmark fixed. Conversely, relative poverty measures change depending on the income level in a country, that is, they are relative to a measure of welfare that reflects changes in living conditions and are useful for tracking how the definition of poverty evolves as countries get richer. Useful references for understanding this difference include Atkinson and Bourguignon (2001); Foster (1998); Jolliffe and Prydz (2017); Ravallion and Chen (2011, 2019); World Bank (2017a).
b. The SPL is estimated as follows: First, the median level of daily per capita consumption (or income) for each national distribution is extracted from PovcalNet (PovcalNet [online analysis tool], World Bank, Washington, DC, http://iresearch.worldbank.org/PovcalNet/). Then each country-year observation is assigned a value of the SPL according to the equation given in the text. If this value exceeds US$1.90, the SPL is passed to PovcalNet to estimate the poverty rate associated with this line. The regional and global values represent population-weighted averages and use the same methodology applied to the IPL aggregate values (see annex 1A). For additional details on how the SPL is defined and how it compares with other measures of relative poverty, see Jolliffe and Prydz (2016, 2017) and chapter 3 in World Bank (2018). Additional seminal work in this field can be found in Atkinson and Bourguignon (2001) and Ravallion and Chen (2011, 2013, 2019).

The multidimensional poverty measure (MPM) shows that the high levels of extreme poverty in Sub-Saharan Africa are compounded by deprivations in nonmonetary dimensions such as access to schooling and basic infrastructure. For example, in Sub-Saharan Africa, almost 20 percent of the population lives in households where at least one school-age child is not in school. Compared with other regions, Sub-Saharan Africa also shows greater overlaps across the different dimensions of poverty: about 40 percent of the region's multidimensionally poor are deprived in all three dimensions (income, education, and access to infrastructure), compared with 11 percent in Latin America and the Caribbean and 22 percent in the Middle East and North Africa.

The data used in this chapter are mainly drawn from PovcalNet, the home of the World Bank's global poverty numbers.[4] The ability to monitor global poverty depends crucially on the availability of household survey data collected by national authorities.[5] The number of recent household surveys has improved somewhat since the first edition of this report (World Bank 2016). In particular, the number of surveys and population coverage have improved in Sub-Saharan Africa, with the improvement in population coverage driven largely by a new survey that recently became available for Nigeria.[6] At the same time, the lack of recent data for India severely hinders global poverty monitoring. Hence, 2017 is the last year for which global poverty estimates are reported, and the series for South Asia ends in 2014 (a range of estimates for 2017 is included in box 1.2), whereas data for all

BOX 1.2 Measuring Poverty in India without Recent Data

Citing concerns over the quality of the data, the government of India decided not to release the 2017/18 All-India Household Consumer Expenditure Survey data from the 75th round, conducted by the National Statistical Office. This decision leaves an important gap in understanding poverty in the country, South Asia, and the world in recent years. The latest comprehensive household consumption expenditure survey data available for estimating poverty for India date to 2011/12, the 68th round of the National Sample Survey.

The 2018 *Poverty and Shared Prosperity* report used the 2014/15 72nd round of the National Sample Survey, which includes some information on household characteristics and expenditures (but not the full consumption module used for poverty measurement) to impute a more comprehensive value of consumption (Newhouse and Vyas 2018; World Bank 2018). The results of this survey-to-survey imputation were used to derive the India estimate that underpins the

2015 global poverty count (see Chen et al. 2018, for details).

Given the relevance of India for global poverty measurement and the lack of more recent data, this box summarizes several methodologies that have been used to approximate a poverty estimate for India to be used in the 2017 global poverty count. All these estimates are subject to strong assumptions; therefore, considerable uncertainty remains over poverty in India in 2017, and this uncertainty can be resolved only if new survey data become available.

The first method is a pass-through exercise similar to the method adopted by the World Bank in its nowcasts and forecasts of global poverty (see below). A pass-through is a discount factor that accounts for the differences in growth rates in per capita household consumption expenditures in national accounts and the mean per capita household consumption expenditures recorded in surveys. Using all comparable consumption surveys available in PovcalNet,

a pass-through rate of 0.67 (with a 95 percent confidence interval of [0.59, 0.75]) is estimated that is to be applied to per capita household final consumption expenditure (HFCE) growth in national accounts.[a] This estimate is in line with many of the pass-through rates available in the literature on this issue (Sen 2000; Datt, Kozel, and Ravallion 2003; Deaton and Kozel 2005; Lakner et al. 2020).

Applying this pass-through estimate to per capita HFCE growth in India as reported in the World Development Indicators using official sources results in a national poverty rate estimate of 10.4 percent in 2017 for the US$1.90 poverty line, which translates into 139 million people living in extreme poverty.[b] This number underpins the global poverty estimate (9.2 percent) for 2017 and the nowcast and forecast exercises shown in the rest of this chapter.

The second approach uses survey-to-survey imputation techniques, similar to the approach used in the 2018 *Poverty and*

(continued)

BOX 1.2 **Measuring Poverty in India without Recent Data** *(continued)*

Shared Prosperity report, to impute consumption into the 2017/18 Social Consumption Survey for Health (National Sample Survey, 75th round). This approach results in a lower national poverty estimate of 9.9 percent in 2017, with a 95 percent confidence interval of between 8.1 and 11.3.

The India and South Asia estimates are reported for the widest range of estimates derived from these methods. For India, the values range between 8.1 percent and 11.3 percent nationally, that is, between 109 million and 152 million people.[c] This value would translate to between 7.7 percent and 10.0 percent poor in South Asia, that is, between 137 million and 180 million people.

Neither approach is without limitations. The pass-through approach assumes that the national accounts estimates of HFCE growth are accurate and that growth is distribution-neutral. Both these assumptions have been the subject of recent debate in India.[d] The survey-to-survey method takes advantage of the variation in the survey data to capture changes in the distribution of welfare. However, if the imputation is done between periods too far apart, it may fail to capture important changes in the behavior of markets. Important structural changes in the Indian economy between 2011 and 2017 may not be captured by these imputation techniques. Thus, the range of poverty estimates could be

even wider than those presented in this report.

The limitations of the methods described add to concerns about the lack of access to survey data to measure standards of living in India. Several economists and policy experts have used public news and media outlets to cite figures from different sources of data leading to opposite views about the direction of poverty rates in India in recent years.[e] The lack of data creates doubts among the general public, obstructs scientific debate, and hinders the implementation of sound, empirically based development policies. There is no alternative to timely, quality-assured, and transparent data for the design and monitoring of antipoverty policies.

a. Further details can be found in Edochie et al. (forthcoming). Because pass-through rates are found to vary systematically between consumption and income surveys (Lakner et al. 2020), only consumption surveys are included in this sample (which is the welfare aggregate used in India). For all regions except Sub-Saharan Africa, HFCE is the national accounts aggregate used by PovcalNet to line up surveys to the reference year (Prydz et al. 2019). To isolate real changes in consumption from one survey to the next, it is important to focus on comparable surveys using the comparability metadata described in Atamanov et al. (2019).
b. See World Development Indicators (database), World Bank, Washington, DC, http://data.worldbank.org/products/wdi.
c. The 95 percent confidence interval for the pass-through estimates gives a range of 10.0 percent to 10.8 percent for the national poverty rate, which is nested within this range.
d. Academics have argued that India's growth in gross domestic product from official sources may be overstated (A. Subramanian 2019), but these findings are disputed (Goyal and Kumar 2019). Regarding changes in inequality, Chanda and Cook (2019) and Chodorow-Reich et al. (2020) find a negative short-term impact of the demonetization introduced in November 2016 among the poorest groups, which dissipates after several months. Lahiri (2020), meanwhile, reports a decline in unemployment shortly after demonetization, which may hide an important decline in labor force participation that the author also indicates is reported by Vyas (2018). Ongoing work with survey data from the Center for Monitoring Indian Economy, which produces a consumption aggregate that is comprehensive (although not fully comparable to the National Sample Survey) shows an increase in real average consumption between 2015 and 2017, but with a drop-off among the bottom quintile of the distribution.
e. For instance, economists S. Subramanian (2019) and Himanshu (2019) argue that poverty rates went up significantly. However, Bhalla and Bhasin (2020) posit that poverty in 2017/18 declined significantly with respect to 2011/12.

other regions extend to 2018. It is important to reiterate that the absence of recent data on India, one of the economies with the largest population of extreme poor, creates substantial uncertainty around current estimates of global poverty.[7] Similarly, lack of data for economies in fragile and conflict-affected situations (FCS) poses an important limitation on the measurement of poverty in those economies, which appears to be somewhat underestimated by existing methods (Corral et al. 2020).[8] This underestimation particularly affects Sub-Saharan Africa and the

Middle East and North Africa, regions where one in five persons lives in proximity to conflict (Corral et al. 2020) and that have seen extreme poverty decreasing slowly or rising.

Monitoring global poverty: Tracking progress toward the 2030 goals

The past 25 years have seen remarkable progress toward ending extreme

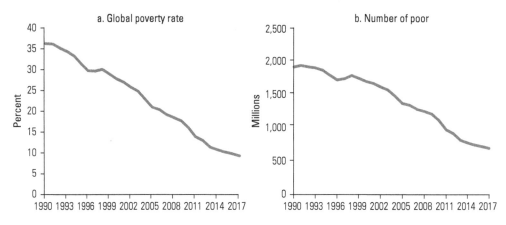

FIGURE 1.1 Global Poverty Rate and Number of Poor at the US$1.90-a-Day Poverty Line, 1990–2017

Source: PovcalNet (online analysis tool), World Bank, Washington, DC, http://iresearch.worldbank.org/PovcalNet/.
Note: The global coverage rule is applied (see annex 1A).

FIGURE 1.2 Number of Poor at the US$1.90-a-Day Poverty Line, by Region, 1990–2017

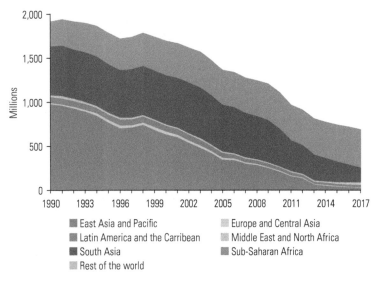

Source: PovcalNet (online analysis tool), World Bank, Washington, DC, http://iresearch.worldbank.org/PovcalNet/.
Note: The height of each area gives the global number of poor in each year, which can be found in table 1A.2. The figure reported for South Asia uses the India estimate that is included in the global headcount (see box 1.2).

poverty. The number of people living below the IPL decreased from 1.9 billion in 1990 to 741 million in 2015. This decreasing trend is confirmed by the data for 2017. Poverty has fallen further, to 689 million (figure 1.1, panel b)—52 million less than in 2015 and 28 million less than in 2016 (see annex 1A,

table 1A.2). Yet the number of people living in extreme poverty remains unacceptably high, and there are several reasons to believe that the target of reducing the share of people living in extreme poverty to below 3 percent by 2030 will not be achieved.

The slowdown in poverty reduction observed in 2015 by the previous *Poverty and Shared Prosperity* report (World Bank 2018) is confirmed in the new poverty figures presented here (figure 1.1, panel a). Between 1990 and 2015, the global rate of extreme poverty fell by about 1 percentage point per year. However, toward the end of that period, the rate of poverty reduction slowed. For example, between 2013 and 2015, the poverty rate fell by about 0.6 percentage point per year. Continuing this trend, the global poverty rate fell by less than a half percentage point per year between 2015 and 2017, with 9.2 percent of the global population still living below the IPL in 2017.

One reason for this deceleration is Sub-Saharan Africa's slower pace of poverty reduction compared with other regions, in line with the forecast that extreme poverty will be a predominantly African phenomenon in the coming decade (Beegle and Christiaensen 2019; World Bank 2018) (also see later in this chapter). Figure 1.2 shows the number of extreme poor in each region in 1990–2017 (see also annex 1A, table 1A.2).[9] Although the number of poor has fallen in many regions, most notably East Asia and Pacific and, more recently, South Asia, there has been no reduction in Sub-Saharan Africa. In fact, the number of people living in extreme poverty in Sub-Saharan Africa rose from 284 million in 1990 to 431 million in 2017. The Middle East and North Africa has also seen an increase in the number of poor in recent years, driven largely by the economies in the region that are affected by conflict.

During this time, the poverty rate has continued to fall in Sub-Saharan Africa, but not fast enough to keep up with rapid population growth in the region (Beegle and Christiaensen 2019). Figure 1.3 shows the trends in the extreme poverty rate by region. The poverty rate in Sub-Saharan Africa declined, but only slightly, from 41.7 percent to 40.2 percent, between 2015 and 2018 (for details, see annex 1A, table 1A.2, panel c). The extreme poverty rate remains greater than 40 percent in the region, with some economies showing poverty rates exceeding 60 percent. Given Sub-Saharan Africa's poor performance in reducing extreme poverty in recent years and its crucial role in reaching the 2030 goal of ending extreme poverty, the final section of this chapter provides a more detailed analysis of the region.

The recent estimates for South Asia are subject to additional uncertainty given the absence of recent data for India, which is why the time series ends in 2014. Using various methods to estimate poverty for India in 2017 results in a range for the regional extreme poverty headcount ratio of between 7.7 percent and 10.0 percent. Box 1.2 provides a summary of the methodologies used to address the lack of recent data on India for the global monetary poverty measures.

The Middle East and North Africa region showed an increase in the extreme poverty rate between 2015 and 2018. The rate rose from 2.3 percent in 2013 to 3.8 percent in 2015 and almost doubled to 7.2 percent in 2018. The conflicts in the Syrian Arab Republic and the Republic of Yemen are among the leading explanations for this increase (Corral et al. 2020).[10] Comparing this trend with trends in other regions, the 2018 estimate indicates that the levels of extreme poverty are higher in the Middle East and North Africa than in Latin America and the Caribbean for the first

FIGURE 1.3 Trends in Poverty Rates at the US$1.90-a-Day Poverty Line, by Region, 1990–2018

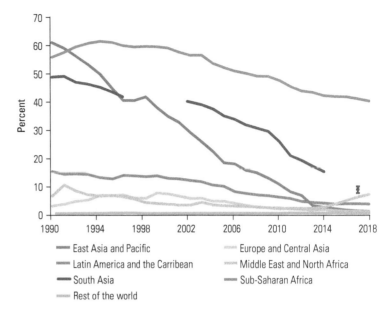

Source: PovcalNet (online analysis tool), World Bank, Washington, DC, http://iresearch.worldbank.org /PovcalNet/.
Note: Lined-up poverty estimates for South Asia are not reported for 1997–2001 and after 2014 because of a lack of population coverage (see box 1.2 on India and annex 1A). For South Asia in 2017, a range [7.7; 10.0] is reported, as described in box 1.2.

time, although the levels are difficult to compare because of the use of different welfare aggregates in the two regions.[11]

Latin America and the Caribbean has seen stagnation in the extreme poverty rate, at about 4 percent, for the sixth straight year. This slowdown in poverty reduction is even clearer if compared with the progress in East Asia and Pacific, where extreme poverty continues to decline. Europe and Central Asia offers a more consistent comparison, given that it has also largely used income surveys in recent years; in contrast to the stagnation in Latin America and the Caribbean, Europe and Central Asia has seen a continued decline in extreme poverty.

Nowcasting global poverty to 2020 and 2021: The impact of COVID-19

Global extreme poverty numbers are reported only through 2017, which is the latest year with sufficient global population coverage of household survey data. The complexity of household surveys results in an inevitable time lag between when national statistics offices collect their data and when results are released. Using information on national accounts growth rates after 2017, it is possible to predict, or *nowcast*, poverty for 2020. However, such an exercise involves additional assumptions about the relationship between national accounts growth and growth in the survey welfare aggregate (measured either as consumption or income). In particular, it is assumed that (1) only 85 percent of national accounts growth is passed through to the survey welfare aggregate, and that (2) growth is distribution neutral, such that all households grow at the same rate (which equals 0.85 times national accounts growth).[12] This method is similar to the approach PovcalNet uses to line up surveys to a common reference year (Prydz et al. 2019; World Bank 2015a).[13]

Nowcasting global poverty to 2020 provides an estimate of the effect of the COVID-19 pandemic on global poverty. The magnitude of this effect is still highly uncertain, but it is clear that the pandemic will lead to the first increase in global poverty since the 1998 Asian financial crisis, when global poverty increased by 0.4 percentage point and 47 million people were pushed into extreme poverty relative to the previous year (see figure 1A.2 for a long-term perspective on global poverty from 1990 to 2030). However, the increase in poverty attributable to COVID-19 is estimated to be considerably larger, between 1.1 and 1.5 percentage points relative to a pre-COVID-19 scenario.[14] Given that current poverty rates are lower than in 1997, the increase in the poverty rate is larger not only in absolute terms but also in relative terms. Figure 1.4 shows the nowcast of global poverty to 2020 and 2021, updating earlier work by Mahler et al. (2020), based on Lakner et al. (2020).[15] To understand the effect of the current crisis on global poverty, this exercise is carried out using three different growth scenarios, while assuming that inequality remains unchanged.[16] The first scenario estimates the nowcast in 2020 and 2021 using gross domestic product (GDP) growth data from the January 2020 edition of the *Global Economic Prospects* (GEP) report (World Bank 2020a), which predates the COVID-19 pandemic. These numbers confirm a continuing slowdown in poverty reduction, yielding an estimated global extreme poverty rate of 7.9 percent in 2020 and 7.5 percent in 2021 (figure 1.4, panel a), corresponding to 615 million and 586 million poor (figure 1.4, panel b).

The second and third scenarios use more recent growth data from the June

FIGURE 1.4 Nowcasts of the Global Poverty Rate and Number of Poor at the US$1.90-a-Day Poverty Line, 2015–21

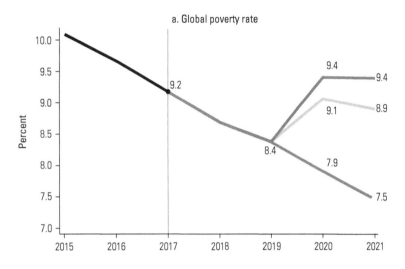

a. Global poverty rate

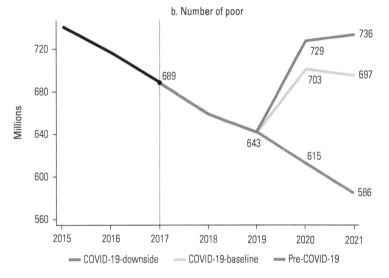

b. Number of poor

— COVID-19-downside   ⋯⋯ COVID-19-baseline   — Pre-COVID-19

Sources: Updated estimates of Mahler et al. 2020, based on Lakner et al. 2020; PovcalNet (online analysis tool), World Bank, Washington, DC, http://iresearch.worldbank.org/PovcalNet/; World Bank 2020a, 2020b.
Note: Three growth scenarios are considered: First, pre-COVID-19 uses the January 2020 *Global Economic Prospects* (GEP) growth forecasts for 2020 and 2021, predating the COVID-19 crisis, and the June 2020 forecasts for 2019. Second and third, COVID-19-downside and COVID-19-baseline use the June 2020 GEP growth forecasts projecting a contraction in global growth in 2020 of 8 percent and 5 percent, respectively. Mahler et al. (2020) use the January 2020 GEP growth forecasts (World Bank 2020a) for the pre-COVID-19 scenario in 2019. They thus find a difference in projected poverty rates under the pre-COVID-19 and COVID-19 scenarios in 2019. To calculate the number of additional poor attributable to COVID-19 in 2020, they use a difference-in-differences methodology. Here, it is sufficient to use the raw difference between the pre-COVID-19 and COVID-19 scenarios for 2020.

FIGURE 1.5 Additional Poor at the US$1.90-a-Day Poverty Line in 2020, per the COVID-19-Baseline, and COVID-19-Downside Scenarios

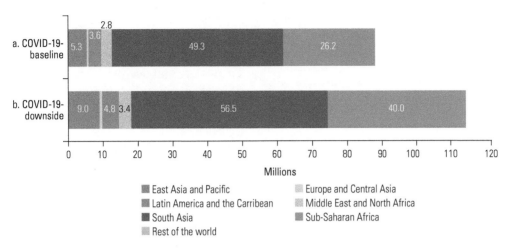

Sources: Updated estimates of Mahler et al. 2020, based on Lakner et al. 2020; PovcalNet (online analysis tool), World Bank, Washington, DC, http://iresearch.worldbank.org/PovcalNet/; World Bank 2020a, 2020b.

2020 edition of the GEP report (World Bank 2020b), which incorporates the effect of COVID-19 on growth. These forecasts indicate that the COVID-19 pandemic will cause a contraction in global per capita GDP growth of between 5 percent and 8 percent in 2020.[17] These scenarios are considered separately in the calculations and translate into a global poverty rate of between 9.1 percent and 9.4 percent in 2020, setting back the clock as much as three years to a level similar to that estimated for 2017.

Using the counterfactual scenario, it is also possible to estimate the additional number of people pushed into extreme poverty by the pandemic in 2020. By comparing the poverty nowcasts using the pre-COVID-19 growth rates with those using the post-COVID-19 growth rates, it is estimated that 88 million people will be pushed into poverty under the baseline scenario and as many as 115 million people under the downside scenario.[18]

These estimates suggest that South Asia will be the region hardest hit, with 49 million additional people (almost 57 million under the downside scenario) pushed into extreme poverty (figure 1.5).[19] Sub-Saharan Africa would be the next most affected region, with between 26 million and 40 million additional people predicted to be pushed into extreme poverty.

At the US$3.20-a-day poverty line discussed below in this chapter, between 175 million and 223 million people are estimated to be pushed into poverty, primarily in South Asia.

The projections in figure 1.4 assume that inequality remains unchanged. At the same time, several authors have argued that COVID-19 will have a disproportionately negative effect on the poor, exacerbating pre-existing inequalities as well as creating new ones (see above). However, in the absence of data on the distributional impacts of the pandemic for a large set of countries, predicting what the effect on inequality will be is difficult.[20] Keeping this uncertainty in mind, Lakner et al. (2020) assess the effect of changes in inequality by modeling scenarios that assume a change in the Gini index of 1 percent and 2 percent per year between 2019 and 2030.

If COVID-19 also increases inequality, in 2020 global poverty under the COVID-19-baseline and COVID-19-downside scenarios would range between 9.2 percent and 9.6 percent (if the Gini index increases by 1 percent in all countries) or between 9.5 percent and 9.8 percent (if the Gini index increases by 2 percent in all countries). Compared with the distribution-neutral scenario, which projects between 703 million and 729 million people living in extreme poverty in 2020 as reported in figure 1.4, panel b, an increase in inequality could see between 717 million and 746 million (if the Gini index increases by 1 percent) or between 734 million and 762 million (if the Gini index increases by 2 percent) people living in extreme poverty in 2020. Figure 1A.3 shows

FIGURE 1.6 **Projection of Global Poverty at the US$1.90-a-Day Poverty Line, to 2030**

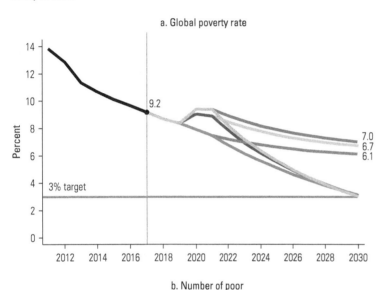

a. Global poverty rate

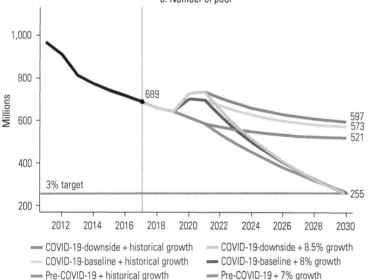

b. Number of poor

— COVID-19-downside + historical growth ···· COVID-19-downside + 8.5% growth
···· COVID-19-baseline + historical growth — COVID-19-baseline + 8% growth
— Pre-COVID-19 + historical growth — Pre-COVID-19 + 7% growth

Sources: Updated estimates of Lakner et al. 2020; PovcalNet (online analysis tool), World Bank, Washington, DC, http://iresearch.worldbank.org/PovcalNet/; World Bank 2020a, 2020b.
Note: All six scenarios use assumptions identical to those used in figure 1.4 until 2021. For 2021–30, scenarios with historical growth use the annualized growth rate for each country between 2008 and 2018. Another set of growth scenarios is chosen such that all economies grow at the same rate between 2021 and 2030, and such that the 2030 target of 3 percent extreme poverty is reached: these growth rates are estimated to be 7 percent for pre-COVID-19, 8 percent for COVID-19-baseline, and 8.5 percent for the COVID-19-downside.

the results of relaxing the distribution-neutral assumption adopted so far and updates the Lakner et al. (2020) estimates to the latest PovcalNet data used in this chapter.

Simulations to 2030: Checking on progress toward ending global poverty by 2030

The simulations of global poverty to 2030 use scenarios similar to those for the nowcasts but also make additional assumptions about national accounts and population growth in the longer term.[21] Any such projection over a long time horizon is subject to considerable uncertainty, compounded now by the lack of recent data on India (see box 1.2) and by the evolving effects of the COVID-19 pandemic on poverty. Until 2021, the growth scenarios are identical to those shown in figure 1.4. After 2021, the growth rate is estimated using the average annual growth for each country in the period between 2008 and 2018 (following Lakner et al. [2020] and similar to World Bank [2018]). These growth rates are then used to project forward the household survey mean until 2030. Another set of growth scenarios is chosen in which all countries grow at the same rate between 2021 and 2030, such that the 2030 target of 3 percent extreme poverty is reached. For example, under the 7 percent scenario, each country grows at 7 percent annually beginning from its position in 2021 under the pre-COVID-19 scenario. The 8 percent and 8.5 percent scenarios start from each country's position in 2021 under the COVID-19-baseline and COVID-19-downside growth rates, respectively.

Figure 1.6 shows that, even using growth rates from before the COVID-19 pandemic, the 3 percent target would not be achieved by 2030. The estimate for global poverty in 2030 would be 6.1 percent (corresponding to 521 million poor). The previous two editions of this report (World Bank 2016, 2018) similarly argue that reaching the 3 percent target requires more than business as usual (also see Ravallion 2020). Reaching the 3 percent target in a scenario without COVID-19 conditions would have required all countries to grow at 7 percent, which for the Sub-Saharan African countries is more than a quadrupling of the growth rates observed between 2008 and 2018.[22]

The remaining scenarios consider the impact of the COVID-19 pandemic. Under the COVID-19-baseline scenario, 6.7 percent of the global population will be living under the IPL by 2030. Using the COVID-19-downside scenario results in an extreme poverty headcount ratio of 7 percent in 2030. Reaching the 2030 target under the two COVID-19 scenarios would require all countries to grow at rates of 8 percent (baseline) or 8.5 percent (downside) per year between 2021 and 2030, which would be equivalent to more than quintuple the historical growth rates in Sub-Saharan Africa.

COVID-19 not only sets back poverty by three years but also implies, as simulated here, about a billion additional person-years spent in extreme poverty over the next decade. The distribution-neutral nowcasts show that between 88 million and 115 million additional people will be pushed into poverty in 2020. For the entire decade 2020 to 2030, the additional new poor due to COVID-19 will range between 831 million (under the baseline scenario) and 1.16 billion (under the downside scenario).[23]

Figure 1A.3, in annex 1A, shows the range of global poverty estimates by relaxing the distribution-neutral assumption. Under the COVID-19-baseline scenario, global poverty in 2030 would rise to 8.2 percent (11.3 percent) if the Gini index rises by 1 percent (2 percent) per year in every country, compared with 6.7 percent in the absence of distributional changes. In contrast, if inequality were to decline, global poverty in 2030 could be as low as 5.6 percent (1 percent decline in the Gini index) or 4.7 percent (2 percent decline in the Gini index). Under the COVID-19-downside scenario, global poverty would rise to between 8.6 percent (with a 1 percent rise in the Gini index) and 11.8 percent (with a 2 percent rise in the Gini index), corresponding to between 732 million (with a 1 percent rise in the Gini index) and 1 billion (with a 2 percent rise in the Gini index) people living in extreme poverty globally. On a more positive note, a decline in the Gini index by 1 percent per year in every country would be one way to offset the increase in poverty as a result of COVID-19.[24] These results illustrate that changes in inequality matter for our ability to end global poverty (see also box 2.3 in chapter 2; Bergstrom 2020; Lakner et al. 2020).

Although the COVID-19 pandemic will have a decisive impact on poverty reduction in the coming decade, other global challenges also hinder the world's progress toward poverty eradication. This report, specifically chapter 3, focuses on two of these challenges—conflict and climate change. Although conflict is already affecting extreme poverty in the Middle East and North Africa and in Sub-Saharan Africa, climate change poses a global threat that is likely to further affect the projections discussed so far. Box 1.3 presents estimates aimed at measuring the impact of climate change on extreme poverty in the next decade.

BOX 1.3 How Is Climate Change Affecting Poverty? Nowcasts and Forecasts

Climate change disproportionately affects the poor, who have fewer resources to mitigate negative impacts and less capacity for adaptation. Quantifying climate-related impacts on poorer households is important for guiding policy and interventions. Jafino, Hallegatte, and Walsh (forthcoming) model the effects of climate conditions on socioeconomic outcomes, applying the method developed for the 2016 World Bank report *Shock Waves: Managing the Impacts of Climate Change on Poverty* (Hallegatte et al. 2016; see also Hallegatte and Rozenberg 2017) to the most recent household surveys.

For each country included in the analysis, the model incorporated information on household size and demographics, urbanization, labor force participation, and household income or consumption. The model is used to create baseline scenarios for the future distribution of household income and poverty for each country in 2030, in the absence of climate change, by combining various assumptions about the socioeconomic and technological drivers of

(continued)

poverty, such as changes in labor productivity in various sectors, structural change in the economy, or improvements in education levels. Among hundreds of scenarios, the analysis selected one set of optimistic baseline scenarios (with inclusive economic growth, low inequality, universal access to basic infrastructure, and steady progress toward achieving the Sustainable Development Goals) and one set of pessimistic baseline scenarios with slower and unequal growth. Then the model is used to assess the expected change in extreme poverty due to climate change via five channels in those baselines: agricultural productivity and prices, food prices, natural disasters, the effect of extreme temperature on outdoor workers' productivity, and health issues, including malaria, diarrhea, and stunting.

The results of this exercise are presented in Jafino, Hallegatte, and Walsh (forthcoming) and can be summarized as follows: The analysis was performed for 86 economies covering 64 percent of the total poor population. In most baseline scenarios and most regions, the largest impact of climate change on extreme poverty comes through higher food prices. In the pessimistic baseline, on average 39 million additional people will be pushed into poverty because of these higher

food prices. To provide a global estimate, the number is scaled up to account for the missing population, resulting in 61 million additional poor people globally. Significant additional impacts arise from worsening health conditions (on average, 43 million additional poor) and natural disasters (more than 25 million additional poor). The effects also vary by region. Food prices play the largest role in pushing people into extreme poverty in Sub-Saharan Africa and South Asia (with an average of 36 million and 18 million additional poor, respectively), whereas health dominates in Latin America and the Caribbean and East Asia and Pacific (5 million and 6 million additional poor, respectively).

If all five climate impact channels are considered simultaneously, 132 million people on average will be pushed into poverty in the pessimistic baseline scenarios; the figure is 68 million on average in the optimistic baseline scenarios. These estimates are consistent, but slightly higher, than the assessment in the *Shock Waves* report (Hallegatte et al. 2016).[a]

These results show the importance of the baseline scenarios for assessing the impacts of climate change and highlight the interdependence of achieving different Sustainable Development Goals. Ensuring that all people

have decent jobs and income, food security, and access to clean water and appropriate health care is an efficient way to reduce climate change vulnerability. At the same time, the impacts of climate change are large enough to make adaptation and risk management a powerful contributor to poverty eradication. In other words, good development (Hallegatte et al. 2016) and poverty reduction help reduce climate change impacts, and reducing climate change impacts contributes to development and poverty reduction.

This analysis shows how good development can contribute to reducing future climate change impacts. However, it considers impacts only to 2030, a short time horizon for climate change impacts. It should be kept in mind that the impacts of climate change on poverty will only be emerging by that date, and the effect will likely be much larger in the longer term. Preventing a continued increase in the impacts of climate change would require stabilizing global temperatures, which in turn requires that global net greenhouse gas emissions be reduced to zero before the end of the twenty-first century (Hallegatte et al. 2016).

a. Because of the different methodologies and data used in the analysis presented in this chapter, the effect of climate change on poverty is considered separately. Specifically, the estimated additional people living in poverty because of climate change should not be read as cumulative to those estimated in the projections discussed elsewhere in the chapter. The climate impact scenarios refer to a separate exercise consisting in measuring the distribution of hundreds of counterfactual exercises between scenarios with climate change (including effects on food prices, productivity, natural disasters, and increased diseases) and a baseline scenario without climate change. The numbers of 68 million and 132 million additional poor refer to the average value of multiple simulation results grouped into optimistic (that is, low poverty) and pessimistic (that is, high poverty) scenarios within cases of high climate change impact. For low climate change impact, the average changes range from 32 million to 42 million people entering poverty compared with the baseline scenario without climate change. Reducing the impact of climate change has clear poverty-reduction effects according to these simulations. Further discussion of methods is available in chapter 1 of Hallegatte et al. (2016) and updated in Jafino, Hallegatte, and Walsh (forthcoming). It can plausibly be argued that many of those pushed into poverty because of COVID-19 will also be those with fewer resources to endure climate change. Many of the poor are exposed to multiple risks, and empirical challenges do not permit accounting simultaneously for all the different factors that affect poverty. Chapter 3 of this report discusses the overlapping of multiple risks and poverty in more detail.

Beyond extreme poverty: The US$3.20-a-day and US$5.50-a-day poverty lines

The World Bank's priority remains eradicating extreme poverty as measured by the IPL. However, achieving the vital goal of lifting all people above the US$1.90 threshold will not end poverty in the world. Poverty evolves as countries grow and develop. Figure 1.7 shows global poverty rates (panel a) and the number of poor (panel b) at the US$1.90, US$3.20, and US$5.50 poverty lines (see box 1.1 for further details on the definition of these lines; also see Jolliffe and Prydz 2016 and World Bank 2018).[25]

About a quarter of the global population is living below the US$3.20 poverty line, and almost half is living below the US$5.50 line, compared with less than a 10th living below US$1.90. These figures translate to 1.8 billion people and 3.3 billion people at the US$3.20 and US$5.50 poverty lines, respectively. The number of people living below US$3.20 today is as high as the number of people in extreme poverty in 1990, the starting point of this analysis, which is perhaps one way to illustrate the scale of the challenge that remains at these higher lines. The number of people living below US$5.50 per person per day has barely declined over the past 25 years.

FIGURE 1.7 Global Poverty Rate and Number of Poor, US$3.20-a-Day and US$5.50-a-Day Poverty Lines, 1990–2017

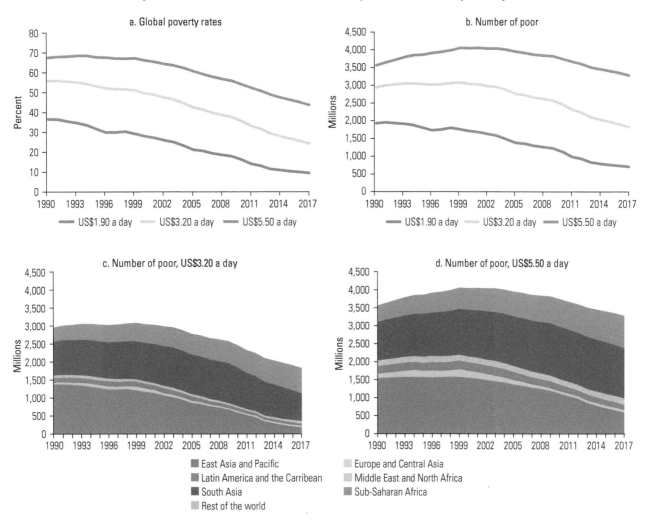

Source: PovcalNet (online analysis tool), World Bank, Washington, DC, http://iresearch.worldbank.org/PovcalNet/.
Note: Panel c shows the geographic distribution of the number of poor at the US$3.20 line and panel d shows the geographic distribution of the number of poor at the US$5.50 line. The figures reported for South Asia use the India estimate included in the global headcount (see box 1.2). The global number for 2017 uses the global coverage rule.

The COVID-19 pandemic and the risks associated with climate change and conflict expose the vulnerability of many millions of individuals who have escaped extreme poverty but can easily fall back.

There is some evidence of a slowdown in poverty reduction at the higher lines, but it is somewhat less dramatic than for the extreme poverty rate. The poverty rate at both these higher lines declined by about 2.5 percentage points between 2015 and 2017, similar to the decrease between 2013 and 2015. However, the poverty rate had fallen by 3.9 percentage points and 3.5 percentage points, respectively, between 2011 and 2013, pointing to stagnation in poverty reduction in the most recent years.

Panels c and d of figure 1.7 show the regional distribution of the global number of poor at these higher lines between 1990 and 2017 (see also tables 1B.1 and 1B.2). Unlike the number of extreme poor, the highest numbers of poor at both the US$3.20 and US$5.50 poverty lines live in South Asia rather than Sub-Saharan Africa. Although extreme poverty is becoming more highly concentrated in Sub-Saharan Africa, this concentration is much less pronounced beyond the US$1.90 threshold.

The regional trends in poverty rates also show important differences when compared with the extreme poverty estimates (figure 1.8). In South Asia, for example, the decrease in poverty has been slower at these higher lines than for extreme poverty. More than half of the region's people lived below the US$3.20 poverty line in 2014, and 96 percent of them lived in lower-middle-income countries, making the US$3.20 poverty line a relevant poverty measure for the region. Thus, millions of individuals still live in poverty in South Asia, notwithstanding the remarkable success in lifting them out of extreme poverty. In contrast, in the East Asia and Pacific region, progress in poverty reduction goes well beyond extreme poverty and all the way up to the US$5.50 poverty line, although at a slower pace at the higher lines.

For many other regions, the results at the higher poverty lines are similar to those for extreme poverty (figure 1.3). The poverty rate is increasing in the Middle East and North Africa at both the US$3.20 and US$5.50 poverty lines. The stagnation in poverty rates in Latin America and the Caribbean is confirmed at these higher lines, with about a quarter of the population living on less than US$5.50 a day (equivalent to 144 million people). Almost 90 percent of the region's population lives in upper-middle-income countries, suggesting that this is a relevant poverty line.

The highest poverty rates are once again in Sub-Saharan Africa. Figure 1.9 shows that almost 70 percent of the region's population is living below the US$3.20

FIGURE 1.8 Poverty Rates at the US$3.20-a-Day and US$5.50-a-Day Poverty Lines, by Region, 1990–2018

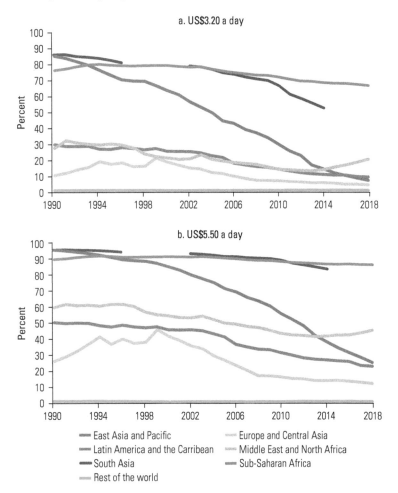

Source: PovcalNet (online analysis tool), World Bank, Washington, DC, http://iresearch.worldbank.org /PovcalNet/.
Note: Additional information on yearly lined-up estimates can be found in tables 1B.1 and 1B.2 in annex 1B. South Asia estimates are not reported for the period 1997–2001 and stop in 2014 because of a lack of population coverage.

poverty line and almost 90 percent is living under the US$5.50 poverty line. As in the case of extreme poverty, given the high rate of population growth in the region, the number of poor has increased over time. Notwithstanding the high concentration of extreme poverty in Sub-Saharan Africa, it should not be assumed that these higher lines are not meaningful measures of poverty in the region. About half of the population lives in countries that are at least lower-middle income, for which the US$3.20 poverty line would be typical.

A relative poverty measure: The societal poverty line

So far, this chapter has reported measures of absolute poverty. One of the original goals of the IPL was to fix the threshold for a person to be defined as poor so that poverty could be monitored over time (Ravallion, Datt, and van de Walle 1991). The previous section explains why the World Bank has added two complementary higher absolute poverty lines that are more typical of the national poverty lines found in lower-middle-income and upper-middle-income countries (Jolliffe and Prydz 2016; World Bank 2018). This section presents results for global and regional societal poverty (see box 1.1; Jolliffe and Prydz 2017; World Bank 2018).

The SPL is not designed to capture the national poverty lines for countries in one income group rather than another. Instead, societal poverty increases with the income level of each country and is thus relevant even in high-income economies, where extreme poverty rates are very close to zero. At the same time, this concept translates into a very different picture for poverty reduction at both the global and regional levels. In contrast to the absolute poverty lines presented in this chapter, the SPL varies across countries and within a country over time, increasing with the level of income as captured by the median. In addition, the SPL, at least in its relative portion, can be seen as a measure of inequality; hence, this section also relates to the discussion on shared prosperity and inequality in chapter 2.

FIGURE 1.9 Poverty Rates and Number of Poor, US$3.20-a-Day and US$5.50-a-Day Poverty Lines, Sub-Saharan Africa, 1990–2018

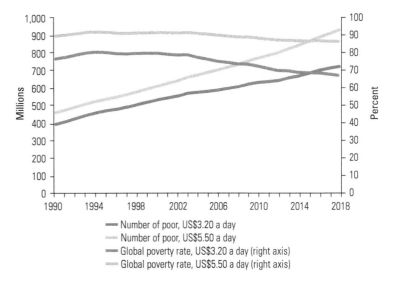

Source: PovcalNet (online analysis tool), World Bank, Washington, DC, http://iresearch.worldbank.org/PovcalNet/.
Note: See tables 1B.1 and 1B.2 for yearly lined-up estimates.

The average value of the SPL at the global level was US$7.20 in 2017, increasing from US$6.90 in 2015 (see annex 1C, table 1C.1). Figure 1.10 compares the different trends for extreme poverty and societal poverty. Given that the SPL increases with median income, it is not surprising that societal poverty has declined at a slower pace than extreme poverty. In 2017, there were still 2 billion people living below their countries' respective SPLs, 14 million less than in 2015 (figure 1.10 panel b). Figure 1.10, panel c, shows the geographical distribution of the number of poor living in societal poverty (see table 1C.1). The richer regions (for example, Europe and Central Asia or the high-income economies falling in the 'Rest of the world' category) account for a larger share of global societal poverty using the SPL than if compared with the absolute poverty lines presented above. Also, the number of poor is fairly stable in most regions, with the exception of East Asia and Pacific, which also shows a noticeable reduction by this poverty measure.

This analysis concludes by examining the differences in societal poverty rates across regions. Although there are differences in the levels of societal poverty across regions,

FIGURE 1.10 Global Societal Poverty Rate and Number of Poor, Compared with International Poverty Line Estimates, 1990–2017

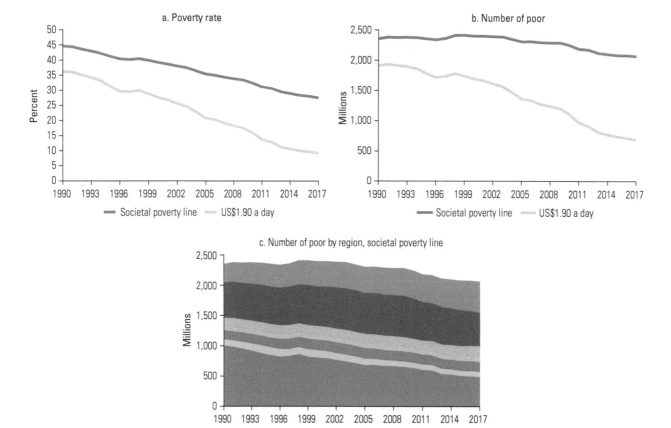

Source: PovcalNet (online analysis tool), World Bank, Washington, DC, http://iresearch.worldbank.org/PovcalNet/.
Note: The coverage rule for the global lined-up estimates is applied to the three panels. Global societal poverty is calculated using a population-weighted average of country-specific societal poverty rates (see table 1C.1 for the full series of yearly lined-up estimates). The treatment of missing economies is identical to the other monetary poverty measures. The figure reported for South Asia uses the India estimate that is included in the global headcount (see box 1.2). IPL = international poverty line.

the trends look similar. In fact, figure 1.11 shows that, although societal poverty is highest in Sub-Saharan Africa and has stagnated there over the past decade, the gap with other regions is much narrower by this measure compared with what was presented in previous sections of this chapter, largely because other regions have higher poverty rates according to the SPL, which by construction is higher in richer countries and regions.

Europe and Central Asia shows one of the lowest values at about 17 percent. In the high-income economies included in the 'Rest of the world' category, 15 percent of the population lives below an SPL, that is, on average, about US$24 a day (see table 1C.1). The trends for other regions in figure 1.11 are similar to what was observed earlier in this chapter: societal poverty is on the rise in the Middle East and North Africa, consistent with the increase in extreme poverty in the region. East Asia and Pacific shows the largest progress in societal poverty reduction, whereas Latin America and the Caribbean has stagnated.

Beyond monetary poverty: The multidimensional poverty measure

Poverty is a complex and multifaceted phenomenon. When poor people are asked in participatory studies what makes them feel poor, they indicate a wide range of deprivations: not having enough to eat, having inadequate housing material, being sick, having limited or no formal education, having no work, and living in unsafe neighborhoods. To reflect this complex experience and inform policies to address it, the multidimensional poverty measure (MPM) incorporates deprivations across several indicators of well-being (see box 1.1; annex 1D; World Bank 2018).

The MPM builds on monetary extreme poverty, which is the focal point of the World Bank's monitoring of global poverty and is included as one of the MPM dimensions, along with access to education and basic infrastructure. The MPM is at least as high as or higher than the monetary poverty headcount in a country, to reflect the additional role of nonmonetary dimensions in increasing multidimensional poverty. Figure 1.12 illustrates this point by plotting the correlation between monetary poverty and multidimensional poverty; the distance from the red 45-degree line highlights in which economies the difference between the two measures is greatest. This difference might be as large as 34 percentage points (Niger) or relatively low as in Tanzania (8.4 percentage points).[26] Although Niger and Tanzania have similar monetary poverty rates (45.4 percent and 49.4 percent, respectively), the multidimensional poverty headcount is considerably higher in Niger (79.3 percent vs. 57.8 percent), suggesting that nonmonetary deprivations play a greater role in Niger. Taking a different perspective, Angola and Uganda show similar levels of multidimensional poverty, although Uganda has lower levels of monetary poverty (41.5 percent vs. 51.8 percent in Angola). Some economies might have low monetary poverty headcounts, but a large share of their populations might be deprived in the other dimensions, for example, Guatemala (9 percent vs. 22 percent) and Mauritania (6 percent vs. 46 percent).

FIGURE 1.11 **Societal Poverty Rates, by Region, 1990–2018**

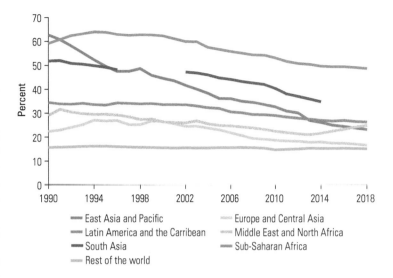

Source: PovcalNet (online analysis tool), World Bank, Washington, DC, http://iresearch.worldbank.org/PovcalNet/.
Note: Each estimate is the population-weighted average of economy-level societal poverty rates by region. Societal poverty lines are estimated at the economy level using the formula in box 1.1. The regional coverage rule is applied and estimates for South Asia are not reported in the period 1997–2001 and after 2014 because of a lack of population coverage.

FIGURE 1.12 **Correlation between Monetary and Multidimensional Poverty Headcount, circa 2017**

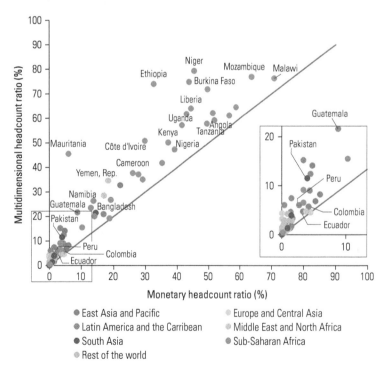

Source: Global Monitoring Database.
Note: The figure shows the relationship between the monetary poverty headcount (horizontal axis) and the multidimensional poverty headcount (vertical axis) for 114 economies. The full list of economies can be found in annex 1D. The red line is the 45-degree line.

The analysis in this section is based on the set of harmonized household surveys compiled in the Global Monitoring Database (GMD) (see annex 1D).[27] The monetary poverty rate in the MPM is not directly comparable to the monetary poverty measures in PovcalNet used elsewhere in the chapter for two primary reasons: first, not all surveys in PovcalNet include the additional indicators required by the MPM, and, second, PovcalNet lines up surveys to a common reference year, whereas the MPM uses the monetary headcount ratio in the survey year.[28]

As with monetary poverty, Sub-Saharan Africa experiences the highest levels of deprivations in multidimensional poverty, with more than half of the population multidimensionally poor (see table 1.1). Although almost 20 percent of the population lives in households in which at least one school-age child is not enrolled in school (table 1.2), this is the dimension under which the lowest share of individuals is deprived in the region, suggesting a possible reduction in multidimensional poverty for future generations.[29]

Although multidimensional poverty is endemic in Sub-Saharan Africa, other regions of the world also show high deprivations in some dimensions. Table 1.2 shows important differences when comparing monetary poverty to deprivations in other dimensions. About a third of those who are multidimensionally deprived are not captured by

TABLE 1.1 Monetary and Multidimensional Poverty Headcount, by Region and the World, circa 2017

Region	Monetary poverty, headcount ratio (%)	Multidimensional poverty, headcount ratio (%)	Number of economies	Population coverage (%)[a]
East Asia and Pacific	4.1	6.2	9	30
Europe and Central Asia	0.3	1.6	25	89
Latin America and the Caribbean	3.4	6.8	16	89
Middle East and North Africa	4.2	6.8	6	58
South Asia	8.1	15.0	5	22
Sub-Saharan Africa	38.5	53.8	31	74
Rest of the world	0.8	1.4	22	69
All regions	**9.1**	**14.0**	**114**	**50[b]**

Source: Global Monitoring Database.
Note: The monetary headcount is based on the international poverty line. Regional and total estimates are population-weighted averages of survey-year estimates for 114 economies and are not comparable to those presented in previous sections. The multidimensional poverty measure headcount indicates the share of the population in each region defined as multidimensionally poor. Number of economies is the number of economies in each region for which information is available in the window between 2014 and 2018, for a circa 2017 reporting year. The coverage rule applied to the estimates is identical to that used in the rest of the chapter and details can be found in annex 1A. Regions without sufficient population coverage are shown in light grey.
a. Data coverage differs across regions. The data cover as much as 89 percent of the population in Latin America and the Caribbean and as little as 22 percent of the population in South Asia. The coverage for South Asia is low because no household survey is available for India between 2014 and 2018. Regional coverage is calculated using the same rules as in the rest of this chapter (see annex 1A). Hence, because of the absence of data on China and India, the regional coverage of South Asia and East Asia and Pacific is insufficient.
b. The table conforms to both coverage criteria for global poverty reporting. The global population coverage is 50 percent and in low-income and lower-middle-income countries it is 51 percent.

TABLE 1.2 Share of Population Deprived in Each Indicator, 114 Economies, circa 2017

Region	Monetary (%)	Educational attainment (%)	Educational enrollment (%)	Electricity (%)	Sanitation (%)	Drinking water (%)
East Asia and Pacific	4.1	7.0	3.0	4.2	13.6	10.2
Europe and Central Asia	0.3	0.8	2.6	1.6	8.8	3.3
Latin America and the Caribbean	3.4	9.3	2.6	1.7	18.8	3.1
Middle East and North Africa	4.2	9.4	8.1	4.7	7.8	2.9
South Asia	8.1	31.4	6.4	15.2	37.3	5.8
Sub-Saharan Africa	38.5	32.3	19.5	46.2	59.9	29.3
Rest of the world	0.8	0.8	0.0	0.0	0.2	0.2
All regions	**9.1**	**15.4**	**5.9**	**11.7**	**23.6**	**9.0**

Source: Global Monitoring Database.
Note: This table shows the share of population living in households deprived in each indicator of the multidimensional poverty measure. The monetary poverty headcount is based on the international poverty line. Regional and total estimates are population-weighted averages of survey-year estimates for 114 economies and are not comparable to those presented in previous sections. The coverage rule applied to the estimates is identical to that used in the rest of the chapter and details can be found in annex 1A. Regions without sufficient population coverage are shown in light grey.

monetary poverty, in line with the findings of the previous edition of this report (World Bank 2018). The gap is particularly striking between sanitation and monetary poverty in Europe and Central Asia, Latin America and the Caribbean, and the Middle East and North Africa; but it is also large when looking at educational attainment. For example, Latin America and the Caribbean and the Middle East and North Africa show a difference of less than 1 percentage point in their monetary headcount, but larger differences in educational enrollment and sanitation. On the one hand, the share of the population living in households with at least one school-age child not enrolled in school is more than three times higher in the Middle East and North Africa than in Latin America and the Caribbean (likely related to the negative effects of conflict in the Middle East and North Africa). On the

other hand, the share of population lacking appropriate sanitation is close to 19 percent in Latin America and the Caribbean, more than twice that of the Middle East and North Africa and of Europe and Central Asia.

There are stark overlaps in the forms of deprivation afflicting households in Sub-Saharan Africa (World Bank 2018). Figure 1.13 shows that 21 percent of the population in Sub-Saharan Africa is deprived in all three dimensions, a figure that equates to about 40 percent of the region's multidimensionally poor.[30] This overlap is lower in other regions; for example, 0.7 percent of the population (that is, only 11 percent of the multidimensionally poor) in Latin America and the Caribbean is deprived in all three dimensions, compared with 1.5 percent of the population (that is, 22 percent of the multidimensionally poor) in the Middle East and North Africa.

FIGURE 1.13 Deprivation in Multiple Dimensions, circa 2017

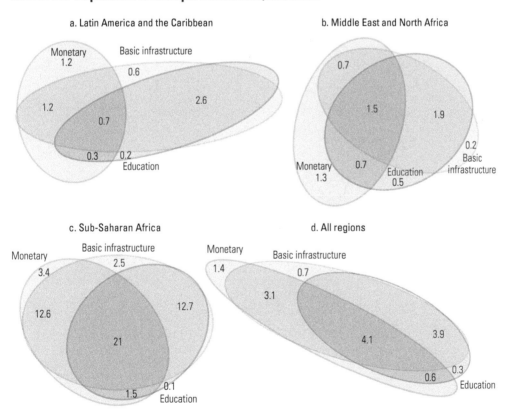

Source: Global Monitoring Database.
Note: The figure shows the overlap in different dimensions of the multidimensional poverty measure at the household level. It shows the share of households (in percent) deprived in all indicators and in each combination of the monetary, education, and basic infrastructure dimensions. Only Latin America and the Caribbean, the Middle East and North Africa, and Sub-Saharan Africa are shown because these regions have sufficient population coverage.

Because of a lack of comparable data over time, changes in the regional and total estimates since 2013 (the reporting year published in World Bank [2018]) cannot be discussed.[31]

A focus on extreme poverty in Sub-Saharan Africa

Whereas global and regional aggregate poverty measures monitor progress toward the 2030 Sustainable Development Goals, policy action needed to eradicate poverty largely happens at the national and subnational levels. Therefore, this section focuses on differences across countries, with an emphasis on Sub-Saharan Africa, the region with the largest concentration of the extreme poor. Chapter 3 takes an additional step, providing an even finer disaggregation of poverty, for example, by place of residence, gender, and age group.

Map 1.1 shows the geographical distribution of poverty rates by economy in 2017. The concentration of high poverty rates in Sub-Saharan Africa recalls the image of a poverty belt extending from Senegal to Ethiopia and from Mali to Madagascar. Of the 44 economies with available poverty estimates in the region, 38 have a rate of extreme poverty higher than 10 percent. Half of the economies have poverty rates higher than 35 percent. These numbers become even more alarming when compared with the levels of extreme poverty in other regions. Of the 20 economies with the largest poverty rates (based on PovacalNet estimates) 18 are in Sub-Saharan Africa, and 2 are in the Middle East and North Africa (Syria and the Republic of Yemen).[32]

MAP 1.1 Poverty Rate at the US$1.90-a-Day Poverty Line, by Economy, 2017

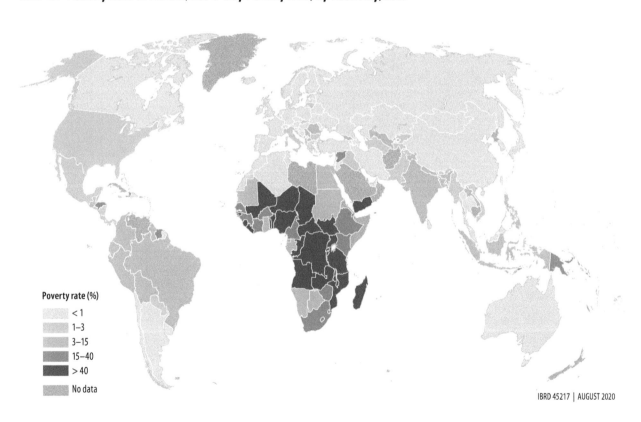

IBRD 45217 | AUGUST 2020

Source: PovcalNet (online analysis tool), World Bank, Washington, DC, http://iresearch.worldbank.org/PovcalNet/.
Note: The map shows the lined-up poverty rates (at the international poverty line) for 2017 for economies with available data in PovcalNet. The figure uses the India estimate included in the global headcount (see box 1.2).

Perhaps even more alarming than having 40 percent of the Sub-Saharan African population living in extreme poverty is the stagnation of poverty at such high levels over the past three decades. Figure 1.14 shows the dispersion in extreme poverty rates between 1990 and 2018 in Sub-Saharan Africa and compares this pattern with the distribution in East Asia and Pacific.[33] East Asia and Pacific has seen a remarkable compression in poverty rates over that period. In contrast, the range of poverty rates in Sub-Saharan Africa has barely narrowed between 1990 and 2018, extending from close to 0 to about 80 percent. This does not mean that individual economies have not seen progress in poverty reduction, but rather that the region still has many economies with poverty rates well above the world average. The reasons for the stagnation in these economies are numerous. Fragility and conflict play a crucial role (Corral et al. 2020), as do the degree of policy effectiveness and institutional stability (World Bank 2018).[34] Many of the economies in figure 1.14 have small populations, thus contributing less to global and regional extreme poverty. However, having such large shares of the national population living below the IPL cannot go unremarked.

An examination of country-level information also reveals different local patterns in poverty rates. Of the 32 economies in Sub-Saharan Africa for which the latest two years of survey data are comparable in PovcalNet, 25 show a decrease in poverty, whereas 7 show an increase.[35] Looking at changes that are greater than 1 percentage point per year, 9 economies show a decline, and 4 economies show an increase. For every economy where poverty increased by more than 1 percentage point per year, there were two economies where it declined. This underscores that progress in poverty reduction has been achieved. Ethiopia registered a decrease of 7 percentage points in its extreme poverty rate between 2004/05 and 2015/16, confirming a virtuous trend since the early 2000s. The share of population living below the IPL decreased from 44 percent to 37 percent between 2005 and 2015 in Kenya and from 23 percent to 13 percent between 2009

FIGURE 1.14 Variation in Poverty Rates, East Asia and Pacific versus Sub-Saharan Africa, 1990–2018

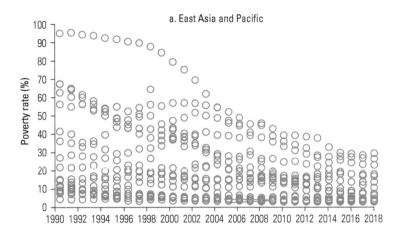

a. East Asia and Pacific

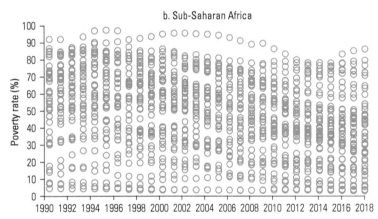

b. Sub-Saharan Africa

Source: PovcalNet (online analysis tool), World Bank, Washington, DC, http://iresearch.worldbank.org/PovcalNet/.
Note: The figure shows the variation in lined-up poverty estimates between 1990 and 2018 for economies in Sub-Saharan Africa and compares it with economies in East Asia and Pacific. Each dot represents the poverty rate estimate for an economy in a lineup year for the two regions. Poverty rates are based on the US$1.90 line.

and 2015 in Namibia. However, because of rapid population growth, the number of poor actually increased in Ethiopia and Kenya during the periods considered. For example, the number of poor in Ethiopia increased by 3 million over this period.

Other economies in Sub-Saharan Africa have been less successful. Angola saw extreme poverty rise by 18 percentage points in the past decade. Extreme poverty increased by 6 percentage points in Uganda between 2012 and 2016. Both examples show a reversal in poverty reduction compared with the previous period. Similarly, remarkable progress in poverty reduction in Tanzania has come to a halt: after an

11-percentage-point drop in poverty between 2007 and 2011, data for 2017 show stagnation at a poverty rate of 49 percent. A similar trend can be observed in Ghana, where poverty rose by 1 percentage point between 2012 and 2016 after having dropped by 12 percentage points between 2005 and 2012. These examples help illuminate the region's limited progress in poverty reduction in recent years.[36]

Map 1.2 provides information on the distribution of extreme poverty at the subnational level in Sub-Saharan Africa. The data show that in some economies, for example, Madagascar and South Sudan, extreme poverty is evenly distributed over the national territory. Other economies, such as Angola and Nigeria, show considerable heterogeneity across subnational areas. In Nigeria, administrative areas in the north and northeast have poverty rates higher than the national average, but poverty rates are lower in areas closer to the coast. In addition, in some places poverty "hot spots" are spread across borders, such as the regions in the Central African Republic bordering the Democratic Republic of Congo and South Sudan.

MAP 1.2 Poverty Rate at the US$1.90-a-Day Poverty Line at the Subnational Level, Lined-Up Estimates, Sub-Saharan Africa, 2018

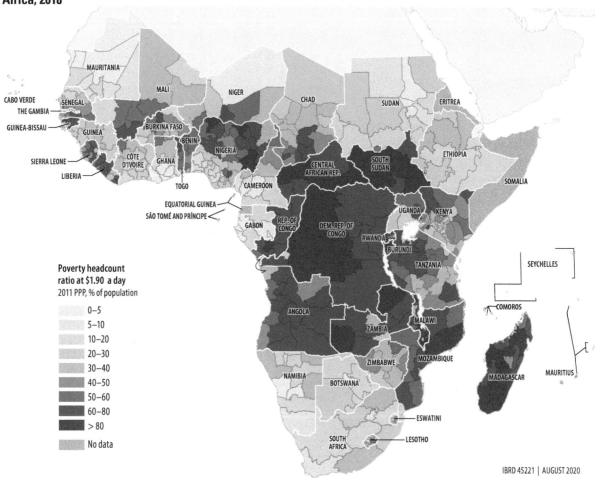

Source: Global Subnational Atlas of Poverty (see annex 3B), based on Global Monitoring Database and PovcalNet (online analysis tool), World Bank, Washington, DC, http://iresearch.worldbank.org/PovcalNet/.
Note: The poverty rates are based on the international poverty line of US$1.90 a day and are shown across areas for which the surveys are representative. The map shows lined-up estimates for 2018.

Figure 1.15 returns to the population-weighted perspective by showing the distribution of the extreme poor across African economies. Nigeria has the largest poor population in Sub-Saharan Africa (79 million extreme poor).[37] It accounts for 20 percent of the total poor in the region. Almost half of poor people in Sub-Saharan Africa live in just five economies: Nigeria (79 million), the Democratic Republic of Congo (60 million), Tanzania (28 million), Ethiopia (26 million), and Madagascar (20 million).

FIGURE 1.15 Distribution of Extreme Poor, by Economy, Sub-Saharan Africa, 2018

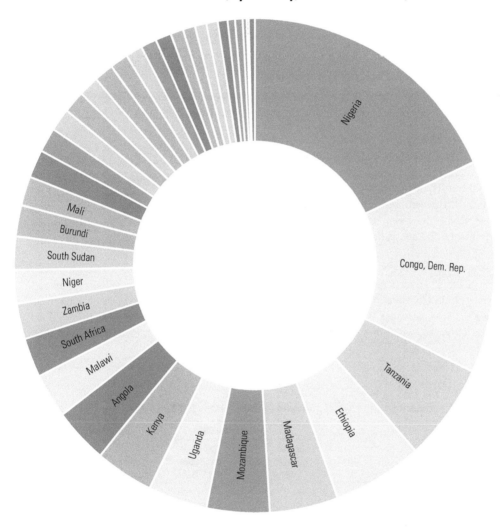

Source: PovcalNet (online analysis tool), World Bank, Washington, DC, http://iresearch.worldbank.org/PovcalNet/.
Note: The estimates are based on the international poverty line of US$1.90 a day. The figure shows the distribution of the number of poor across economies in Sub-Saharan Africa. The poverty estimates are for the 2018 lineup year and include an estimate of the number of poor for economies with missing data in PovcalNet (calculated using the regional population-weighted average of the poverty rate following the aggregation methodology explained in annex 1A) to reflect the regional total.

Annex 1A

PovcalNet data and methodology for measuring extreme poverty

Data source

Most of the data for this chapter come from PovcalNet, the online analysis tool for global poverty monitoring produced by the World Bank (Chen and Ravallion 2010; Ferreira et al. 2016; World Bank 2015a). PovcalNet was developed to enable public replication of the World Bank's poverty measures for the IPL. It contains poverty estimates from more than 1,600 household surveys spanning 166 economies.[38] In recent years, most of the surveys in PovcalNet have been taken from the Global Monitoring Database, the World Bank's repository of household surveys. For general documentation on PovcalNet, see the website and the Global Poverty Monitoring Technical Notes published there.[39]

The surveys report welfare aggregates in local currency, which are adjusted for price differences within countries over time using the local consumer price index (CPI) (Lakner et al. 2019) and for price differences across countries using purchasing power parities (PPPs). Throughout this chapter, the revised 2011 PPPs, which were published in May 2020, are used. As explained by Atamanov et al. (2020) and Castaneda et al. (2020), the impact of the PPP revisions on global and regional poverty estimates is minor.

Data availability: Progress and setbacks in monitoring global poverty

Table 1A.1 compares population coverage of the poverty estimates for 2013 with those for 2017. It is important to note that population coverage for 2013 is calculated using the data

TABLE 1A.1 Data Coverage, by Region and Income Group, 2013 and 2017

Region	Reference year 2013		Reference year 2017	
	Number of economies	Share of population covered (%)	Number of economies	Share of population covered (%)
East Asia and Pacific	11	94	10	97
Europe and Central Asia	26	90	26	90
Latin America and the Caribbean	18	91	18	90
Middle East and North Africa	3	25	6	58
South Asia	6	98	5	22
Sub-Saharan Africa	26	55	33	79
Rest of the world	23	75	26	78
Total	**113**	**83**	**124**	**71**
Low- and lower-middle-income countries	52	79	55	52
Fragile and conflict-affected economies	15	40	14	43

Source: PovcalNet (online analysis tool), World Bank, Washington, DC, http://iresearch.worldbank.org/PovcalNet/.
Note: The columns for reference year 2013 refer to the data available when reference year 2013 was first reported (World Bank 2016; PovcalNet vintage published in October 2016). For each reference year, coverage is calculated using economies with survey data within a three-year window either side of a reference year. Economies are assigned the classifications low-income or lower-middle-income countries, or fragile and conflict-affected economies.

that were available when the reference year 2013 was first reported (World Bank [2016] using the PovcalNet vintage published in October 2016). This calculation differs from today's population coverage for reference year 2013 because new survey data have been received since then.[40]

The total number of economies with recent survey data increased by about 10 percent between 2013 and 2017, from 113 to 124. The developments in Sub-Saharan Africa, which is a focus of the World Bank's efforts to improve data coverage in poorer economies, are particularly encouraging.[41] The region added data for seven economies and increased the population coverage by more than 20 percentage points, driven largely by new data for Nigeria, the most populous country in the region.[42] Improvements in data availability are also seen in the Middle East and North Africa, namely for the Arab Republic of Egypt, West Bank and Gaza, and the Republic of Yemen, increasing population coverage in the region to 58 percent from 25 percent. The population coverage of fragile and conflict-affected economies has improved slightly but remains at less than half.

In contrast to these positive developments, the population coverage for South Asia has fallen dramatically, from 98 percent to 22 percent between 2013 and 2017. This drop in coverage reflects the absence of recent survey data for India, which also drives the decline in population coverage for low- and lower-middle-income countries (dropping to 52 percent from 79 percent) and for the world (decreasing to 71 percent from 83 percent), despite an increase in the number of countries with surveys.[43] These estimates illustrate how the ability to monitor global poverty depends on the availability of data for populous countries, especially countries with large populations of extreme poor, and how India and Nigeria show opposite developments in the availability of data.[44]

Population coverage for the MPM in 2017 reported in the main text (see table 1.1) is worse than the population coverage reported in table 1A.1. Only a monetary welfare aggregate (consumption or income) is required to measure monetary poverty, but the estimation of the MPM requires additional indicators that capture nonmonetary deprivations.[45]

Welfare aggregates

Household surveys measure either consumption or income. In the current 2017 global estimate, about 60 percent of economies use consumption, with the rest using income. The differences between income and consumption matter for comparing trends and levels of poverty. For example, because most poverty estimates for Latin America and the Caribbean use income as a measure of welfare, it is difficult to compare the trend in poverty rates with the trend in other regions that use consumption, such as East Asia and Pacific. This difference is relevant, given that in recent years East Asia and Pacific shows lower poverty rates than Latin America and the Caribbean (see figure 1.3) pointing to stagnation in poverty reduction in Latin America and the Caribbean. Economies typically choose the concept that can be more accurately measured and that is more relevant to the country context, while balancing concerns about respondent burden. On the one hand, consumption measures of poverty require a wide range of questions and are thus more time-consuming. Income measures, on the other hand, are difficult to obtain when a large fraction of the population works in the informal sector or is self-employed, which is frequently the case in poorer economies, which therefore often opt to use consumption. Also, when households produce their own food with limited market interactions, it is harder to measure income than consumption. It should be noted that, because PovcalNet focuses on extreme poverty, it chooses consumption over income when both welfare measures are available.

Both approaches to measuring poverty have advantages and disadvantages. The consumption approach is arguably more directly connected to economic welfare. Income measures of poverty also suffer from the disadvantage that incomes might be very low—even negative—in a given period, whereas consumption is smoothed to safeguard against such shocks.[46] Consumption-based measures of poverty, conversely, are often more time intensive and require detailed price data and often post-fieldwork adjustments. Also, the design of consumption questionnaires varies widely and, as shown by numerous experiments, can have significant effects on final poverty estimates (Beegle et al. 2012; Deaton 2001; Jolliffe 2001). Income measures often rely on no more than a handful of questions and can, at times, be verified from other sources.

Moreover, given that incomes can be very low or negative, poverty rates are typically higher when income is used rather than consumption. For a given poverty rate, poor households also tend to be further below the poverty line when income is used, as explained by the earlier point about very low incomes: although it is plausible for households to have zero income in a given period, subsistence requires a minimum level of consumption, which is strictly above zero (World Bank 2018). Moreover, because richer households tend to save larger shares of their income, inequality measures based on consumption tend to result in lower levels of inequality (Lakner et al. 2016; World Bank 2016).

The differences also matter for nowcasting and making poverty projections for the future. Such projections are typically made by assuming a fixed growth rate of household consumption or income over time. Households with zero income will never be projected to move out of poverty regardless of how large the growth rates are assumed to be (World Bank 2018).

To express the national welfare aggregates in comparable units, CPIs and PPPs are applied (Atamanov et al. 2018; Lakner et al. 2019). National CPIs are used to deflate the welfare aggregate to the PPP reference year (currently 2011). Therefore, all within-country comparisons over time depend only on national CPIs. PPPs are then used to adjust for cross-country price differences (see the detailed discussion below). In addition, PovcalNet uses rural and urban PPPs for China, India, and Indonesia to take into account the urban bias in the International Comparison Program (ICP)

price data collection (Castaneda et al. 2020; Chen and Ravallion 2010; Ferreira et al. 2016; World Bank 2018).

Comparisons of country trends should also account for whether household surveys remain comparable over time. Since September 2019, PovcalNet has published a comparability data set tracking this information over time for each economy with available survey data (Atamanov et al. 2019). Comparability depends on various characteristics such as the sampling process, questionnaire, methodological changes in the construction of welfare aggregates, consistent price deflation over time and space, and so on. The full data set can be found online.[47]

Finally, global poverty estimates use data on household consumption or income per capita to measure poverty, and the IPL is expressed in per capita terms. This means that the welfare measures do not reflect differences in the distribution of income or consumption within the household and do not account for economies of scale in larger households. This approach is subject to criticism because important differences in intrahousehold allocation matter for monitoring drivers of poverty by gender, age, or economic activity. These issues are discussed in detail in chapter 5 of World Bank (2018).

Revised 2011 Purchasing Power Parities

Purchasing power parities (PPPs) are used in global poverty estimates. PPPs are price indexes that measure how much it costs to purchase a basket of goods and services in one country relative to purchasing the same basket in a reference country. They express how much of a country's currency can be exchanged for one unit of the currency of a reference country, typically the United States, in real terms. Market exchange rates do not take account of nontradable services, which are often cheaper in developing countries where factors of production (for example, labor) are not as expensive as in rich countries (the Balassa-Samuelson effect).

All the poverty estimates included in this chapter adjust for differences in relative price levels across countries using the revised 2011 PPPs released by the ICP in May 2020.[48] The original 2011 PPPs were revised mainly in light of the rebasing of national accounts data in several countries. The underlying price data remain unchanged. Because the PPPs are multilateral price indexes, revisions to national accounts weights in one or a few countries translate into changes in PPP estimates for all countries.

The revision of the 2011 PPPs has a relatively small effect on global poverty estimates. The global poverty numbers change slightly when the global income or consumption distribution is updated with the revised 2011 PPPs. The global poverty headcount ratio increases by 0.24 percentage point (equivalent to 17.7 million more poor people) in 2017. Compared with the adoption of the 2005 PPPs, which increased global poverty by 400 million people, this change in poverty is quite small (Chen and Ravallion 2010). Historically, ICP rounds have reflected not only new price information but also changes in ICP methodologies (for example, the change from 2005 to 2011 PPPs). With this concern in mind, the Atkinson Commission on Global Poverty (World Bank 2017a) has recommended against adopting future ICP rounds. Thus, the 2017 PPPs, which were published together with the revised 2011 PPPs, are not currently used for global poverty measurement and will require more analysis. However, it is necessary to adopt the revised 2011 PPPs because they incorporate new information from national accounts. This approach is similar to how PovcalNet periodically revises its other input data, such as CPI, GDP, or population estimates, to reflect the most accurate information.

PPPs are also used in the derivation of the global poverty lines. When updated with the revised 2011 PPPs, the IPL becomes US$1.87, which still rounds to US$1.90 per person per day (Atamanov et al. 2020). The higher lines—US$3.20 and US$5.50 per person per day—are derived as the median implicit national poverty lines corresponding to lower-middle-income countries and upper-middle-income countries, respectively (Jolliffe and Prydz 2016). When updated with the revised 2011 PPPs, the US$3.20 line also remains unchanged, but the US$5.50 line increases by approximately US$0.15 (Atamanov et al. 2020). Over time the World Bank's global poverty lines have been widely used in the development community, such that they could be considered to be parameters in estimating global poverty, and there is a cost to revising them frequently. Although changes in PPPs could result in a different estimate, it is important to recognize that the poverty line is a parameter chosen, using a reasonable method, to monitor progress in different parts of the global distribution of income or consumption. To this end, the World Bank has decided to keep all global poverty lines unchanged.

More details on how the revised 2011 PPPs affect the measurement of global poverty can be found in Atamanov et al. (2020) and Castaneda et al. (2020).

Derivation of regional and global estimates

Because the frequency and timing of household surveys vary across economies, regional estimates that cover as many economies as possible require projecting the survey data to the reference year for which global poverty is expressed, in this report 2017 for the global estimates. When the timing of surveys does not align with the reference year, PovcalNet "lines up" the survey estimates to the reference year using growth in national accounts consumption or GDP and assuming no changes in the distribution (Prydz et al. 2019; World Bank 2018). Thus, a lined-up estimate is available in every year for which national accounts data are available (see Castaneda et al. [2020] for updated information on national accounts data sources).

To arrive at regional and global estimates of poverty, population-weighted average poverty rates are calculated for each region. Some economies have no household survey data that can be used to monitor poverty (or they lack the national accounts data for a particular reference year). For the regional and global aggregations, these economies are assigned the population-weighted average for the region based on the economies with data available. Population data are taken from the World Bank's World Development Indicators.[49] Regions are defined using the PovcalNet classification, which differs from the regional classifications typically used by the World Bank. Some economies, mostly high-income economies, are excluded from the geographical regions and are included as a separate group (referred to as other high-income, industrialized economies, or rest of the world in earlier publications). The list of economies included in each region can be found on the PovcalNet website.[50]

Coverage rule

In September 2020, PovcalNet began reporting annual lined-up global and regional poverty numbers. Before then, poverty estimates were reported at varying intervals and for the following years: 1981, 1984, 1987, 1990, 1993, 1996, 1999, 2002, 2005, 2008, 2010–13, and 2015. This change in reporting annual numbers is documented by Castaneda et al. (2020). Together with introducing annual lined-up estimates, the coverage rule used to report regional and global numbers has also been slightly revised (with very limited impacts on reporting, as discussed by Castaneda et al. 2020). This rule is used to determine whether a particular lineup year has sufficient population coverage to allow the estimation of regional and global poverty aggregates to be made. It is important to highlight that this change does not affect how these aggregates are estimated; it affects only whether an estimate is displayed. As noted previously, an estimate is always calculated provided that survey and national accounts data are available.

The coverage rule now includes data for survey years within three years either side of a lineup year. This change makes the rule slightly more lenient but represents a small change compared with the old rule.[51] The second change increases the threshold of population coverage at the regional level from 40 percent to 50 percent of the population. For regions in which the surveys within three years either side of the lineup year account for less than half of the regional population, the regional poverty estimate is not reported. This is a stricter parameter compared with the previous version of the coverage rule, and it balances the previous requirement. The third additional requirement addresses the goal of focusing the measurement of global poverty on economies where most of the poor live. Specifically, it tries to avoid a situation in which the global population threshold is met by having recent data in the high-income countries, East Asia and Pacific, and Latin America and the Caribbean, which together account for a very small share of the global extreme poor. Under this requirement, global poverty estimates are reported only if data are representative of at least 50 percent of the population in low-income and lower-middle-income countries, because most of the poor live in these groups of countries. This requirement is applied only to the global poverty estimate, not at the regional level. The World Bank classification of economies according to income groups in the lineup year is used.[52]

Using these new rules, the global extreme poverty rate stops in 2017, even though information is available up to 2018 for individual regions—except for South Asia where the regional estimate is reported only through 2014. Reporting the most recent regional estimates for which the coverage rule is satisfied is an attempt to provide the most up-to-date poverty estimates and recognizes the immense effort by countries to collect timely household survey data with which to monitor global poverty.

TABLE 1A.2 Global and Regional Extreme Poverty

a. Global poverty rate at the US$1.90-a-day poverty line, 1990–2017

Year	Poverty rate (%)	Poverty gap (%)	Squared poverty gap (%)	Number of poor (millions)	Global population (millions)
1990	36.2	12.8	6.2	1,912.4	5,280.1
1993	34.3	12.1	5.8	1,897.9	5,537.5
1996	29.7	9.9	4.7	1,718.9	5,789.6
1999	28.9	9.6	4.6	1,741.3	6,034.5
2002	25.7	8.4	3.9	1,613.9	6,272.7
2005	20.9	6.4	2.9	1,362.9	6,511.7
2008	18.4	5.5	2.5	1,243.1	6,756.9
2011	13.8	4.1	1.9	969.1	7,002.9
2014	10.7	3.2	1.5	773.8	7,254.2
2015	10.1	3.1	1.4	741.4	7,339.0
2016	9.7	3.0	1.4	716.9	7,424.3
2017	9.2	2.9	1.4	689.1	7,509.1

b. Poverty rates (%) at the US$1.90-a-day poverty line, by region, 1990–2018

	1990	1993	1996	1999	2002	2005	2008	2011	2014	2015	2016	2017	2018
East Asia and Pacific	60.9	53.2	40.4	37.9	29.1	18.3	14.8	8.1	2.6	2.1	1.7	1.4	1.2
Europe and Central Asia	3.1	5.2	7.0	7.7	5.7	4.7	2.7	2.0	1.8	1.5	1.3	1.3	1.1
Latin America and the Caribbean	15.2	14.2	13.9	13.7	12.1	10.0	7.0	5.7	4.1	3.8	3.9	3.9	3.8
Middle East and North Africa	6.6	7.1	6.3	4.0	3.4	3.2	2.8	2.3	2.7	3.8	5.1	6.3	7.2
South Asia	48.7	46.2	41.6	–	39.8	34.9	30.6	20.9	15.2	–	–	–[a]	–
Sub-Saharan Africa	55.7	60.6	59.8	59.4	56.4	52.0	49.0	45.3	42.1	41.8	41.7	41.0	40.2
Rest of the world	0.4	0.5	0.6	0.5	0.5	0.5	0.5	0.6	0.6	0.7	0.6	0.6	0.6

c. Number of poor (millions) at the US$1.90-a-day poverty line, by region, 1990–2018

	1990	1993	1996	1999	2002	2005	2008	2011	2014	2015	2016	2017	2018
East Asia and Pacific	976.9	891.5	702.1	681.8	538.4	346.2	285.9	159.7	53.3	42.2	35.3	29.3	24.5
Europe and Central Asia	14.4	24.5	33.0	36.2	26.7	22.1	12.9	9.7	8.7	7.3	6.2	6.5	5.6
Latin America and the Caribbean	66.3	65.6	67.6	69.8	64.4	55.3	39.9	33.7	25.2	23.6	24.5	24.4	24.2
Middle East and North Africa	15.0	17.4	16.6	10.9	10.0	9.7	9.0	8.0	9.8	13.8	19.1	24.0	28.0
South Asia	551.9	559.3	536.0	–	574.0	529.8	486.6	347.9	262.4	–	–	–[a]	–
Sub-Saharan Africa	283.8	335.0	358.4	384.8	395.1	394.4	403.4	404.2	407.9	416.4	426.8	430.8	433.4
Rest of the world	4.1	4.6	5.2	4.9	5.1	5.5	5.5	6.0	6.5	7.1	6.9	6.5	6.5

Source: PovcalNet (online analysis tool), World Bank, Washington, DC, http://iresearch.worldbank.org/PovcalNet/.

Note: Panel a shows the global poverty numbers for selected lineup years. The poverty rate refers to the percentage of the population living on less than the international poverty line (IPL) of US$1.90 a day. The poverty gap is the average consumption shortfall of the population where the nonpoor have no shortfall. Number of poor is the number of people living below the IPL calculated using the poverty rate and population data from the World Bank World Development Indicators. Population is the global total population in each year. Panels b and c show the regional lined-up poverty estimates at the IPL for selected years between 1990 and 2018. The regional coverage rule is applied, and poverty estimates for South Asia are not reported for the period 1997–2001 and after 2014 because of a lack of population coverage. See PovcalNet for a full series of yearly lined-up estimates. – = not available.

a. See box 1.2 for an estimate of poverty in South Asia in 2017.

FIGURE 1A.1 Global Distribution at the US$1.90-a-Day Poverty Line, by Region and Economy, 2017

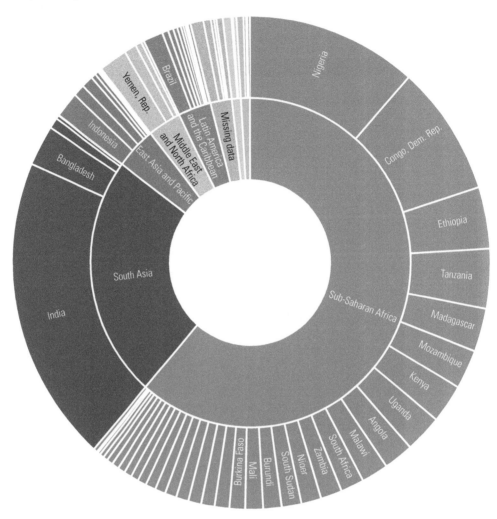

Source: PovcalNet (online analysis tool), World Bank, Washington, DC, http://iresearch.worldbank.org/PovcalNet/.
Note: For each economy, the number of poor is calculated using the lined-up poverty estimate and the population in 2017. The figure uses the India estimate that is included in the global poverty headcount (see box 1.2). The estimate for the number of poor in economies with no available data in PovcalNet is included under the missing data category. For these economies, the number of poor is calculated using the regional (population-weighted) poverty headcount ratio. More details can be found in the "Derivation of regional and global estimates" section of this annex.

TABLE 1A.3 Poverty Rate at the US$1.90-a-Day Poverty Line, by Economy, Most Recent Survey Year

Economy	Survey year	Number of poor (millions)	Poverty rate (%)	Poverty gap (%)	Ratio of poverty gap to poverty rate (%)[a]
Albania	2017	0.0	1.3	0.2	15.3
Algeria	2011.2	0.2	0.4	0.2	33.6
Angola	2018.2	15.9	51.8	23.9	46.1
Argentina	2018	0.5	1.3	0.5	34.9
Armenia	2018	0.0	1.4	0.2	16.7
Australia	2014	0.1	0.5	0.4	74.9
Austria	2017	0.0	0.3	0.2	74.9
Azerbaijan	2005	0.0	0.0	0.0	

(continued)

Economy	Survey year	Number of poor (millions)	Poverty rate (%)	Poverty gap (%)	Ratio of poverty gap to poverty rate (%)[a]
Bangladesh	2016	22.9	14.5	2.7	18.3
Belarus	2018	0.0	0.0	0.0	
Belgium	2017	0.0	0.1	0.1	80.0
Belize	1999	0.0	13.9	6.0	43.3
Benin	2015	5.2	49.6	22.4	45.2
Bhutan	2017	0.0	1.5	0.2	15.9
Bolivia	2018	0.5	4.5	1.7	37.7
Bosnia and Herzegovina	2011	0.0	0.1	0.0	34.4
Botswana	2015.8	0.3	14.5	3.9	26.8
Brazil	2018	9.3	4 4	1.6	37.1
Bulgaria	2017	0.1	1.4	0.4	32.7
Burkina Faso	2014	7.7	43.8	11.2	25.5
Burundi	2013.5	7.2	72.8	31.1	42.7
Cabo Verde	2015	0.0	3.4	0.7	21.3
Cameroon	2014	5.9	26.0	8.4	32.5
Canada	2017	0.1	0.2	0.1	34.3
Central African Republic	2008	2.8	65.9	32.8	49.8
Chad	2011	4.7	38.1	15.2	39.9
Chile	2017	0.1	0.3	0.2	57.3
China (rural)	2016	5.9	1.0	0.2	20.2
China (urban)	2016	1.3	0.2	0.0	28.8
China (national)	2016	7.2	0.5	0.1	21.8
Colombia	2018	2.1	4.2	1.7	40.2
Comoros	2014	0.1	19.1	6.8	35.6
Congo, Dem. Rep.	2012.4	53.3	77.2	39.3	50.9
Congo, Rep.	2011	1.7	38.2	15.4	40.3
Costa Rica	2018	0.1	1.5	0.6	38.6
Côte d'Ivoire	2015	6.9	29.8	9.8	32.7
Croatia	2017	0.0	0.5	0.3	60.8
Cyprus	2017	0.0	0.0	0.0	35.3
Czech Republic	2017	0.0	0.0	0.0	
Denmark	2017	0.0	0.1	0.1	62.6
Djibouti	2017	0.2	17.0	5.6	33.0
Dominican Republic	2018	0.0	0.4	0.1	33.8
Ecuador	2018	0.6	3.3	1.0	30.5
Egypt, Arab Rep.	2017.8	3.7	3.8	0.6	16.9
El Salvador	2018	0.1	1.5	0.3	22.2
Estonia	2017	0.0	0.3	0.2	65.0
Eswatini	2016.2	0.3	29.2	9.8	33.5
Ethiopia	2015.5	33.8	32.6	9.4	28.9
Fiji	2013.2	0.0	0.5	0.1	16.3
Finland	2017	0.0	0.1	0.1	94.1
France	2017	0.0	0.0	0.0	39.2
Gabon	2017	0.1	3.4	0.8	24.8
Gambia, The	2015.3	0.2	10.3	2.3	22.0
Georgia	2018	0.2	4.5	1.2	26.9
Germany	2016	0.0	0.0	0.0	
Ghana	2016.8	3.8	13.0	4.6	35.5
Greece	2017	0.1	0.9	0.4	48.7
Guatemala	2014	1.3	8.8	2.6	29.1

(continued)

Economy	Survey year	Number of poor (millions)	Poverty rate (%)	Poverty gap (%)	Ratio of poverty gap to poverty rate (%)[a]
Guinea	2012	3.8	36.1	10.6	29.4
Guinea-Bissau	2010	1.0	68.4	32.0	46.8
Guyana	1998	0.1	11.7	4.0	34.3
Haiti	2012	2.5	24.5	8.0	32.5
Honduras	2018	1.6	16.9	6.8	40.3
Hungary	2017	0.1	0.6	0.3	58.5
Iceland	2015	0.0	0.0	0.0	13.1
India (rural)	2011.5	227.4	26.3	5.4	20.6
India (urban)	2011.5	56.9	14.2	2.9	20.4
India (national)	2011.5	284.6	22.5	4.6	20.6
Indonesia (rural)	2018	4.6	3.9	0.5	13.0
Indonesia (urban)	2018	5.1	3.4	0.5	14.1
Indonesia (national)	2018	9.7	3.6	0.5	13.6
Iran, Islamic Rep.	2017	0.3	0.3	0.1	16.0
Iraq	2012	0.5	1.7	0.3	15.4
Ireland	2016	0.0	0.1	0.1	66.9
Israel	2016	0.0	0.2	0.0	18.6
Italy	2017	0.9	1.4	1.1	78.5
Jamaica	2004	0.0	1.7	0.4	22.2
Japan	2013	0.9	0.7	0.2	22.6
Jordan	2010.2	0.0	0.1	0.0	25.1
Kazakhstan	2017	0.0	0.0	0.0	28.4
Kenya	2015.7	18.2	37.1	11.7	31.6
Kiribati	2006	0.0	12.9	3.3	25.6
Korea, Rep.	2012	0.1	0.2	0.1	45.1
Kosovo	2017	0.0	0.4	0.2	35.7
Kyrgyz Republic	2018	0.0	0.6	0.1	15.5
Lao PDR	2012.3	1.4	21.2	4.9	22.9
Latvia	2017	0.0	0.8	0.3	42.7
Lebanon	2011.8	0.0	0.0	0.0	
Lesotho	2017.1	0.6	27.8	9.6	34.6
Liberia	2016	2.0	44.4	14.5	32.6
Lithuania	2017	0.0	1.0	0.8	79.5
Luxembourg	2017	0.0	0.3	0.2	56.2
Madagascar	2012	17.3	77.4	38.7	50.0
Malawi	2016.3	12.2	70.8	29.8	42.1
Malaysia	2015.3	0.0	0.0	0.0	13.5
Maldives	2016	0.0	0.0	0.0	
Mali	2009.9	7.6	50.3	15.8	31.4
Malta	2017	0.0	0.2	0.1	55.7
Mauritania	2014	0.2	6.0	1.4	23.8
Mauritius	2017	0.0	0.2	0.0	12.2
Mexico	2018	2.2	1.7	0.5	28.1
Micronesia, Fed. Sts.	2013	0.0	15.4	5.5	36.1
Moldova	2018	0.0	0.0	0.0	5.2
Mongolia	2018	0.0	0.5	0.1	11.7
Montenegro	2015	0.0	1.4	0.3	18.3
Morocco	2013.5	0.3	0.9	0.2	17.9
Mozambique	2014.4	16.7	63.7	28.6	44.9
Myanmar	2017	0.7	1.4	0.2	15.3
Namibia	2015.3	0.3	13.8	4.8	34.7

(continued)

Economy	Survey year	Number of poor (millions)	Poverty rate (%)	Poverty gap (%)	Ratio of poverty gap to poverty rate (%)[a]
Nepal	2010.2	4.0	15.0	3.0	20.3
Netherlands	2017	0.0	0.2	0.1	36.8
Nicaragua	2014	0.2	3.4	0.8	22.2
Niger	2014	8.7	45.4	13.7	30.2
Nigeria	2018.8	78.5	39.1	12.5	31.9
North Macedonia	2017	0.1	4.6	1.9	40.6
Norway	2017	0.0	0.3	0.2	71.0
Pakistan	2015.5	8.1	4.0	0.5	12.8
Panama	2018	0.1	1.7	0.5	30.3
Papua New Guinea	2009.7	2.8	38.0	14.8	30.9
Paraguay	2018	0.1	1.4	0.3	24.8
Peru	2018	0.9	2.7	0.7	25.5
Philippines	2015	7.8	7.6	1.4	18.5
Poland	2017	0.1	0.3	0.2	54.7
Portugal	2017	0.0	0.4	0.2	50.9
Romania	2017	0.6	3.1	1.2	39.4
Russian Federation	2018	0.0	0.0	0.0	16.4
Rwanda	2016.8	6.8	56.5	20.9	36.9
Samoa	2013.3	0.0	1.1	0.1	12.4
São Tomé and Príncipe	2017	0.1	35.6	13.1	36.7
Senegal	2011.3	5.0	38.5	13.1	34.0
Serbia	2018	0.0	0.0	0.0	10.6
Seychelles	2013	0.0	1.2	0.5	39.8
Sierra Leone	2018	3.3	43.0	11.7	27.2
Slovak Republic	2016	0.1	1.3	1.2	86.4
Slovenia	2017	0.0	0.0	0.0	
Solomon Islands	2013	0.1	25.1	6.8	27.2
South Africa	2014.8	10.4	18.7	6.1	32.7
South Sudan	2009	4.1	44.7	20.1	45.1
Spain	2017	0.3	0.7	0.5	79.4
Sri Lanka	2016	0.2	0.9	0.1	11.6
St. Lucia	2016	0.0	4.6	2.6	56.9
Sudan	2014	4.6	12.2	2.8	22.9
Suriname	1999	0.1	23.4	16.6	71.0
Sweden	2017	0.0	0.2	0.1	54.8
Switzerland	2017	0.0	0.0	0.0	
Syrian Arab Republic	2004	0.3	1.7	0.2	14.5
Taiwan, China	2016	0.0	0.0	0.0	
Tajikistan	2015	0.3	4.1	0.9	21.0
Tanzania	2017.9	27.8	49.4	15.9	32.1
Thailand	2018	0.0	0.0	0.0	14.8
Timor-Leste	2014	0.3	22.0	4.4	20.2
Togo	2015	3.7	51.1	20.7	40.5
Tonga	2015	0.0	1.0	0.2	18.9
Trinidad and Tobago	1992	0.0	3.2	0.8	25.2
Tunisia	2015.4	0.0	0.2	0.0	13.1
Turkey	2018	0.0	0.0	0.0	20.7
Turkmenistan	1998	2.2	49.0	18.0	36.8

(continued)

TABLE 1A.3 Poverty Rate at the US$1.90-a-Day Poverty Line, by Economy, Most Recent Survey Year *(continued)*

Economy	Survey year	Number of poor (millions)	Poverty rate (%)	Poverty gap (%)	Ratio of poverty gap to poverty rate (%)[a]
Tuvalu	2010	0.0	3.3	0.4	12.2
Uganda	2016.5	16.5	41.5	13.1	31.6
Ukraine	2018	0.0	0.0	0.0	16.6
United Arab Emirates	2014.4	0.0	0.0	0.0	
United Kingdom	2016	0.1	0.2	0.1	68.9
United States	2016	3.2	1.0	0.9	88.8
Uruguay	2018	0.0	0.1	0.0	51.5
Uzbekistan	2003	15.7	61.6	21.8	35.4
Vanuatu	2010	0.0	13.2	3.3	24.8
Venezuela, RB	2006	2.8	10.3	7.1	69.5
Vietnam	2018	1.8	1.9	0.4	18.8
West Bank and Gaza	2016.8	0.0	0.8	0.1	15.7
Yemen, Rep.	2014	4.7	18.3	4.2	23.2
Zambia	2015	9.3	58.7	30.7	52.2
Zimbabwe	2017	4.8	33.9	9.3	27.3

Source: PovcalNet (online analysis tool), World Bank, Washington, DC, http://iresearch.worldbank.org/PovcalNet/.

Note: The year column refers to the latest survey available. For economies that use European Union Statistics on Income and Living Conditions surveys, the survey year is backdated by one year to align with the reference period for the income data in the survey (for example, the 2016 survey is listed as 2015). The decimal year notation is used if data are collected over two calendar years. The number before the decimal point refers to the first year of data collection, and the number after the decimal point shows the proportion of data collected in the second year. For example, the Algerian survey (2011.2) was conducted in 2011 and 2012, with approximately 20 percent of the data collected in 2012. If both consumption and income measures are available in PovcalNet, consumption is reported. The poverty rate is the percentage of the population living on less than the international poverty line of US$1.90 a day. The poverty gap is the average consumption shortfall of the population, where the nonpoor have no shortfall. The ratio of the poverty gap to the poverty rate is the average consumption shortfall of the poor.

a. Differences between the ratio and the indicators presented in the table are due to rounding.

a. Global poverty rate

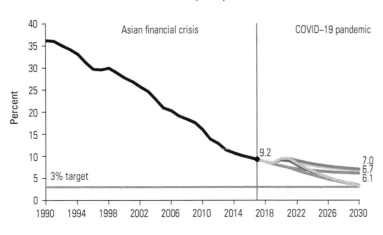

b. Number of poor

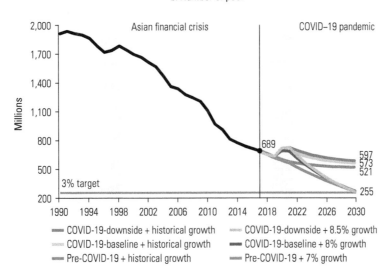

Source: Lakner et al. 2020.
Note: See figure 1.6.

FIGURE 1A.3 Projection of Global Poverty at the US$1.90-a-Day Poverty Line to 2030 with Changes in the Gini Index

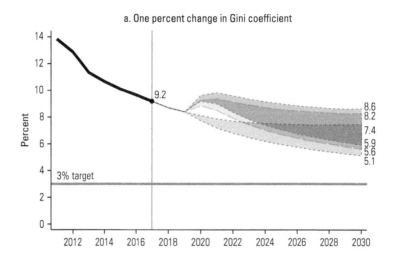

a. One percent change in Gini coefficient

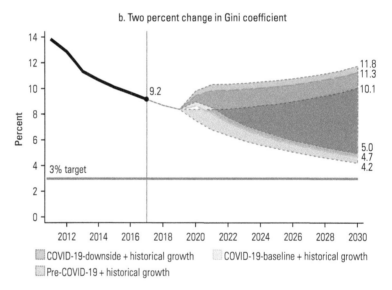

b. Two percent change in Gini coefficient

- COVID-19-downside + historical growth
- COVID-19-baseline + historical growth
- Pre-COVID-19 + historical growth

Source: Lakner et al. 2020.
Note: The assumption of distribution neutrality is relaxed, and a change in the Gini index of 1 percent (panel a) or 2 percent (panel b) per year is included in the projections to reflect the effect of a change in inequality during the period of analysis. See figure 1.6.

Annex 1B

Higher poverty lines: US$3.20 and US$5.50 a day

TABLE 1B.1 Global and Regional Poverty at the US$3.20-a-Day Poverty Line

a. Global poverty at the US$3.20-a-day poverty line, 1990–2017

Year	Poverty rate (%)	Poverty gap (%)	Squared poverty gap (%)	Number of poor (millions)
1990	55.5	26.9	15.7	2,931.2
1993	54.8	25.9	14.9	3,033.8
1996	51.9	23.0	12.8	3,003.3
1999	50.8	22.4	12.5	3,065.9
2002	47.3	20.3	11.0	2,965.9
2005	42.3	17.0	8.9	2,754.1
2008	38.5	15.2	7.8	2,602.3
2011	32.9	12.1	6.0	2,303.2
2014	27.8	9.8	4.8	2,013.9
2015	26.6	9.3	4.6	1,950.4
2016	25.4	8.9	4.4	1,886.6
2017	24.1	8.5	4.2	1,811.1

b. Poverty rates (%) at the US$3.20-a-day poverty line, by region, 1990–2018

	1990	1993	1996	1999	2002	2005	2008	2011	2014	2015	2016	2017	2018
East Asia and Pacific	85.0	79.4	70.2	66.6	56.6	44.5	37.0	25.8	14.5	12.0	10.3	8.7	7.2
Europe and Central Asia	10.3	15.3	18.2	21.2	15.0	11.5	7.2	6.4	5.7	5.3	4.7	4.7	4.3
Latin America and the Caribbean	29.5	28.5	27.8	27.2	25.2	21.5	15.8	13.1	10.9	10.5	10.5	9.5	9.3
Middle East and North Africa	27.3	29.9	29.3	22.1	20.6	19.2	17.1	13.7	13.8	15.3	16.7	18.5	20.3
South Asia	82.4	81.1	78.0	–	76.2	72.2	68.8	60.1	52.4	–	–	–	–
Sub-Saharan Africa	76.1	79.5	79.1	79.3	78.3	75.8	73.2	70.6	68.4	68.1	68.0	67.3	66.6
Rest of the world	0.7	0.8	0.8	0.8	0.7	0.7	0.7	0.8	0.8	0.9	0.9	0.8	0.8

c. Number of poor (millions) at the US$3.20-a-day poverty line, by region, 1990–2018

	1990	1993	1996	1999	2002	2005	2008	2011	2014	2015	2016	2017	2018
East Asia and Pacific	1,364.0	1,329.2	1,220.5	1,198.6	1,046.8	843.5	717.4	510.6	293.1	243.8	211.6	179.1	148.9
Europe and Central Asia	47.8	71.6	85.3	99.7	70.1	54.0	34.2	30.7	27.6	25.9	23.1	23.0	21.2
Latin America and the Caribbean	129.0	131.8	135.2	138.2	133.6	118.6	90.2	77.4	66.7	64.9	65.6	59.8	59.4
Middle East and North Africa	62.3	73.5	76.8	61.1	60.0	58.9	55.3	46.8	49.9	56.2	62.7	70.6	78.6
South Asia	933.7	980.6	1,004.1	–	1,100.0	1,096.5	1,095.6	998.7	904.9	–	–	–	–
Sub-Saharan Africa	387.5	439.5	474.0	514.2	548.6	575.0	602.2	630.7	662.8	678.4	695.5	706.5	718.3
Rest of the world	6.8	7.7	7.5	7.4	6.8	7.5	7.6	8.3	9.0	9.7	9.7	9.0	9.0

Source: PovcalNet (online analysis tool), World Bank, Washington, DC, http://iresearch.worldbank.org/PovcalNet/.
Note: Panel a shows the lined-up global poverty estimates at the US$3.20 line for select years in the period 1990–2017. Poverty rate is the percentage of the population living on less than US$3.20 per person per day. Poverty gap is the average consumption shortfall of the population, where the nonpoor have no shortfall. Number of poor is the number of people living below the US$3.20 line calculated using the poverty rate and population data from the World Bank World Development Indicators. The global coverage rule is applied. Panels b and c show the regional lined-up poverty estimates at the US$3.20 line for selected years between 1990 and 2018. The regional coverage rule is applied and poverty estimates for South Asia are not reported for the period 1997–2001 and after 2014 because of a lack of population coverage. See PovcalNet for a full series of yearly lined-up estimates. – = not available.

TABLE 1B.2 Global and Regional Poverty at the US$5.50-a-Day Poverty Line

a. Global poverty at the US$5.50-a-day poverty line, 1990–2017

Year	Poverty rate (%)	Poverty gap (%)	Squared poverty gap (%)	Number of poor (millions)
1990	67.3	41.8	29.0	3,552.4
1993	68.3	41.3	28.2	3,779.8
1996	67.4	38.9	25.7	3,902.4
1999	67.0	38.2	25.2	4,044.9
2002	64.2	35.6	23.1	4,028.0
2005	60.5	31.9	20.0	3,939.3
2008	56.6	29.2	18.0	3,826.4
2011	52.2	25.3	15.0	3,655.7
2014	47.4	21.8	12.6	3,440.0
2015	46.2	21.0	12.0	3,391.1
2016	45.0	20.3	11.6	3,337.6
2017	43.6	19.5	11.1	3,270.9

b. Poverty rates (%) at the US$5.50-a-day poverty line, by region, 1990–2018

	1990	1993	1996	1999	2002	2005	2008	2011	2014	2015	2016	2017	2018
East Asia and Pacific	95.1	93.1	89.2	86.8	79.7	71.3	63.4	51.9	38.0	34.3	31.2	28.2	25.0
Europe and Central Asia	25.8	36.4	39.7	45.5	35.4	26.5	16.8	15.0	13.7	13.9	13.3	12.6	11.9
Latin America and the Caribbean	49.9	49.5	48.3	47.3	45.4	41.0	33.2	29.5	26.6	26.0	25.6	23.1	22.6
Middle East and North Africa	59.3	60.8	61.2	54.8	52.9	49.6	46.7	42.1	41.4	42.0	42.1	43.4	45.0
South Asia	95.5	95.3	94.1	–	93.1	91.3	90.2	87.0	83.4	–	–	–	–
Sub-Saharan Africa	89.3	91.2	90.8	91.0	90.9	90.2	88.6	87.4	86.4	86.3	86.4	86.1	86.0
Rest of the world	1.6	1.7	1.6	1.3	1.3	1.3	1.2	1.3	1.4	1.4	1.4	1.3	1.3

c. Number of poor (millions) at the US$5.50-a-day poverty line, by region, 1990–2018

	1990	1993	1996	1999	2002	2005	2008	2011	2014	2015	2016	2017	2018
East Asia and Pacific	1,526.6	1,559.0	1,550.8	1,561.8	1,474.1	1,351.8	1,229.4	1,026.8	769.0	699.8	640.9	583.0	519.8
Europe and Central Asia	119.4	170.6	186.2	213.8	165.6	124.3	79.1	71.7	66.5	67.4	64.9	62.0	58.8
Latin America and the Caribbean	218.4	228.5	234.7	240.6	241.0	226.4	190.1	174.8	162.6	160.5	159.9	145.6	143.9
Middle East and North Africa	135.3	149.4	160.1	151.5	154.4	152.5	151.3	143.9	149.7	154.7	157.9	165.3	174.5
South Asia	1,083.0	1,152.5	1,212.0	–	1,343.0	1,386.7	1,435.2	1,445.2	1,440.2	–	–	–	–
Sub-Saharan Africa	454.9	504.1	543.7	590.0	637.4	684.9	729.3	780.1	837.4	859.5	883.0	904.7	927.1
Rest of the world	14.8	15.7	14.9	12.8	12.6	12.8	12.0	13.3	14.6	15.0	14.9	14.0	14.0

Source: PovcalNet (online analysis tool), World Bank, Washington, DC, http://iresearch.worldbank.org/PovcalNet/.
Note: Panel a shows the lined-up global poverty estimates at the US$5.50 line for select years in the period 1990–2017. Poverty rate is the percentage of the population living on less than US$5.50 per person per day. Poverty gap is the average consumption shortfall of the population, where the nonpoor have no shortfall. Number of poor is the number of people living below the US$5.50 line calculated using the poverty rate and population data from the World Bank World Development Indicators. The global coverage rule is applied. Panels b and c show the regional lined-up poverty estimates at the US$5.50 line for selected years between 1990 and 2018. The regional coverage rule is applied and poverty estimates for South Asia are not reported for the period 1997–2001 and after 2014 because of a lack of population coverage. See PovcalNet for a full series of yearly lined-up estimates. – = not available.

Annex 1C

Societal poverty line

TABLE 1C.1 **Global and Regional Societal Poverty**

a. Global societal poverty, 1990–2017

Year	Poverty rate (%)	Average societal poverty line (US$, 2011 PPP)	Number of poor under the societal poverty line (millions)
1990	44.6	5.3	2355.2
1991	44.4	5.2	2383.5
1992	43.6	5.2	2377.8
1993	43.0	5.1	2379.2
1994	42.3	5.1	2374.4
1995	41.3	5.2	2355.9
1996	40.4	5.3	2339.5
1997	40.2	5.3	2361.8
1998	40.6	5.3	2414.9
1999	40.0	5.4	2412.3
2000	39.3	5.5	2400.3
2001	38.8	5.6	2400.7
2002	38.1	5.6	2389.9
2003	37.6	5.7	2386.9
2004	36.5	5.8	2348.1
2005	35.4	5.9	2308.4
2006	35.0	6.0	2309.9
2007	34.4	6.2	2294.4
2008	33.9	6.3	2290.3
2009	33.5	6.3	2288.4
2010	32.5	6.4	2249.8
2011	31.2	6.5	2187.0
2012	30.7	6.6	2173.8
2013	29.5	6.7	2118.4
2014	29.0	6.8	2103.5
2015	28.4	6.9	2085.9
2016	28.1	7.1	2084.2
2017	27.6	7.2	2071.4

b. Average societal poverty line (US$, 2011 PPP), by region, 1990–2018

	East Asia and Pacific	Europe and Central Asia	Latin America and the Caribbean	Middle East and North Africa	South Asia	Sub-Saharan Africa	Rest of the world
1990	2.0	5.9	3.8	3.5	1.9	2.1	17.8
1991	2.0	5.5	4.0	3.4	1.9	2.1	18.0
1992	2.0	5.2	4.0	3.5	1.9	2.1	18.1
1993	2.0	4.9	4.0	3.5	1.9	2.0	18.2
1994	2.1	4.6	4.1	3.6	2.0	2.0	18.3
1995	2.1	4.8	4.1	3.6	2.0	2.0	18.5
1996	2.2	4.7	4.0	3.5	2.0	2.0	18.8
1997	2.2	4.8	4.0	3.5	–	2.1	19.1
1998	2.2	4.8	4.1	3.8	–	2.1	19.3

(continued)

	East Asia and Pacific	Europe and Central Asia	Latin America and the Caribbean	Middle East and North Africa	South Asia	Sub-Saharan Africa	Rest of the world
1999	2.3	4.4	4.1	3.8	–	2.1	19.7
2000	2.3	4.6	4.1	3.8	–	2.1	20.2
2001	2.4	4.7	4.2	3.9	–	2.1	20.6
2002	2.5	4.9	4.1	4.0	2.0	2.1	20.9
2003	2.6	5.1	4.2	4.0	2.1	2.1	21.0
2004	2.7	5.5	4.3	4.2	2.1	2.1	21.4
2005	2.9	5.7	4.5	4.3	2.1	2.1	21.6
2006	3.0	6.0	4.9	4.3	2.1	2.1	22.0
2007	3.1	6.5	5.1	4.5	2.2	2.1	22.5
2008	3.2	7.0	5.2	4.5	2.2	2.1	22.3
2009	3.3	6.9	5.3	4.5	2.2	2.2	22.1
2010	3.6	7.1	5.5	4.6	2.3	2.2	22.3
2011	3.8	7.3	5.7	4.7	2.4	2.2	22.3
2012	4.0	7.4	5.9	4.7	2.4	2.2	22.3
2013	4.3	7.6	6.1	4.7	2.5	2.2	22.2
2014	4.6	7.7	6.1	4.7	2.6	2.2	22.5
2015	4.9	7.5	6.1	4.6	–	2.3	22.9
2016	5.1	7.7	6.2	4.6	–	2.3	23.4
2017	5.3	8.2	6.4	4.7	–	2.3	23.7
2018	5.7	8.4	6.5	4.5	–	2.3	24.1

c. Societal poverty rates (%), by region, 1990–2018

Year	East Asia and Pacific	Europe and Central Asia	Latin America and the Caribbean	Middle East and North Africa	South Asia	Sub-Saharan Africa	Rest of the world
1990	62.7	22.3	34.4	29.0	51.7	59.1	15.6
1991	60.7	22.9	33.8	31.6	51.9	60.7	15.7
1992	58.0	24.0	33.7	30.4	50.7	62.4	15.9
1993	55.2	25.1	34.1	29.7	50.4	63.1	16.1
1994	52.3	27.0	33.5	29.4	49.8	63.9	16.2
1995	49.6	26.7	33.3	29.5	49.1	63.7	16.1
1996	47.4	26.9	34.2	29.1	48.1	62.8	15.9
1997	47.4	25.1	34.0	28.4	–	62.5	15.8
1998	48.5	25.1	33.9	27.3	–	62.7	15.6
1999	45.8	26.6	34.0	27.5	–	62.7	15.6
2000	44.5	26.4	33.5	26.3	–	62.2	15.5
2001	43.5	25.5	33.5	26.0	–	61.0	15.4
2002	41.6	24.4	33.4	25.9	47.2	59.8	15.4
2003	40.1	24.5	32.9	26.7	46.7	59.8	15.4
2004	38.3	23.7	32.1	25.4	45.9	57.4	15.4
2005	36.1	23.0	31.9	24.8	44.6	56.5	15.5
2006	36.0	21.8	30.5	24.6	44.1	55.7	15.5
2007	35.0	20.6	30.1	24.2	43.2	55.0	15.6
2008	34.5	19.4	29.4	23.8	42.6	54.2	15.5
2009	33.6	19.1	29.3	23.2	42.0	54.1	15.3
2010	32.5	18.7	28.9	22.4	40.4	53.0	14.7
2011	30.7	18.3	28.3	21.9	38.0	51.5	14.9
2012	30.0	18.2	27.8	21.4	37.0	50.7	15.0
2013	26.9	17.8	27.4	21.1	35.9	50.3	15.4
2014	26.1	18.0	26.9	21.6	34.8	49.6	15.2
2015	24.9	17.4	26.7	22.4	–	49.4	15.2
2016	24.4	17.4	26.9	23.2	–	49.4	15.3
2017	23.8	17.1	26.5	24.2	–	49.1	15.2
2018	23.2	16.6	26.3	24.9	–	48.7	15.1

(continued)

TABLE 1C.1 **Global and Regional Societal Poverty** *(continued)*

d. Number of poor (millions) according to the societal poverty line, by region, 1990–2018

	East Asia and Pacific	Europe and Central Asia	Latin America and the Caribbean	Middle East and North Africa	South Asia	Sub-Saharan Africa	Rest of the world
1990	1,006.3	103.5	150.7	66.2	586.5	301.0	141.0
1991	989.4	106.6	150.7	73.9	601.3	317.7	143.3
1992	958.3	112.1	153.0	72.9	600.4	335.7	145.4
1993	923.9	117.1	157.3	73.0	609.5	349.2	148.6
1994	887.1	126.7	157.1	73.9	615.9	363.2	150.5
1995	852.4	125.3	159.1	75.7	619.8	371.9	151.7
1996	824.7	126.3	166.2	76.2	619.0	376.3	150.7
1997	834.4	117.9	168.0	75.8	–	384.1	151.0
1998	864.0	118.2	160.0	74.1	–	395.9	150.3
1999	824.1	824.1	173.0	76.1	–	406.1	150.6
2000	809.2	124.0	172.9	74.1	–	413.7	150.9
2001	797.1	119.4	175.5	74.6	–	416.5	151.4
2002	770.0	114.4	177.3	75.6	680.5	419.4	152.7
2003	747.4	114.8	176.9	79.1	685.7	430.3	153.5
2004	720.1	111.0	175.2	76.8	686.0	424.5	154.6
2005	684.7	107.7	175.8	76.2	678.1	428.8	157.1
2006	688.0	102.2	170.1	76.9	680.1	434.2	158.3
2007	672.6	96.8	170.3	77.1	677.1	440.6	159.9
2008	668.4	91.4	168.1	77.1	677.9	446.3	161.1
2009	655.7	90.3	169.7	76.5	678.5	457.8	160.0
2010	639.8	88.6	169.4	75.3	661.4	460.8	154.6
2011	608.5	87.3	167.6	74.9	631.4	460.3	157.1
2012	598.7	87.1	166.2	74.5	622.4	465.1	159.8
2013	540.6	85.8	165.7	74.8	612.7	474.7	164.3
2014	528.3	87.1	164.7	78.1	600.9	480.3	164.2
2015	508.2	84.8	165.0	82.6	–	491.6	165.2
2016	502.2	84.9	168.0	87.0	–	504.9	166.8
2017	491.8	83.8	167.1	92.3	–	515.6	166.9
2018	482.2	81.9	167.5	96.4	–	525.1	166.6

Source: PovcalNet (online analysis tool), World Bank, Washington, DC, http://iresearch.worldbank.org/PovcalNet/.

Note: Panel a shows the lined-up global societal poverty estimates for the period 1990–2017. Poverty rate is the share of the population living below each economy's specific societal poverty line (SPL). The average SPL indicates the population-weighted average. Number of poor is the number of people living below each economies' SPL and is calculated using the societal poverty rate and population data from the World Bank World Development Indicators. The global coverage rule is applied. Panels b through d show the lined-up regional societal poverty estimates for the period 1990–2018. The average SPL is the population-weighted regional average of the economy-specific SPL. The regional coverage rule is applied, and estimates for South Asia are not reported in the period 1997–2001 and after 2014 because of a lack of population coverage. See PovcalNet for a full series of yearly median consumption or income values used to calculate the SPL using the formula in box 1.1. – = not available; PPP = purchasing power parity.

Annex 1D

Multidimensional poverty

The estimates of multidimensional poverty (tables 1.2, 1.3, and 1D.2) are largely derived from household surveys included in the World Bank's GMD for circa 2017. These surveys account for most of the welfare aggregates included in PovcalNet in recent years (Luxembourg Income Study [LIS] data are the other main source of information included in PovcalNet).[53] These harmonized surveys collect information on total household consumption or income for monetary poverty estimation as well as information on a host of other topics, including education enrollment, adult education attainment, and access to basic infrastructure services, which permits the construction of the MPM. However, there is considerable heterogeneity in how the questions are worded, how detailed the response choices are, and how closely they match the standard definitions of access (for example, as defined by the Joint Monitoring Programme for Water Supply and Sanitation.)[54] Despite best efforts to harmonize country-specific questionnaires to the standard definition, discrepancies with measures reported elsewhere could arise.

Therefore, the estimates must be viewed as the best possible estimates under the stringent data requirement of jointly observing monetary and nonmonetary dimensions of well-being. Finally, both education indicators are household-level indicators (for example, the number of individuals living in a household in which one child is not attending school), meaning that the table of each country's educational deprivations (see table 1D.2) presented in the chapter cannot be directly compared with official estimates of the United Nations Educational, Scientific, and Cultural Organization, which are based on individual-level indicators.

Not all indicators are applicable to every household. For example, not every household has a child younger than the school age for grade 8 (necessary for the school enrollment indicator). In these cases, the weight of the missing indicator is shifted to other indicators within the dimension so that each dimensional weight is unchanged (see table 1D.1 for weights of the indicators). The same process occurs if the information on an indicator for a household is missing, even if the indicator is applicable. Because of this reweighting process, few households are ignored because of missing data. Only households for which information is missing on all the indicators that constitute a dimension are not considered in the analysis.

In addition to the economies included from the GMD, three economies (Germany, Israel, and the United States) are used from the LIS database. Including these economies improves the country and data coverage for the analysis of multidimensional poverty. However, including them raises two issues. First, there is no information on the infrastructure variables in the LIS data. This is similar to the European Union Statistics on Income and Living Conditions[55] data, which lack information on electricity. However, data from the World Bank's World Development Indicators suggest that 99 percent or more of the population in these economies has access to electricity, safely managed drinking water, and basic sanitation in the latest survey year (2016). So universal coverage is assumed for these economies in the infrastructure indicators. PovcalNet uses LIS data for several additional economies; however, because their coverage in the World Development Indicators is lower than 99 percent or missing, they are not used in the MPM. Second, school enrollment is not available in the LIS data because there is no education information for the 6–14 age group. Thus, in estimating the MPM, the school enrollment indicator is set to "missing" and all the weight for the education dimension is shifted to the educational attainment indicator. This is also how the data are used for economies in the European Union Statistics on Income and Living Conditions, given that there is no schooling information for children younger than 15.

TABLE 1D.1 Multidimensional Poverty Measure Indicators and Weights

Dimension	Parameter	Weight
Monetary poverty	Daily consumption or income is less than US$1.90 per person.	1/3
Education	At least one school-age child up to the age of grade 8 is not enrolled in school.	1/6
	No adult in the household (age of grade 9 or above) has completed primary education.	1/6
Access to basic infrastructure	The household lacks access to limited-standard drinking water.	1/9
	The household lacks access to limited-standard sanitation.	1/9
	The household has no access to electricity.	1/9

Source: World Bank 2018.

TABLE 1D.2 Individuals in Households Deprived in Each Indicator, 114 Economies, circa 2017

Economy	Survey year	Monetary (%)	Educational attainment (%)	Educational enrollment (%)	Electricity (%)	Sanitation (%)	Drinking water (%)	Multidimensional poverty headcount ratio (%)
Albania	2017	1.3	0.3	–	0.1	7.0	9.3	1.5
Angola	2018	51.8	29.8	27.4	52.6	53.6	32.1	59.2
Argentina	2018	1.3	1.3	0.7	0.0	0.5	0.3	1.3
Armenia	2018	1.4	0.0	1.7	0.1	5.1	0.4	1.4
Austria	2017	0.3	0.0	–	0.0	0.7	0.5	0.3
Bangladesh	2016	14.5	22.0	8.4	23.6	54.5	2.8	21.4
Belarus	2018	0.0	0.0	–	–	5.3	4.4	4.3
Belgium	2017	0.3	1.9	–	0.0	0.9	0.3	2.1
Benin	2015	49.6	61.6	25.5	69.0	70.7	26.9	71.8
Bhutan	2017	1.5	40.8	4.1	1.9	13.7	0.4	3.9
Bolivia	2018	4.5	15.3	1.6	7.2	19.4	9.4	12.4
Botswana	2015	14.1	8.2	4.2	35.5	52.0	3.7	20.0
Brazil	2018	4.4	13.9	0.5	0.3	35.7	1.8	9.0
Bulgaria	2017	1.4	0.7	–	0.0	15.3	9.4	2.0
Burkina Faso	2014	43.8	64.7	58.0	85.2	63.3	20.6	74.8
Cabo Verde	2015	3.4	11.7	2.7	9.9	30.2	11.1	6.5
Cameroon	2014	26.0	24.4	15.9	1.2	38.9	23.2	37.7
Chile	2017	0.3	4.0	0.4	0.3	0.6	0.1	0.4
Colombia	2018	4.2	5.5	2.6	1.5	8.3	2.5	5.7
Comoros	2014	19.1	15.3	7.3	28.5	67.2	6.4	26.7
Costa Rica	2018	1.5	4.9	1.0	0.4	1.8	0.1	1.8
Côte d'Ivoire	2015	29.8	53.2	25.6	37.4	59.5	23.3	50.8
Croatia	2017	0.6	0.3	–	0.0	1.3	1.2	0.8
Cyprus	2017	0.0	1.4	–	0.0	0.5	0.5	1.4
Czech Republic	2017	0.1	0.0	–	0.0	0.5	0.3	0.1
Denmark	2017	0.5	0.4	–	0.0	0.4	1.9	0.9
Djibouti	2017	17.0	30.1	18.0	39.8	45.4	7.1	28.5
Dominican Republic	2018	0.4	14.4	26.7	1.1	6.7	1.1	6.0
Ecuador	2018	3.3	3.9	2.3	1.3	3.1	4.4	4.7
Egypt, Arab Rep.	2017	3.8	10.6	4.2	0.5	3.2	0.8	4.7
El Salvador	2018	1.5	24.7	4.0	3.0	9.3	3.8	7.4
Estonia	2017	0.5	0.0	–	0.0	5.3	6.6	0.5
Eswatini	2016	29.1	10.7	0.3	35.7	46.5	27.9	35.1
Ethiopia	2015	32.6	66.7	31.2	64.1	95.9	42.7	73.8
Finland	2017	0.1	1.5	–	0.0	0.4	0.4	1.6
France	2017	0.1	1.5	–	0.0	0.5	0.6	1.6
Gabon	2017	3.4	11.3	7.9	8.6	68.2	11.5	9.1
Gambia, The	2015	10.3	29.9	6.1	8.0	58.2	8.2	15.5

(continued)

Economy	Survey year	Deprivation rate (share of population)						Multidimensional poverty headcount ratio (%)
		Monetary (%)	Educational attainment (%)	Educational enrollment (%)	Electricity (%)	Sanitation (%)	Drinking water (%)	
Georgia	2018	4.5	0.0	1.1	0.0	1.5	8.6	4.5
Germany	2016	0.1	0.3	–	0.0	0.0	0.0	0.1
Ghana	2016	13.0	15.1	9.0	19.5	79.9	40.8	23.5
Greece	2017	1.2	1.7	–	0.0	0.3	0.5	2.9
Guatemala	2014	8.8	24.8	18.3	16.5	46.7	8.4	21.6
Honduras	2018	16.9	12.5	12.4	8.4	7.7	8.4	20.9
Hungary	2017	0.7	0.0	–	0.0	3.8	3.6	0.7
Iceland	2015	0.1	0.0	–	0.0	0.0	0.2	0.2
Indonesia	2016	5.3	5.0	1.7	2.4	16.5	10.7	6.8
Iran, Islamic Rep.	2017	0.3	4.4	1.0	0.0	2.0	1.6	0.5
Ireland	2016	0.1	0.6			0.0	0.1	0.2	0.7
Israel	2016	0.0	0.3	–	0.0	0.0	0.0	0.0
Italy	2017	1.6	1.3	–	0.0	0.6	0.5	2.9
Kazakhstan	2017	0.0	0.0	–	0.0	0.9	1.5	1.0
Kenya	2015	37.1	22.5	6.1	56.9	69.0	32.2	50.1
Kosovo	2017	0.4	0.5	23.6	0.2	1.4	0.7	0.8
Kyrgyz Republic	2018	0.6	0.0	–	1.8	0.1	8.9	0.6
Latvia	2017	1.0	0.1	–	0.0	10.0	11.9	1.2
Lesotho	2017	27.8	18.1	4.8	58.7	55.1	13.7	37.1
Liberia	2016	44.4	30.5	54.1	79.7	61.8	25.7	64.0
Lithuania	2017	1.1	0.2	–	0.0	10.6	9.9	1.4
Luxembourg	2017	0.6	0.8	–	0.0	0.0	0.2	1.4
Malawi	2016	70.8	56.2	3.1	6.7	48.1	12.9	76.3
Malaysia	2015	0.0	0.7	0.6	0.6	13.2	1.6	0.2
Maldives	2016	0.0	2.2	1.5	0.0	0.4	0.9	0.0
Malta	2017	0.2	0.2	–	0.0	0.1	0.1	0.4
Mauritania	2014	6.0	54.3	8.3	54.1	49.3	38.6	45.5
Mauritius	2017	0.2	7.2	0.2	0.2	–	–	0.4
Mexico	2018	1.7	4.3	2.5	0.5	6.2	4.2	3.3
Moldova	2017	0.1	0.1	0.4	0.0	0.0	0.5	0.1
Mongolia	2016	0.5	6.0	3.2	0.2	9.6	12.8	1.3
Mozambique	2014	63.7	54.9	33.3	72.8	71.3	40.8	76.9
Myanmar	2015	4.8	17.7	13.7	16.2	18.2	29.4	14.1
Namibia	2015	13.8	11.3	6.1	53.8	68.3	9.2	26.3
Netherlands	2017	0.5	1.1	–	0.0	0.0	0.1	1.6
Nicaragua	2014	3.4	14.1	8.1	20.0	42.7	12.5	15.2
Niger	2014	45.4	70.6	11.7	87.0	83.7	48.5	79.3
Nigeria	2018	39.1	17.6	20.3	39.4	44.9	27.5	47.3
North Macedonia	2016	4.4	0.4	–	0.0	5.2	–	4.7
Norway	2017	0.4	2.1	–	0.0	0.0	0.3	2.4
Pakistan	2015	4.0	41.4	5.1	10.1	28.0	7.7	11.5
Paraguay	2018	1.4	6.3	2.7	0.5	10.4	2.8	4.6
Peru	2018	2.7	5.7	0.6	4.8	12.2	6.8	6.0
Philippines	2015	6.0	4.5	4.4	9.1	6.8	10.6	8.2
Poland	2016	0.0	0.1	3.0	0.0	2.7	0.4	0.0
Portugal	2017	0.4	2.4	–	0.0	0.8	0.9	2.9
Romania	2016	0.0	0.3	2.9	0.9	21.6	1.6	0.8
Russian Federation	2015	0.0	0.2	0.4	4.5	10.7	5.5	3.2
Rwanda	2016	56.5	36.9	4.3	64.0	28.1	24.5	61.1

(continued)

TABLE 1D.2 Individuals in Households Deprived in Each Indicator, 114 Economies, circa 2017 *(continued)*

Economy	Survey year	Deprivation rate (share of population)						Multidimensional poverty headcount ratio (%)
		Monetary (%)	Educational attainment (%)	Educational enrollment (%)	Electricity (%)	Sanitation (%)	Drinking water (%)	
São Tomé and Príncipe	2017	35.2	20.2	4.2	27.4	62.1	8.8	41.8
Serbia	2018	0.0	3.2	0.7	0.1	2.1	0.2	0.1
Sierra Leone	2018	43.0	28.7	18.7	68.7	87.2	33.8	61.7
Slovak Republic	2016	1.5	0.0	—	0.0	1.5	0.9	1.5
Slovenia	2017	0.0	0.0	—	0.0	0.2	0.2	0.0
South Africa	2014	18.7	2.3	1.5	4.1	4.7	8.2	19.2
Spain	2017	0.9	3.4		0.0	0.2	0.2	4.2
Sri Lanka	2016	0.9	3.8	4.0	2.5	1.2	11.0	1.3
Sweden	2017	0.6	0.9	—	0.0	0.0	0.1	1.3
Switzerland	2017	0.1	0.0	—	0.0	0.0	0.1	0.1
Tajikistan	2015	4.1	0.3	26.8	2.0	3.5	26.3	5.0
Tanzania	2018	49.4	13.2	19.5	44.3	71.5	29.2	57.8
Thailand	2017	0.0	14.8	0.6	0.1	0.2	0.9	0.1
Timor-Leste	2014	22.0	21.2	0.3	27.2	48.6	22.1	32.7
Togo	2015	51.3	26.7	2.3	—	51.8	40.6	62.1
Tonga	2015	1.0	—	0.8	0.0	1.8	0.1	1.7
Tunisia	2015	0.2	20.2	2.1	0.2	6.5	2.1	1.6
Turkey	2018	0.0	3.1	3.4	0.0	5.6	0.1	0.3
Uganda	2016	41.5	34.8	14.0	61.2	77.6	22.9	57.2
Ukraine	2014	0.0	0.5	2.5	0.0	21.5	0.0	0.1
United Kingdom	2015	0.7	0.5	—	0.0	0.4	0.6	1.2
United States	2016	1.1	0.2	—	0.0	0.0	0.0	1.1
Uruguay	2018	0.1	2.2	0.7	0.2	0.9	0.4	0.1
Vietnam	2014	2.6	5.9	1.3	0.9	19.8	7.1	3.8
West Bank and Gaza	2016	0.8	1.2	5.8	0.0	0.1	3.2	0.9
Yemen, Rep.	2014	18.3	15.9	44.5	33.9	41.2	14.0	34.6
Zambia	2015	58.7	24.4	30.4	69.2	59.8	30.7	64.5

Source: Global Monitoring Database.

Note: Estimates are based on the harmonized household surveys in 114 economies, circa 2017, Global Monitoring Database, Global Solution Group on Welfare Measurement and Capacity Building, Poverty and Equity Global Practice, World Bank, Washington, DC. The definitions of the indicators and the deprivation thresholds are as follows. Monetary poverty: a household is deprived if income or expenditure, in 2011 purchasing power parity US dollars, is less than US$1.90 per person per day. The estimates in this table for Germany, Israel, and the United States are based on the microdata available from the Luxembourg Income Study, whereas table 1A.3 is based on 400 bins, which gives rise to differences in the first decimal on monetary poverty. Educational attainment: a household is deprived if no adult (grade 9 equivalent age or older) has completed primary education. Educational enrollment: a household is deprived if at least one school-age child up to the (equivalent) age of grade 8 is not enrolled in school. Electricity: a household is deprived if it does not have access to electricity. Sanitation: a household is deprived if it does not have access to limited-standard sanitation. Drinking water: a household is deprived if it does not have access to limited-standard drinking water. The data reported refer to the share of people living in households deprived according to each indicator. — = not available.

Notes

1. The global poverty numbers reported in this chapter extend to 2017, which is the latest year with sufficient population coverage to estimate global poverty. The coverage rule behind this choice is explained in annex 1A and by Castaneda et al. (2020).

2. Nowcast refers to the poverty estimates forecast up to the current time, which for this report is 2020. Because nowcasting relies largely on realized growth rates and population figures, it should, in principle, be more reliable than a forecast. At the same time, because few household surveys are available after 2017, the nowcast needs to make additional assumptions (in particular, that survey growth can be approximated by growth in national accounts and that this growth is distribution neutral). Furthermore, a lack of recent data for India and the evolving effects of COVID-19 create further uncertainty around the nowcast poverty estimates. Forecasts refer to projections that are further into the future, up to 2030.

Forecasts are based on assumed growth rates and predictions of population figures and are subject to even greater uncertainty. The nowcasts in panels a and b of figure 1.4 also show estimates for 2021 to assess the effect of the projected recovery on global poverty.

3. The estimated poverty rate in 2020, between 9.1 percent and 9.4 percent, is based on the June 2020 *Global Economic Prospects* (GEP) growth forecasts (World Bank 2020b). This range is in line with the poverty rate in 2017 of 9.2 percent. Depending on the trajectory of the still-evolving COVID-19 pandemic, the setback to poverty reduction could be longer than three years.

4. See PovcalNet (online analysis tool), World Bank, Washington, DC, http://iresearch. worldbank.org/PovcalNet/. This report uses the data as published in September 2020. See annex 1A for more details about sources of data, country and population coverage, definition of welfare aggregates, changes in purchasing power parity rates, and other technical issues.

5. The World Bank supports national authorities in their survey collection efforts, for example, through the longstanding Living Standards Measurement Study program (Living Standards Measurement Study, database, World Bank, Washington, DC, https:// www.worldbank.org/en/programs/lsms). One of the goals of the World Bank in the past decades has been to improve data coverage in poorer countries, particularly Sub-Saharan Africa (Beegle and Christiaensen 2019).

6. New data for Nigeria were eagerly anticipated given that the last data on poverty date to 2009. The Nigerian Living Standards Survey for 2018/19 was released in June 2020 and is used to update the Nigeria poverty estimates in this report. The latest survey is not comparable to the 2009/10 data because of changes in the survey design (Castaneda et al. 2020; NBS 2020).

7. The poverty rate for India is estimated based on the uniform reference period welfare aggregate (World Bank 2018). Using the consumption aggregate based on the modified mixed reference period results in considerably lower measured levels of poverty. As explained in box 1.2, the number of poor in India in 2017 is estimated at 139 million, with a range between 109 million and 152 million using the uniform reference period aggregate, making India the country with the highest number of poor (Nigeria's number of poor is estimated at 79 million in 2017). However, using the modified mixed reference period aggregate would likely push the number of poor in India to less than Nigeria's level.

8. Corral et al. (2020) suggest that extreme poverty in FCS is underestimated by some 0.5 percentage point, corresponding to 33 million extra poor. For countries with no household survey data at any time, that is, countries for which the lineup exercise cannot be applied, the headcount is assumed to be the regional population-weighted average calculated over the countries with data. Figure 1A.1 illustrates the relevance of missing data in poverty measurement. It shows the geographical distribution of the extreme poor, including a category of countries with missing data. The estimate of the extreme poor for countries with no data in PovcalNet (15 million) accounts for a larger share of the global poor than Europe and Central Asia. For additional methodological details on how PovcalNet deals with countries with missing data, see annex 1A and "PovcalNet: Methodology," World Bank, Washington, DC, http://iresearch.world-bank.org/PovcalNet/methodology.aspx.

9. The total number of poor adds up to the global figure. Thus, the global coverage rule is adopted, and the estimates are shown until 2017. For this reason, figure 1.2, panels c and d of figure 1.7, and figure 1.10 show an estimated number of poor for South Asia until 2017. For South Asia, poverty estimates are reported only until 2014, following the regional coverage rule explained in detail in annex 1A and hindered by the absence of recent data on India (see box 1.2).

10. However, conflicts also limit the availability of recent household survey data in these countries. Corral et al. (2020) discuss the relevance of data deprivation in FCS for poverty monitoring. They show that many economies in this category either lack poverty estimates completely, for example, Afghanistan, or have severely outdated poverty estimates that predate entering FCS, for example, Syria. The authors show that, notwithstanding the attempts to calculate a poverty estimate using the regional average for countries with no microdata or using national

accounts for the yearly lineup, poverty is underestimated in FCS. They estimate that, in 2015, poverty was underestimated by 0.5 percentage point because of data deprivation, accounting for 33 million extra poor, 17 million of whom are living in FCS.

11. Surveys in the Middle East and North Africa largely use consumption expenditures, whereas surveys in Latin America and the Caribbean use income. The poverty levels in the two regions are therefore not comparable. High-income countries (largely falling into the rest of the world category) also primarily use income data. Economies in Europe and Central Asia are roughly evenly split into income and consumption surveys, and all other regions use consumption almost exclusively. Whether consumption or income is used can have important effects on the measurement of poverty (Deaton 2001), making it difficult to compare the trends in Latin America and the Caribbean to those in other regions. For example, income can be zero or negative, but consumption (which includes the monetization of own-produced food in most household surveys) must be positive (see annex 1A). PovcalNet uses consumption measures rather than income if both are available.

12. This share is determined by comparing past growth in national accounts and household surveys (see the discussion in box 1.2). For the global sample of comparable surveys, this pass-through is estimated at 0.85 percent following the methodology in Lakner et al. (2020).

13. There are, however, some subtle differences. The lineup uses a range of methods, including interpolations and extrapolations as described in Prydz et al. (2019). For surveys that are extrapolated, a pass-through of 1 is assumed.

14. The poverty impacts of the Asian financial crisis and COVID-19 are estimated somewhat differently. The impact of the Asian financial crisis is relative to the previous year (1998 relative to 1997). The COVID-19 impact is relative to a counterfactual scenario estimated for 2020, which is consistent with the other COVID-19 impacts reported throughout this chapter. In 2020, COVID-19 is estimated to increase poverty by between 0.7 (under baseline growth assumption) and 1.0 percentage points (under downside growth assumption) relative to 2019.

15. Mahler et al. (2020) use the January 2020 edition of GDP growth forecasts from GEP (World Bank 2020a) for the pre-COVID-19 scenario and the June 2020 edition (World Bank 2020b) for the COVID-19 scenarios for 2019 through 2021. This report uses the June GEP growth forecasts for all scenarios in 2019, the June 2020 GEP forecasts for the COVID-19 scenarios in 2020 and 2021, and the January 2020 GEP forecasts for the pre-COVID-19 scenario in 2020 and 2021. According to Mahler et al. (2020), the difference in poverty rates between the pre-COVID-19 and COVID-19 scenarios in 2020 arises as a result of differences in growth rates in 2019 as well as the effect of COVID-19 in 2020. To account for this difference, the authors use a difference-in-differences methodology to calculate the new poor caused by COVID-19 in 2020. The 2019 poverty estimates in this report are the same across all scenarios. Hence, to calculate the new poor caused by COVID-19, it is sufficient to look at the raw difference in 2020. Until 2018, which is the latest reference year shown, surveys are lined up following the standard procedure. The nowcasts begin in 2019 using the various growth rates discussed previously. Numbers for 2021 are shown to assess the effect of the projected recovery on global poverty.

16. The economic consequences of COVID-19 could disproportionately affect the poor and thus raise inequality in several ways. Because the poor are more likely to be employed informally or self-employed, they lack unemployment insurance (Loayza 2020; Loayza and Pennings 2020). Because the poor spend a larger share of their expenditures on food and because they are more likely to work in agriculture, the food price shocks associated with the pandemic would affect them disproportionately (Hernandez et al. 2020; Sulser and Dunston 2020). Brown, Ravallion, and van de Walle (2020) show that 90 percent of households in the developing world lack adequate home environments for protection from COVID-19. Simulating different changes in inequality, Lakner et al. (2020) show that the number of people pushed into extreme poverty would increase by half if the Gini index increases by 2 percent in all countries.

17. ADB (2020) estimates that COVID-19 could slow global GDP by as much as 6.4 percent to

9.7 percent. Both are larger contractions than those used in this analysis, and they would result in higher poverty rates.

18. The values in figure 1.4 may not add up to these numbers because of rounding. These estimates are somewhat greater than those presented by Mahler et al. (2020), who report an additional 71 million in the baseline scenario and 100 million under the downside scenario. This difference is primarily explained by the revised lineup estimate for India. Assuming that the growth rates of all countries decline by 20 percent, Sumner, Ortiz-Juárez, and Hoy (2020) estimate that the number of people in poverty in 2020 could be as high as 400 million more than in 2019 under the US$1.90-a-day line.

19. Poverty estimates for South Asia in recent years are subject to considerable uncertainty because of the absence of recent survey data for India. Figure 1.5 decomposes the total global change due to COVID-19, thus incorporating the main pass-through estimate on India that is included in the global headcount (see box 1.2). India is lined up until 2018 using growth in per capita household final consumption expenditure with a 0.67 pass-through. From 2019 onward, as with all countries, the Indian distribution is projected forward using the GDP growth scenarios from GEP and the global 0.85 pass-through.

20. One could argue that, if the safety nets put in place by governments successfully protect the income of the poorest, inequality might not increase. However, given that policy support might not be sufficient to offset the negative shock and that the crisis might have long-lasting effects on different outcomes (for example, incomes, human capital accumulation, health), seeing a decrease in inequality is unlikely.

21. This is the crucial factor distinguishing the nowcasts from the forecasts that go to 2030. From the latest global lineup year (2017) until 2021, national accounts data, which may be actual data or near-term forecasts, are published in the World Development Indicators or the GEP. Beyond 2021 the scenarios are based on historical growth rates, given that no forecasts are readily available in standard sources of national accounts data.

22. The average annualized historical per capita growth rate between 2008 and 2018 is 3.1 percent for economies in East Asia and Pacific, 2.7 percent for economies in Europe and Central Asia, 1.6 percent for economies in Latin America and the Caribbean, 0.1 percent for economies in the Middle East and North Africa, 3.8 percent for economies in South Asia, 1.5 percent for economies in Sub-Saharan Africa, and 0.8 percent for the economies in the rest of the world. The estimated averages by income group are as follows: 1.2 percent for high-income economies, 1.7 percent for upper-middle-income economies, 2.8 percent for lower-middle-income economies, and 1.0 percent for low-income economies. The global average annual growth rate over the same period is 1.7 percent per year.

23. This is the difference between the number of poor under the COVID-19 scenarios and the pre-COVID-19 scenario summed over the years between 2020 and 2030.

24. The distribution-neutral scenario using the pre-COVID-19 growth rates results in a poverty rate of 6.1 percent in 2030, which is almost the same as the projected poverty rate of 5.9 percent using the COVID-19-downside growth rates and allowing the Gini index to decline by 1 percent per year.

25. As in figure 1.1, estimates are reported through 2017, applying the same coverage rule as is applied to the IPL global estimates (annex 1A).

26. Detailed information on the multidimensional and monetary poverty headcount of each economy can be found in annex 1D, table 1D.2.

27. The GMD is an ex post harmonization effort based on available multitopic household surveys, including household budget surveys and the Living Standards Measurement Study. The data are stored on secure servers accessible only to subscribed or approved users.

28. Of the 166 economies in the PovcalNet data set, only 114 have a household survey in the period between 2014 and 2018 with enough information to calculate the MPM (that is, indicators capturing education and access to infrastructure). In particular, the two most populous economies in the world, China and India, are not included in the MPM. China lacks data on the covariates. India lacks recent household survey data, as discussed earlier in this chapter. Moreover, and unlike the regional estimates presented so far, the MPM is not calculated at lineup years but uses

the information for survey years. Thus, the regional poverty rates summarized in table 1.1 cannot be directly compared with the regional poverty headcounts presented in table 1A.1.

29. Given the much higher shares of population deprived in each dimension, it is difficult to compare Sub-Saharan Africa with other regions. The only estimates that are similar are for educational attainment in Sub-Saharan Africa and South Asia. However, given the low data coverage for South Asia, this comparison should be interpreted with caution.

30. Figure 1.13 shows the share of households deprived in multiple dimensions. It focuses on Latin America and the Caribbean, the Middle East and North Africa, and Sub-Saharan Africa, which are the regions with sufficient population coverage.

31. The countries included in the circa 2017 MPM reported here are not the same as those included in the previous report, preventing meaningful comparisons of regional estimates. The same is true for the monetary poverty measures presented at the beginning of the chapter. However, in the case of the monetary poverty measures, lining up survey-year estimates to a common reference year ensures that the same numbers of countries are available in all years, although it requires additional assumptions. Moreover, the estimates published in World Bank (2018) were reported for a circa 2013 reference year, including surveys in the period between 2010 and 2016, which overlaps with the 2014 to 2018 period used for the 2017 reference year. Therefore, for some countries the same survey-year estimate would be used in both reference years. These limitations hinder the possibility of comparing these MPM values to those published in the previous edition.

32. This discussion excludes countries for which no household survey can be used for global poverty monitoring, such as the Democratic Republic of Korea and Somalia. These comparisons use the lined-up estimates to be able to compare poverty rates in the same year across as many countries as possible.

33. Rather than showing economy-level information, figure 1.14 is meant to illustrate the change in the variation in poverty rates across economies over time. Each dot in the figure represents the lined-up poverty estimate of an economy in East Asia and Pacific (panel a) and Sub-Saharan Africa (panel b). Put differently, the figure should not be read as tracking the same economy over time, but as a visualization of the variation in poverty rates across economies within each region over time.

34. The previous edition of this report discusses in detail the negative correlation between poverty and strength of institutions measured using different indicators: financial penetration, business climate, rule of law, and perceived corruption. That analysis concluded that countries in FCS score much worse under all these dimensions (World Bank 2018; see also World Bank 2017b).

35. This exercise takes for each economy the latest two comparable survey-year observations, calculates the difference in headcounts between the two periods, and divides that difference by the number of years between the two observations. The lag between the two survey years can be as large as 10 years, as in Angola and Kenya, or as small as 2 years in Liberia and Madagascar. Moreover, the latest year of available data is 2009 in Mali and 2018 in Angola and Sierra Leone. The average yearly changes in poverty headcounts are as follows: Guinea (−4.8), Chad (−3.1), Republic of Congo (−2.8), Democratic Republic of Congo (−2.1), Eswatini (−1.9), Niger (−1.7), Sierra Leone (−1.7), Namibia (−1.6), Zambia (−1.4), Mozambique (−1.0), Togo (−0.9), Benin (−0.9), Burundi (−0.8), Cameroon (−0.8), Mauritania (−0.8), Kenya (−0.7), Mali (−0.5), Ethiopia (−0.5), Rwanda (−0.4), Botswana (−0.4), Madagascar (−0.4), Malawi (−0.2), Côte d'Ivoire (−0.08), Mauritius (−0.07), Tanzania (−0.04), Senegal (0.04), Ghana (0.34), South Africa (0.6), Liberia (1.3), Uganda (1.4), Angola (1.7), and Zimbabwe (2.1). Data on comparable poverty measures can be found at "Comparability Over Time at the Country Level for International Poverty Measures," World Bank, Washington, DC, https://datacatalog.worldbank.org/dataset/comparability-over-time-country-level-international-poverty-measures. For some of these economies, the last available information is severely outdated. See table 1A.3 for the full list of economies in the last survey year and see PovcalNet for the full data set.

36. Beegle and Christiaensen (2019) provide an in-depth analysis of Africa's slow poverty

reduction. They identify three notable factors that have contributed to this phenomenon: persistent high fertility and population growth hindering per capita economic output growth, high initial levels of poverty, and the increasing reliance on natural resources and modest performance of the agriculture and manufacturing sectors.

37. A comparison with other economies in the world is complicated by a lack of recent data for India. Using the estimate for India described in box 1.2 (estimated 139 million poor in 2017 with a range between 109 million and 152 million) would suggest that Nigeria has the second-highest number of poor in the world (it is the seventh most populous country in the world). As discussed in World Bank (2018), the poverty rate for India is estimated using the uniform reference period welfare aggregate. Using the consumption aggregate based on the modified mixed reference period results in considerably lower measured levels of poverty, and likely puts India's number of poor at less than Nigeria's (using the methods described in box 1.2 to estimate poverty in India in 2017).

38. This is the number of economies with at least one survey at any point in time that allows PovcalNet to apply the lineup methodology, provided that national accounts data are available, and to calculate a poverty estimate for that economy.

39. PovcalNet (online analysis tool), World Bank, Washington, DC, http://iresearch.worldbank.org/PovcalNet/.

40. The rule for defining population coverage has been revised slightly, such that the coverage figures reported here for 2013 may be slightly different from those published in World Bank (2016).

41. The World Bank committed to ensuring that the poorest countries have household-level surveys every three years, with the first round completed by 2020. In light of important gaps in poverty data in the past decade, and specifically for African countries (see Beegle et al. 2016), in 2015 the World Bank announced stronger support to address these gaps (World Bank 2015b). For a detailed analysis of progress in data availability in Africa, see Beegle and Christiaensen (2019).

42. The poverty estimates in this report include newly released data for Nigeria for 2018/19.

The previous data used by PovcalNet date back to 2009/10, which is outside the plus- or minus-three-year data coverage window for 2013.

43. The last survey for India is from 2011/12, which is included in the calculation of population coverage for 2013 but is outside the range for 2017. See box 1.2 for further details on India.

44. The relevance of these two economies for the global population coverage can be better understood using a thought experiment that calculates coverage for the world without these two countries. Considering the world without India, global coverage would have increased from 79 percent in 2013 to 86 percent in 2017. If India and Nigeria were excluded from the world, global coverage would have increased from 82 percent in 2013 to 85 percent in 2017. In sum, if we lived in a world that excluded India (and Nigeria), population coverage would have increased, highlighting the progress in the availability of surveys elsewhere.

45. These indicators are missing from the data used for several economies, notably China, which depresses the population coverage for the MPM in East Asia and Pacific. See annex 1D for detailed information on the MPM data source.

46. PovcalNet's current practice is to drop observations with negative welfare, although zeros are included.

47. "Comparability Over Time at the Country Level for International Poverty Measures," World Bank, Washington, DC, https://datacatalog.worldbank.org/dataset/comparability-over-time-country-level-international-poverty-measures.

48. ICP (International Comparison Program) (database), World Bank, Washington, DC, http://www.worldbank.org/en/programs/icp.

49. WDI (World Development Indicators) (database), World Bank, Washington, DC, http://data.worldbank.org/products/wdi.

50. PovcalNet: Data (database), World Bank, Washington, DC, http://iresearch.worldbank.org/PovcalNet/data.aspx.

51. Under the old rule, a country was included if the distance of the survey year was less than three years from the lineup year. Under the new rule, a country is considered covered if the distance to the lineup year is less than or equal to three years.

52. For details on income classification, see Fantom and Serajuddin (2016) and "Data: World Bank Country and Lending Groups," World Bank, Washington, DC, https://datahelpdesk.worldbank.org/knowledgebase/articles/906519-world-bank-country-and-lending-groups.

53. LIS Database (Luxembourg Income Study Database), LIS Cross-National Data Center in Luxembourg, Luxembourg, http://www.lisdatacenter.org/our-data/lis-database/.

54. The Joint Monitoring Programme for Water Supply and Sanitation is the official United Nations mechanism tasked with monitoring progress toward Sustainable Development Goal Number 6. See the website at https://washdata.org/.

55. EU-SILC (European Union Statistics on Income and Living Conditions) (database), Eurostat, European Commission, Luxembourg, http://ec.europa.eu/eurostat/web/microdata/european-union-statistics-on-income-and-living-conditions.

References

ADB (Asian Development Bank). 2020. "Updated Assessment of the Potential Economic Impact of COVID-19." ADB Briefs 133 (May), ADB, Manila.

Atamanov, Aziz, Raul Andres Castaneda Aguilar, Carolina Diaz-Bonilla, Dean Mitchell Jolliffe, Christoph Lakner, Daniel Gerszon Mahler, Jose Montes, et al. 2019. "September 2019 PovcalNet Update: What's New." Global Poverty Monitoring Technical Note 10 (September), World Bank, Washington, DC.

Atamanov, Aziz, Dean Mitchell Jolliffe, Christoph Lakner, and Espen Beer Prydz. 2018. "Purchasing Power Parities Used in Global Poverty Measurement." Global Poverty Monitoring Technical Note 5 (September), World Bank, Washington, DC.

Atamanov, Aziz, Christoph Lakner, Daniel Gerszon Mahler, Samuel Kofi Tetteh Baah, and Judy Yang. 2020. "The Effect of New PPP Estimates on Global Poverty: A First Look." Global Poverty Monitoring Technical Note 12 (May), World Bank, Washington, DC.

Atkinson, Anthony B., and François J. Bourguignon. 2001. "Poverty and Inclusion from a World Perspective." In *Governance, Equity, and Global Markets: The Annual Bank Conference on Development Economics, Europe*, edited by Joseph E. Stiglitz and Pierre-Alain Muet, 151–66. Oxford: Oxford University Press.

Beegle, Kathleen, and Luc Christiaensen, eds. 2019. *Accelerating Poverty Reduction in Africa*. Washington, DC: World Bank.

Beegle, Kathleen, Luc Christiaensen, Andrew L. Dabalen, and Isis Gaddis. 2016. *Poverty in a Rising Africa*. Africa Poverty Report. Washington, DC: World Bank.

Beegle, Kathleen, Joachim De Weerdt, Jed Friedman, and John Gibson. 2012. "Methods of Household Consumption Measurement through Surveys: Experimental Results from Tanzania." *Journal of Development Economics* 98 (1): 3–18.

Bergstrom, Katy. 2020. "The Role of Inequality for Poverty Reduction." World Bank Policy Research Working Paper 9409, Washington, DC: World Bank.

Bhalla, Surjit S., and Karan Bhasin. 2020. "Separating Fact from Economic Fiction: Growth Slowed beyond Expectations Starting Late 2018." *Indian Express*, January 25, 2020. https://indianexpress.com/article/opinion/columns/economy-slowdown-gdp-growth-5-trillion-nirmala-sitharaman-6234056/.

Brown, Caitlin S., Martin Ravallion, and Dominique van de Walle. 2020. "Can the World's Poor Protect Themselves from the New Coronavirus?" NBER Working Paper 27200 (May), National Bureau of Economic Research, Cambridge, MA.

Castaneda Aguilar, Raul Andres, Tony Henri Mathias Jany Fujs, Dean Mitchell Jolliffe, Christoph Lakner, Daniel Gerszon Mahler, Minh C. Nguyen, Marta Schoch, et al. 2020. "September 2020 PovcalNet Update: What's New." Global Poverty Monitoring Technical Note 14 (September), World Bank, Washington, DC.

Chanda, Areendam, and C. Justin Cook. 2019. "Who Gained from India's Demonetization? Insights from Satellites and Surveys." Department of Economics Working Paper 2019-06, Department of Economics, Louisiana State University, Baton Rouge, LA.

Chen, Shaohua, Dean Mitchell Jolliffe, Christoph Lakner, Kihoon Lee, Daniel Gerszon Mahler, Rose Mungai, Minh C. Nguyen, et al. 2018. "September 2018 PovcalNet Update: What's New." Global Poverty Monitoring Technical

Note 2 (updated March 2019), World Bank, Washington, DC.

Chen, Shaohua, and Martin Ravallion. 2010. "The Developing World Is Poorer Than We Thought, but No Less Successful in the Fight against Poverty." *Quarterly Journal of Economics* 125 (4): 1577–625.

Chodorow-Reich, Gabriel, Gita Gopinath, Prachi Mishra, and Abhinav Narayanan. 2020. "Cash and the Economy: Evidence from India's Demonetization." *Quarterly Journal of Economics* 135 (1): 57–103.

Corral, Paul, Alexander Irwin, Nandini Krishnan, Daniel Gerszon Mahler, and Tara Vishwanath. 2020. *Fragility and Conflict: On the Front Lines of the Fight against Poverty*. Washington, DC: World Bank.

Datt, Gaurav, Valerie Kozel, and Martin Ravallion. 2003. "A Model-Based Assessment of India's Progress in Reducing Poverty in the 1990s." *Economic and Political Weekly* 38 (4): 355–61.

Deaton, Angus S. 2001. "Counting the World's Poor: Problems and Possible Solutions." *World Bank Research Observer* 16 (2): 125–47.

Deaton, Angus S., and Valerie Kozel. 2005. "Data and Dogma: The Great Indian Poverty Debate." *World Bank Research Observer* 20 (2): 177–99.

Edochie, Ifeanyi Nzegwu, Samuel Freije-Rodriguez, Christoph Lakner, Laura Moreno Herrera, David Locke Newhouse, Pedro Olinto, Sutirtha Sinha Roy, Nishant Yonzan, and Nobuo Yoshida. Forthcoming. "What Do We Know about Poverty in India in 2017/2018?" Policy Research Working Paper, World Bank, Washington, DC.

Fantom, Neil James, and Umar Serajuddin. 2016. "The World Bank's Classification of Countries by Income." Policy Research Working Paper 7528, World Bank, Washington, DC.

Ferreira, Francisco H. G., Shaohua Chen, Andrew L. Dabalen, Yuri Dikhanov, Nada Hamadeh, Dean Mitchell Jolliffe, Ambar Narayan, et al. 2016. "A Global Count of the Extreme Poor in 2012: Data Issues, Methodology, and Initial Results." *Journal of Economic Inequality* 14 (2): 141–72.

Foster, James E. 1998. "Absolute versus Relative Poverty." *American Economic Review* 88 (2): 335–41.

Goyal, Ashima, and Abhishek Kumar. 2019. "Indian Growth Is Not Overestimated: Mr. Subramanian, You Got It Wrong." Working Paper 2019-019, Indira Gandhi Institute of Development Research, Mumbai, India.

Hallegatte, Stéphane, Mook Bangalore, Laura Bonzanigo, Marianne Fay, Tamaro Kane, Ulf Narloch, Julie Rozenberg, David Treguer, and Adrien Vogt-Schilb. 2016. *Shock Waves: Managing the Impacts of Climate Change on Poverty*. Climate Change and Development Series. Washington, DC: World Bank.

Hallegatte, Stéphane, and Julie Rozenberg. 2017. "Climate Change through a Poverty Lens." *Nature Climate Change* 7 (4): 250–56.

Hernandez, Manuel, Soonho Kim, Brendan Rice, and Bob Vos. 2020. "IFPRI's New COVID-19 Food Price Monitor Tracks Warning Signs of Stress in Local Markets." *IFPRI Blog*, May 5, 2020. https://www.ifpri.org/blog/ifpris-new-covid-19-food-price-monitor-tracks-warning-signs-stress-local-markets.

Himanshu. 2019. "Opinion: What Happened to Poverty during the First Term of Modi?" *Live Mint*, August 15, 2019. https://www.livemint.com/opinion/columns/opinion-what-happened-to-poverty-during-the-first-term-of-modi-1565886742501.html.

Jafino, Bramka Arga, Stéphane Hallegatte, and Brian James Walsh. Forthcoming. "Revised Estimates of the Future impact of Climate Change on Poverty by 2030." Policy Research Working Paper, World Bank, Washington, DC.

Jolliffe, Dean Mitchell. 2001. "Measuring Absolute and Relative Poverty: The Sensitivity of Estimated Household Consumption to Survey Design." *Journal of Economic and Social Measurement* 27 (1–2): 1–23.

Jolliffe, Dean Mitchell, and Espen Beer Prydz. 2016. "Estimating International Poverty Lines from Comparable National Thresholds." Policy Research Working Paper 7606, World Bank, Washington, DC.

Jolliffe, Dean Mitchell, and Espen Beer Prydz. 2017. "Societal Poverty: A Relative and Relevant Measure." Policy Research Working Paper 8073, World Bank, Washington, DC.

Lahiri, Amartya. 2020. "The Great Indian Demonetization." *Journal of Economic Perspectives* 34 (1): 55–74.

Lakner, Christoph, Daniel Gerszon Mahler, Mario Negre, and Espen Beer Prydz. 2020. "How Much Does Reducing Inequality Matter for Global Poverty?" Global Poverty Monitoring Technical Note 13 (June), World Bank, Washington, DC.

Lakner, Christoph, Daniel Gerszon Mahler, Minh C. Nguyen, João Pedro Azevedo,

Shaohua Chen, Dean Mitchell Jolliffe, Espen Beer Prydz, and Prem Sangraula. 2019. "Consumer Price Indices Used in Global Poverty Measurement." Global Poverty Monitoring Technical Note 4 (update, March), World Bank, Washington, DC.

Lakner, Christoph, Mario Negre, José Cuesta, and Ani Silwal. 2016. "Measuring Inequality Isn't Easy or Straightforward: Here's Why." World Bank Blogs: Let's Talk Development, November 3, 2016. https://blogs.worldbank.org/developmenttalk/measuring-inequality-isn-t-easy-or-straightforward-here-s-why.

Loayza, Norman V. 2020. "Costs and Trade-Offs in the Fight against the COVID-19 Pandemic: A Developing Country Perspective." Research and Policy Brief 35 (May 15), World Bank, Kuala Lumpur, Malaysia.

Loayza, Norman V., and Steven Pennings. 2020. "Macroeconomic Policy in the Time of COVID-19: A Primer for Developing Countries." Research and Policy Brief 28 (March 26), World Bank, Kuala Lumpur, Malaysia.

Mahler, Daniel Gerszon, Christoph Lakner, Raul Andres Castaneda Aguilar, and Haoyu Wu. 2020. "Updated Estimates of the Impact of COVID-19 on Global Poverty." World Bank Blogs: Data Blogs, June 8, 2020. https://blogs.worldbank.org/opendata/updated-estimates-impact-covid-19-global-poverty.

NBS (National Bureau of Statistics, Nigeria). 2020. "2019 Poverty and Inequality in Nigeria: Executive Summary." May, NBS, Abuja, Nigeria.

Newhouse, David Locke, and Pallavi Vyas. 2018. "Nowcasting Poverty in India for 2014–15: A Survey to Survey Imputation Approach." Global Poverty Monitoring Technical Note 6 (September), World Bank, Washington, DC.

Prydz, Espen Beer, Dean Mitchell Jolliffe, Christoph Lakner, Daniel Gerszon Mahler, and Prem Sangraula. 2019. "National Accounts Data Used in Global Poverty Measurement." Global Poverty Monitoring Technical Note 8 (March), World Bank, Washington, DC.

Ravallion, Martin. 2020. "SDG1: The Last Three Percent." CGD Working Paper 527 (March 30), Center for Global Development, Washington, DC.

Ravallion, Martin, and Shaohua Chen. 2011. "Weakly Relative Poverty." Review of Economics and Statistics 93 (4): 1251–61.

Ravallion, Martin, and Shaohua Chen. 2013. "A Proposal for Truly Global Poverty Measures." Global Policy 4 (3): 258–65.

Ravallion, Martin, and Shaohua Chen. 2019. "Global Poverty Measurement When Relative Income Matters." Journal of Public Economics 177 (September): 104046.

Ravallion, Martin, Shaohua Chen, and Prem Sangraula. 2009. "Dollar a Day Revisited." World Bank Economic Review 23 (2): 163–84.

Ravallion, Martin, Gaurav Datt, and Dominique van de Walle. 1991. "Quantifying Absolute Poverty in the Developing World." Review of Income and Wealth 37 (4): 345–61.

Sen, Abhijit. 2000. "Estimates of Consumer Expenditure and Its Distribution: Statistical Priorities after NSS 55th Round." Economic and Political Weekly 35 (51): 4499–501.

Subramanian, Arvind. 2019. "India's GDP Mis-estimation: Likelihood, Magnitudes, Mechanisms, and Implications." CID Faculty Working Paper 354 (June), Center for International Development, Harvard University, Cambridge, MA.

Subramanian, S. 2019. "What Is Happening to Rural Welfare, Poverty, and Inequality in India?" India Forum, updated December 12, 2019. https://www.theindiaforum.in/article/what-happened-rural-welfare-poverty-and-inequality-india-between-2011-12-and-2017-18.

Sulser, Timothy, and Shahnila Dunston. 2020. "COVID-19-Related Trade Restrictions on Rice and Wheat Could Drive up Prices and Increase Hunger." IFPRI Blog, May 15, 2020. https://www.ifpri.org/blog/covid-19-related-trade-restrictions-rice-and-wheat-could-drive-prices-and-increase-hunger.

Sumner, Andy, Eduardo Ortiz-Juárez, and Chris Hoy. 2020. "Precarity and the Pandemic: COVID-19 and Poverty Incidence, Intensity, and Severity in Developing Countries." WIDER Working Paper 2020/77, United Nations University–World Institute for Development Economics Research, Helsinki.

Vyas, Mahesh. 2018. "Using Fast Frequency Household Survey Data to Estimate the Impact of Demonetization on Employment." Review of Market Integration 10 (3): 159–83.

World Bank. 2015a. A Measured Approach to Ending Poverty and Boosting Shared Prosperity: Concepts, Data, and the Twin Goals. Policy Research Report. Washington, DC: World Bank.

World Bank. 2015b. "World Bank's New End-Poverty Tool: Surveys in Poorest Countries." Press Release, October 15, https://www.worldbank.org/en/news/press-release/2015/10/15/world-bank-new-end-poverty-tool-su rveys-in-poorest-countries.

World Bank. 2016. *Poverty and Shared Prosperity 2016: Taking On Inequality*. Washington, DC: World Bank.

World Bank. 2017a. *Monitoring Global Poverty: Report of the Commission on Global Poverty*. Washington, DC: World Bank.

World Bank. 2017b. *World Development Report 2017: Governance and the Law*. Washington, DC: World Bank.

World Bank. 2018. *Poverty and Shared Prosperity 2018: Piecing Together the Poverty Puzzle*. Washington, DC: World Bank.

World Bank. 2020a. *Global Economic Prospects, January 2020: Slow Growth, Policy Challenges*. Washington, DC: World Bank.

World Bank. 2020b. *Global Economic Prospects, June 2020*. Washington, DC: World Bank.

Shared Prosperity: Monitoring Inclusive Growth

Shared prosperity focuses on the poorest 40 percent of the population in each economy (the bottom 40) and is defined as the annualized growth rate of their mean household per capita income or their consumption. The shared prosperity premium is the difference between this and the annualized growth rate for the whole population. Shared prosperity and the shared prosperity premium are important indicators of inclusion and well-being in any economy and correlate with reductions in poverty and inequality. Growth has been inclusive for the period circa 2012–17: out of a total of 91 economies with available data, 74 economies had positive shared prosperity, and 53 had positive shared prosperity premiums. But the gains are uneven: shared prosperity and shared prosperity premiums are lower, on average, in conflict-afflicted and fragile and low-income economies than in middle- and high-income economies. These measures for 68 economies can be compared with an estimate of shared prosperity for an earlier period (circa 2010–15), revealing a downward trend in shared prosperity in half the economies with available data. A preliminary outlook projects that the global COVID-19 (coronavirus) pandemic will reduce shared prosperity and the shared prosperity premium in most economies in coming years with the likely consequence, based on the patterns of shared prosperity in recent years, of increases in poverty and inequality in the near future.

Introduction: Shared prosperity—Focusing on the bottom 40

Shared prosperity measures the extent to which economic growth is inclusive by focusing on household income or consumption growth among the population at the bottom of the income distribution rather than on the average or on those at the top. Philosophers and economists have argued that focusing on the least advantaged persons provides an important measure of progress on prosperity (Ferreira, Galasso, and Negre 2018; Rawls 1971). US President Franklin D. Roosevelt (1937) said, "The test of our progress is not whether we add more to the abundance of those who have much; it is whether we provide enough for those who have too little." In a speech to the World Bank and International Monetary Fund Boards of Governors in 1972, World Bank president Robert McNamara (1972, 22) said, "this poverty of the poorest 40 percent of the citizenry is of immense urgency since their condition is in fact far worse than national averages suggest."

Promoting shared prosperity is one of the twin goals of the World Bank Group (together with eradicating extreme poverty). The shared prosperity indicator was introduced to shine a constant light on the growth in living standards of the relatively less well-off segments of the population in any economy. Shared prosperity has no target or finish line, because the aim is to continuously improve the well-being of those at the bottom of the distribution. In good times and bad, in low- and high-income economies alike, shared prosperity captures trends in well-being for the bottom 40 percent of the population (the bottom 40) in each nation that is monitored. Tracking the income and consumption growth of the bottom 40, as well as the growth of this population segment relative to the mean, is a way to consider and strive for equitable outcomes.

The shared prosperity measure focuses on their rank in household per capita income (or consumption) and represents the annualized growth rate of their mean household per capita income (or consumption). Growth in the average income of the bottom 40 can stem from the rising mean income of the overall population, increases in the share of overall income that accrues to the bottom 40, or both. Shared prosperity can thus be decomposed into growth of the mean income and growth of the income share of the bottom 40. The second term in this sum (or equivalently, the difference between growth of the bottom 40 and growth of the mean) may be considered the *sharing* term that measures changes in the proportion of total income growth that accrues to the bottom 40. This is defined as the shared prosperity premium.[1]

Why does shared prosperity focus on the bottom 40? Basu (2001, 2006) argues for a focus on the bottom quintile income. However, there is typically more data error at the bottom of the distribution, and the chosen bottom segment should not be too small. The selection of the bottom 40 as a group for monitoring is a compromise between competing considerations; the bottom 40 still focuses on the bottom of the distribution but is not too small or at risk of introducing measurement errors.

In this report, measures of shared prosperity and the shared prosperity premium are for the period circa 2012–17 as much as possible across economies (see annex 2B). However, because not all economies have survey data for 2012 and 2017, the exact period of measurement of shared prosperity varies from 2009–15 for Botswana and Namibia to 2014–18 for Indonesia and Thailand. Unlike global and regional population-weighted poverty estimates, global and regional means of shared prosperity are simple averages. Data deprivation is an issue in measuring and understanding shared prosperity. Of the

world's 218 economies, shared prosperity is measured for the 91 that have comparable household surveys circa 2012 and 2017, and these economies cover only 60 percent of the world's population.

This chapter first describes measures of shared prosperity and the shared prosperity premium for the most recent period with available data. It then compares this recent batch with a previous round of indicators and subsequently provides an outlook on the impact that the COVID-19 pandemic is expected to have on inclusive growth in coming years. The chapter concludes by comparing shared prosperity with other measures of inclusion such as the median, followed by a description of the demographic characteristics of the bottom 40 that serves as a connection to chapter 3, which elaborates on a more extensive profile of the global poor.

The most recent estimates of shared prosperity and the shared prosperity premium

Annualized income growth among the bottom 40 ranges from −5.3 percent in Benin to 10.2 percent in Romania (figure 2.1).[2] These growth rates represent rare extremes. Most economies (52 out of 91) experienced shared prosperity rates between 0 and 4 percent. Incomes of the bottom 40 grew during this period for 74 of 91 economies. However, 17 of the 91 economies experienced declining growth among the bottom 40. By region, negative values of shared prosperity are most likely to be found in the Middle East and North Africa, where three of the four economies with available data experienced negative shared prosperity. In Sub-Saharan Africa, 6 out of 15 economies experienced negative shared prosperity. Of 14 economies in Latin America, 2 experienced negative shared prosperity, as did 4 of 24 in Europe and Central Asia. In the East Asia and Pacific and South Asia regions, shared prosperity is positive for all economies where it can be measured, that is, 7 and 4 economies, respectively (figure 2.1).

The 91 economies with available data represent 42 percent of the world's economies and 60 percent of the world's population. But the average hides much heterogeneity in coverage across groups of economies (table 2.1).

FIGURE 2.1 **Shared Prosperity and the Shared Prosperity Premium, by Economy, circa 2012–17**

Source: Global Database of Shared Prosperity (7th edition, circa 2012–17), World Bank, Washington, DC. https://www.worldbank.org/en/topic/poverty/brief/global-database
-of-shared-prosperity.
Note: The figure includes 91 economies.

Little more than one-third of the population of lower-income groups is included, while around 80 percent in upper-middle- and high-income economies is included. Fragile and conflict-affected economies are the least represented. Only three economies, representing less than 3 percent of the population in the group, are included in this database. An often neglected problem of conflict-affected economies is that the lack of data makes the plight in these economies less well documented (box 2.1).

BOX 2.1 Data Challenges: Shared Prosperity Cannot Be Measured in Some of the Most Deprived Economies

Shared prosperity is a measure of changes in consumption (or income) between two years, meaning that calculating it requires at least two surveys within the benchmark period. Because of the limited number of surveys produced on a regular cycle in many economies, shared prosperity and the shared prosperity premium can be calculated, in this report, for only 91 of 218 economies, corresponding to 60 percent of the world's population.

Europe and Central Asia is the only region where the majority of economies have shared prosperity indicators (24 of 30 economies) (table B2.1.1). Although the population coverage of East Asia and Pacific appears high, it is driven by the fact that China comprises two-thirds of the region's total population, and the economies not being measured are less populous small island economies. In South Asia, shared prosperity indicators cover about half of the economies but only 21.8 percent of the population, driven by India's absence. Sub-Saharan Africa is the only region where coverage is lower than one-third in both the number of economies represented and the share of total population. When examining population and economy coverage, it becomes evident that shared prosperity indicators are providing only a partial picture of changes in household consumption and income among the bottom 40.

Limited economy coverage also raises the concern that shared prosperity may be poorly understood in the settings where tracking shared prosperity is most important: poorer, fragile, and small economies. Low-income

TABLE B2.1.1 Data Coverage Summary, Global Database of Shared Prosperity, Seventh Edition

	Population, millions			Number of economies		
	All economies	Economies with poverty rate	Economies with SP	All economies	Economies with poverty rate	Economies with SP
East Asia and Pacific	2,081.7	2,039.7	1,966.7	24	19	7
Europe and Central Asia	493.8	493.8	425.6	30	21	24
Latin America and the Caribbean	636.9	625.1	429.0	31	21	14
Middle East and North Africa	382.9	376.2	196.4	13	12	4
South Asia	1,814.4	1,777.2	396.0	8	7	4
Sub-Saharan Africa	1,078.2	1,058.4	334.4	47	44	15
Rest of the world	1,106.4	1,034.5	798.0	65	42	23
Fragile and conflict-affected states	744.0	681.6	20.9	37	32	3
International Development Association	1,640.2	1,568.0	726.1	76	68	19
Low income	705.4	624.2	265.7	31	27	8
Lower-middle income	3,022.9	3,006.7	1,106.4	47	46	20
Upper-middle income	2,655.6	2,635.9	2,273.5	60	51	28
High income	1,210.3	1,138.2	900.4	80	42	35
Total	**7,594.3**	**7,405.0**	**4,546.1**	**218**	**166**	**91**

Sources: Global Database of Shared Prosperity (7th edition, circa 2012–17), World Bank, Washington, DC, http://www.worldbank.org/en/topic/poverty/brief/global-database-of-shared-prosperity; PovcalNet (online analysis tool), World Bank, Washington, DC, http://iresearch.worldbank.org/PovcalNet/; World Development Indicators (database), World Bank, Washington, DC, http://data.worldbank.org/products/wdi.

Note: Shared prosperity growth rates are annualized. Averages across economies are simple averages, not population weighted, SP = shared prosperity indicator.

(continued)

economies not only have the lowest representation among economies for which shared prosperity can be measured, but also the worst performance. Shared prosperity can be measured for only about a quarter of all low-income economies, representing 37.7 percent of the population across this income group. And among economies for which shared prosperity rates are available, average shared prosperity is lowest in the low-income economies, at 0.2 percent. This is also the only income group for which the average shared prosperity premium is negative.

Population coverage and economy coverage are also low in economies affected by fragility, conflict, and violence (FCV) and in those receiving support from the

World Bank's fund for the poorest economies, the International Development Association (IDA). The existence of conflict often prohibits the data collection that is necessary for welfare measurement. Globally, 744 million people live in FCV economies. Poverty can be estimated in 32 FCV economies covering 681.6 million people, but shared prosperity can only be calculated in 3 economies covering 20.9 million. Chapter 3 discusses in more detail the relationship between poverty and conflict. Among the few FCV and IDA economies for which shared prosperity can be measured, more than half have negative values for both shared prosperity and the shared prosperity premium.

Despite these limitations, this round of shared prosperity

estimates represents progress compared with initial efforts. The first two rounds of shared prosperity estimators, in 2014 and 2015, covered 65 and 85 economies, respectively, whereas this round includes 91 economies. The expansion of household surveys is ongoing as part of World Bank efforts to help poorer economies increase data coverage, particularly in Sub-Saharan Africa (Beegle and Christiaensen 2019). This work will further increase country coverage in forthcoming rounds of shared prosperity estimates. A detailed discussion of the different periods of shared prosperity databases and their global and regional coverage is included in annex 2B.

In global terms, the average shared prosperity across 91 economies is 2.3 percent during the period under study. By income class category, upper-middle- and high-income economies have the highest average shared prosperity. Although average shared prosperity is still positive among low- and lower-middle-income economies, it is noticeably lower. Upper-middle-income economies experienced an average shared prosperity of 2.9 percent, followed by high-income economies with 2.7 percent, lower-middle-income economies with 1.8 percent, and low-income economies with only 0.2 percent (see table 2.1). Turning to economies affected by fragility, conflict, and violence (FCV), the result is even lower: a decline of 0.8 percent in the income (or consumption) of those in the bottom 40. As indicated previously, there is also significant heterogeneity across regions. Average shared prosperity ranges from 4.9 and 3.5 percent in the East Asia and Pacific and Europe and Central Asia regions, respectively, to 0.7 and 0.5 percent in Sub-Saharan Africa and the Middle East and North Africa, respectively.[3]

Shared prosperity can be interpreted as the sum of growth in average incomes (or consumption) and growth in the income share of the bottom 40. Average growth is thus an important component of shared prosperity. Figure 2.2 shows the distribution of economies in the sample by average annual growth in mean income or consumption (on the horizontal axis) and their respective measures of shared prosperity (on the vertical axis). The analysis finds that 69 out of 91 economies have positive mean income growth and shared prosperity (figure 2.2, top right quadrant), whereas 8 economies have negative mean income growth and negative shared prosperity (figure 2.2, bottom left quadrant). The remaining 14 economies have either negative shared prosperity or negative mean growth, most with very small differences. Overall, figure 2.2 shows the high correlation between mean growth and shared prosperity.[4]

In economies with positive shared prosperity premiums (above the diagonal in figure 2.2), the income growth of the bottom 40 is growing more quickly than the average

TABLE 2.1 Shared Prosperity and Shared Prosperity Premium: Summary

	Data coverage, economies		Data coverage, population	Economies, number				Simple average across economies			
								Average SP	Average SP premium	Growth of the mean	Growth of the median
	Economies with SP	Percentage of total economies	Percentage of total population	SP > 0	Growth in median > 0	Growth in mean > 0	SPP > 0	(%)	(percentage points)	(%)	(%)
East Asia and Pacific	7	29.2	94.5	7	7	7	6	4.9	1	3.9	4.7
Europe and Central Asia	24	80.0	86.2	20	19	20	19	3.5	0.8	2.7	3.0
Latin America and the Caribbean	14	45.2	67.4	12	12	12	11	2.2	1	1.3	2.0
Middle East and North Africa	4	30.8	51.3	1	3	2	1	0.5	−0.4	0.9	0.8
South Asia	4	50.0	21.8	4	4	4	0	2.5	−0.6	3.1	2.9
Sub-Saharan Africa	15	31.9	31.0	9	12	11	5	0.7	−0.5	1.2	1.5
Rest of the world	23	43.8	74.4	21	22	22	11	1.6	0.1	1.5	1.6
Fragile and conflict-affected states	3	8.1	2.8	1	2	1	1	−0.8	0	−0.7	−1.0
IDA and Blend	19	25.0	44.3	13	17	16	7	0.6	−0.5	1.1	1.2
Low income	8	25.8	37.7	5	7	6	3	0.2	−0.6	0.8	1.0
Lower-middle income	20	42.6	36.6	14	16	16	8	1.8	0.1	1.7	2.0
Upper-middle income	28	46.7	85.6	23	23	23	21	2.9	0.8	2.0	2.5
High income	35	43.8	74.4	32	33	33	21	2.7	0.3	2.4	2.5
Total	**91**	**41.7**	**59.9**	**74**	**79**	**78**	**53**	**2.3**	**0.3**	**2.0**	**2.3**

Sources: Global Database of Shared Prosperity (7th edition, circa 2012–17), World Bank, Washington, DC. https://www.worldbank.org/en/topic/poverty/brief/global-database-of-shared-prosperity; PovcalNet (online analysis tool), World Bank, Washington, DC, http://iresearch.worldbank.org/PovcalNet/; World Development Indicators (database), World Bank, Washington, DC, http://data.worldbank.org/products/wdi.
Note: Averages across economies are simple averages, not population weighted. Shared prosperity, that is, growth in the mean of the bottom 40, is annualized. The number of total economies in the world is 218 based on World Development Indicators. IDA = International Development Association; Blend = IDA-eligible economies but also creditworthy for some borrowing from the International Bank for Reconstruction and Development; SP = shared prosperity indicator; SPP = shared prosperity premium.

population. This is the case of the majority of economies with available data. In total, 53 of 91 economies are above the diagonal. These are the economies in which economic growth has benefited those at the bottom of the distribution more than proportionately.

The shared prosperity premium exhibits considerable heterogeneity. A simple average of this premium across 91 economies is 0.3 percentage points (as compared with overall shared prosperity of 2.3 percent). This means that consumption or income among the bottom 40 is growing, on average, 0.3 percentage points more quickly than at the mean. But the regional averages range from 1.0 percentage points in the East Asia and Pacific and Latin America and the Caribbean regions to negative values in three other regions: Middle East and North Africa (−0.4), South Asia (−0.5), and Sub-Saharan Africa (−0.6). FCV economies suffer a double impact. Two of the three FCV economies in the sample have both negative shared prosperity and negative shared prosperity premiums. More than half of International Development Association (IDA) economies have negative shared prosperity premiums. The average shared prosperity premium in this group is −0.5 percentage points. The shared prosperity premium is also more likely to be negative in low- and lower-middle-income economies than in upper-middle- or high-income economies.

A worrisome number of economies in Sub-Saharan Africa have negative shared prosperity or negative shared prosperity premiums. In 10 of the 15 economies in the region with shared prosperity data, the growth of the bottom 40 is lower than the growth of the mean (figure 2.3). Almost half of the economies globally in which both shared prosperity and the shared prosperity premium are negative are in Sub-Saharan Africa (6 out of 14 economies). This outcome is related to a variety of challenges facing the region, including climate, conflict, and institutional factors. For example, in Uganda, the negative shared prosperity premium is related to a drought in northern Uganda that affected farmers, who are among the country's poorest people (World Bank 2018a). Moreover, Merotto (2019) indicates that agricultural productivity has been stagnant for several years, and job transitions out of agriculture have been too slow, all of which hampers inclusive growth.

On the positive side, growth has been rapid in some economies, and the bottom 40 is catching up. Economies with positive values of shared prosperity and the shared prosperity premium include North Macedonia and the Philippines. Inclusive growth patterns and social policies contributed to these trends. In North Macedonia, expanding job opportunities through investments in infrastructure, active labor market policies, and Special Economic

FIGURE 2.2 Correlation between Shared Prosperity and Growth in Mean Incomes, 91 Economies, circa 2012–17

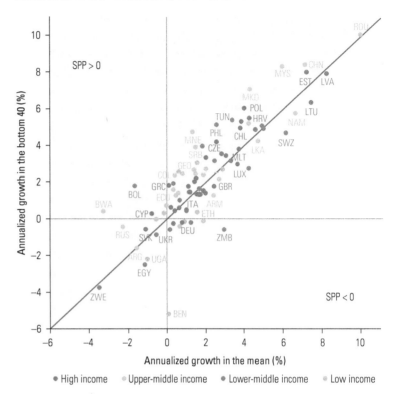

Source: Global Database of Shared Prosperity (7th edition, circa 2012–17), World Bank, Washington, DC, https://www.worldbank.org/en/topic/poverty/brief/global-database-of-shared-prosperity.
Note: SPP = shared prosperity premium.

Zones, as well as new public employment all benefited the bottom 40 (World Bank 2018b). In the Philippines, the trend can be attributed to the transition of workers in agriculture to better-paying services sector jobs, in addition to an increase in government spending on social programs—notably the expanded coverage of the country's conditional cash transfer program (Pantawid Pamilyang Pilipino Program) (World Bank 2019a).

Trends in shared prosperity and its premium over rounds of data

How has shared prosperity changed over time, and are there any large changes by economy or region? The comparisons in this section are based on shared prosperity calculated in the fifth (circa 2010–15) and seventh (circa 2012–17) editions (or "rounds") of the Global Database of Shared Prosperity (GDSP). Comparisons and trends for shared prosperity and its premium can be made for

FIGURE 2.3 Positive and Negative Values for Shared Prosperity and the Shared Prosperity Premium

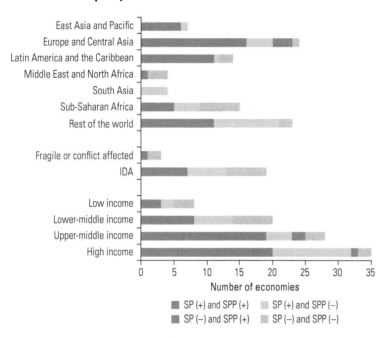

Source: Global Database of Shared Prosperity (7th edition, circa 2012–17), World Bank, Washington, DC, https://www.worldbank.org/en/topic/poverty/brief/global-database-of-shared-prosperity.
Note: SP = shared prosperity; SPP = shared prosperity premium; (+) indicates the indicator is greater than zero; (-) indicates the indicator is less than zero.

68 economies (covering 29.8 percent of the world's population) where data are available for both periods.[5] However, even with this smaller sample, the economy-level stories are illustrative and informative. (See annex 2C for details on comparing shared prosperity across rounds.)

Comparing across two rounds, about half the economies had higher shared prosperity, and the other half had lower (figure 2.4, panel a). Higher shared prosperity on average persists over time: most economies with positive shared prosperity in the previous period also have positive shared prosperity in the most recent period. However, there are exceptions: a few economies with negative shared prosperity in the past now have positive indexes (for example, Greece, Montenegro, and Serbia); in addition, 10 economies with positive shared prosperity in the past now have negative indexes (for example, the Arab Republic of Egypt and Uganda). The shared prosperity premium, however, reveals no clear cross-period pattern (figure 2.4, panel b). Economies are spread across the four quadrants of the figure, indicating that the shared

prosperity premium is not persistent over time. Economies that had high growth in average income or consumption in the first period were more likely to have it in the second, but the same does not hold for the shared prosperity premium.

Although the average change in shared prosperity is positive, there are large differences across regions. On average, shared prosperity was larger in the more recent period (2.3 percent) than in the previous period (1.8 percent). This increase is concentrated in only three regions: East Asia and Pacific, Europe and Central Asia, and the rest of the world (mostly high-income economies). In contrast, the remaining regions show a decline in shared prosperity. The small sample of economies in the Middle East and North Africa, South Asia, and Sub-Saharan Africa all had lower shared prosperity and shared prosperity premiums circa 2012–17 than circa 2010–15. These declines range from 5.4 percentage points in Sub-Saharan Africa to 0.11 percentage points in South Asia.[6]

Growth explains many of the changes in the level of shared prosperity between the two rounds. Economies with higher shared prosperity in the more recent round are those coming out of recessions. Although shared prosperity and growth in the mean seem persistent over time, at least as shown in the two rounds of data compared in this exercise, there are reversals of fortune that may cause both indicators to worsen (discussed in "Outlook: COVID-19 and prospects for shared prosperity" section below). For 10 of 68 economies, shared prosperity was positive in the previous period and negative in the more recent period. The economies concerned span four regions.[7] About half are economies for which the more recent round of shared prosperity was measured during a recession or financial crisis. In some cases, such as Egypt and Uganda, the reversal is due not to general shocks but to country-specific conditions. Uganda's rate of shared prosperity declined the most because a severe drought affected the country in 2016 and 2017. Since the events of the Arab Spring, Egypt has not yet regained the GDP growth rates pre-2011. Moreover, there is evidence that in 2012–15, the bottom quintile of the distribution experienced income losses, whereas the top quintile saw income gains, which explains the declining shared prosperity and

FIGURE 2.4 **Shared Prosperity and the Shared Prosperity Premium across Rounds**

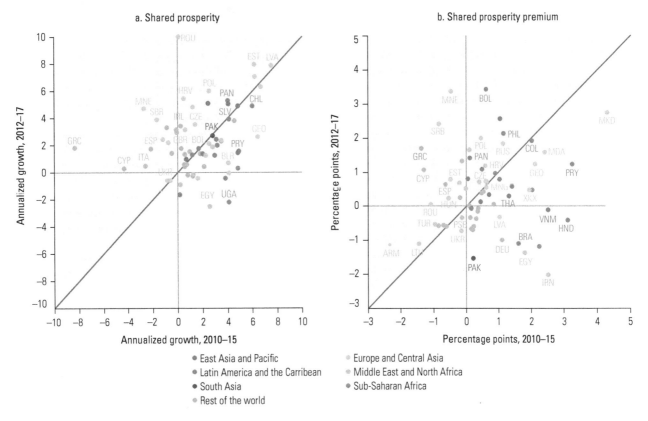

Source: Global Database of Shared Prosperity (5th edition, circa 2010–2015; 7th edition, circa 2012–17), World Bank, Washington, DC, https://www.worldbank.org/en/topic /poverty/brief/global-database-of-shared-prosperity.
Note: The figure covers economies that are in the fifth and seventh editions of the Global Database of Shared Prosperity and have updated shared prosperity. There are 75 recurring economies in the fifth and seventh editions, but seven economies use the same shared prosperity periods and are excluded from the comparison. The areas shaded in yellow contain the economies that experienced higher shared prosperity or a higher shared prosperity premium in the recent round compared with the previous round. Full data are available in annex 2C.

shared prosperity premium between the two rounds of data (World Bank 2019b).

Financial crises can also have region-wide impacts as experienced by the Latin America and the Caribbean region. In 10 of 13 economies in Latin America and the Caribbean, shared prosperity was lower circa 2012–17 than circa 2010–15 because the region experienced broad economic stagnation. Circa 2012–17, Argentina and Brazil experienced both negative shared prosperity and negative shared prosperity premiums.[8] Brazil's 2014–16 crisis and recovery are a stark departure from the previous decade. As millions of jobs were lost, Brazil's expansive social protection system was unable to serve effectively as a countercyclical protection system. The 2014–16 crisis proved to be severe across all income groups, and recovery following the crisis

was uneven and slow (Ciaschi et al. 2020; Dutz 2018). Argentina experienced a similarly stark economic downturn (World Bank 2018c). During the crisis period, job creation in Argentina slowed considerably, and labor productivity declined. These examples suggest that the global economic recession caused by the COVID-19 pandemic will also have strong negative impacts on shared prosperity.

In contrast, several economies that went from negative to positive shared prosperity experienced the impact of the aftermath of the international financial crisis of 2007–09 and then rebounded. These include several European countries in the database, such as Albania, Greece, Italy, Serbia, Slovenia, and Spain, and most of them also saw an increase in their shared prosperity premium, which indicates that the recovery benefited the bottom 40 more than proportionately.

Outlook: COVID-19 and prospects for shared prosperity

COVID-19 has led to a massive collapse in growth as economies around the world have imposed severe containment measures to control the spread of the virus. These demand and supply shocks have spilled across borders, hampering trade and shrinking economic activity globally. By reducing growth in average incomes, COVID-19 has already led to major declines in shared prosperity, which will persist until the virus is controlled, lockdown measures are eased, and growth eventually resumes. There is considerable uncertainty about how long the current recession will last, and thus how large the reduction in shared prosperity will be. Moreover, existing evidence indicates substantial heterogeneity in the economic effects of COVID-19 that will likely have long-term distributional consequences, as the least well-off and most vulnerable members of society are disproportionately affected.

Figure 2.5 gives a sense of the magnitude of COVID-19's blow to shared prosperity. The figure shows projected average annual growth in mean incomes in 2019–21 from the baseline scenario described in chapter 1 (on the vertical axis) and shared prosperity over 2012–17 (on the horizontal axis). This exercise assumes the shared prosperity premium is zero, that is, the bottom 40 experience the same annualized growth as the average population. This projection is also—as in previous iterations of this report—based on a neutral distribution projection of shared prosperity for 2019 through 2021. Most of the 91 economies are below the diagonal. Given the high correlation between growth in mean incomes (or consumption) and shared prosperity, as documented in figure 2.2, figure 2.5 indicates that most economies will see substantially lower shared prosperity as a result of the pandemic. Average shared prosperity was 2.3 percent in the period 2012–17; if shared prosperity were to be equal to growth in the mean (again, assuming a zero shared prosperity premium in all economies), the new average shared prosperity for 2019–21 would be −0.02 percent, that is, virtually no growth among the bottom 40. The longer the current contraction lasts, the larger this decline in shared prosperity will be. As usual, averages hide regional differences. The least affected region would be East Asia and Pacific, which would have an average shared prosperity of 1.92 percent (almost 3 percentage points lower than in the 2012–17 round), and the most affected would be the Middle East and North Africa, with shared prosperity of −1.5 (2 percentage points lower than the 2012–17 round) and Latin America and the Caribbean, with a projected average shared prosperity of −1.0 (3.2 percentage points lower than the 2012–17 round).

FIGURE 2.5 **Projected Growth in Mean Incomes, 2019–21, and Past Shared Prosperity, circa 2012–17**

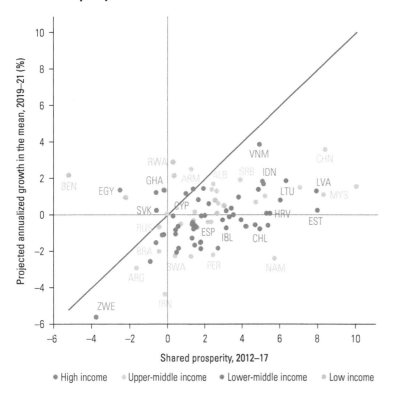

● High income ● Upper-middle income ● Lower-middle income ● Low income

Sources: COVID-19 baseline growth simulations for the period 2019–21 are from figure 1.4 in chapter 1 of this report. Global Database of Shared Prosperity (7th edition, circa 2012–17), World Bank, Washington, DC, https://www.worldbank.org/en/topic/poverty/brief/global-database-of-shared-prosperity.
Note: The projected growth in mean incomes is equivalent to 85 percent of the projected average annualized GDP per capita growth for 2019, 2020, and 2021.

The deceleration in economic activity will likely hit the poorest hardest, implying a lower shared prosperity premium as well. A neutral distribution projection is already an assumption of a lower shared prosperity premium because for 2012–17, it was 0.3 on average and positive for more than half the economies in the sample. Although forecasts of future shared prosperity premiums are not available, it is likely that the data in figure 2.5 substantially understate the decline in shared prosperity by not factoring in an even lower shared prosperity premium.[9] The rest of this section discusses past and emerging evidence on the likely adverse distributional effects of COVID-19 that are expected to contribute to this fall in the shared prosperity premium.

Historical data on major epidemics from the past two decades (including SARS in 2003, H1N1 in 2009, MERS in 2012, Ebola in 2014, and Zika in 2016) indicate that disease outbreaks raise income inequality and significantly diminish employment prospects among those with basic education. More specifically, in the five years following these epidemics, on average, the Gini coefficient increased by nearly 1.5 points, the income shares of the lowest deciles fell, and the employment-to-population ratio decreased for those with basic education relative to those with higher education. Evidence also indicates that, despite government efforts to redistribute income to mitigate the effects of pandemics, inequality increases, reflecting the extent of the long-term effects caused by job losses, income shocks, and diminished job opportunities (Furceri et al. 2020). Emerging evidence on the effects of COVID-19 echoes these trends.

Labor incomes of households in low-income deciles and of low-skilled workers are disproportionately affected by the adverse health and economic costs of the COVID-19 pandemic. In some cases, the impact is direct and immediate: poor workers who are more likely to suffer from health conditions, are older, and who cannot afford protective equipment are more likely to contract COVID-19, stop working, and lose earnings. In other cases, the impact is indirect but with long-lasting effects: poor workers are less able to cope with the effects of prolonged income shocks attributable to diminished employment prospects as economies go into recession (Schmitt-Grohé, Teoh, and Uribe 2020).

Another divide is due to differences in working conditions for the rich versus the poor. Workers in low-income deciles have less ability to work from home than those in higher deciles, threatening their job security and ability to adhere to social distancing measures (Avdiu and Nayyar 2020; Papageorge et al. 2020). Likewise, in developing economies, a larger share of workers are in occupations and sectors that are less compatible with social distancing (for example, construction, labor-intensive manufacturing, and small retail), increasing their risk of exposure to COVID-19 and the ubiquity of job loss (Dingel and Neiman 2020; Gerard, Imbert, and Orkin 2020; Gottlieb, Grobovsek, and Poschke 2020; Hatayama, Viollaz, and Winkler 2020). If containment measures are strictly enforced, the poor working in these sectors are more likely to lose their jobs. And if containment measures are ineffective, the poor are at greater risk of exposure to the virus. Either way, the poor are the hardest hit.

Because of the size of the global recession caused by the pandemic, households along the entire distribution are experiencing negative labor market impacts. In Cambodia, 84 percent and 83 percent of the bottom 40 and top 60, respectively, experienced a reduction in household income (World Bank 2020a). In Indonesia, the evidence seems to indicate that urban centers are more prone to experiencing increases in poverty because these areas were harder hit economically. Those who work in industry and the services sector, and those with relatively low levels of education, are the most vulnerable (World Bank 2020b). The bottom 40 also has fewer strategies to cope with severe shocks, having less savings and an inability to sell assets, which will magnify the negative impacts they experience. This evidence comes from early results from rapid-response phone surveys. Given the swift evolution of the pandemic, the diversity of economic and social structures, and the variety of country-specific policies adopted, close monitoring of the situation is needed, and useful, timely,

To monitor the impacts of the COVID-19 (coronovirus) pandemic on household welfare, from food security and education, to employment and access to social policies, the World Bank has initiated, in collaboration with several institutions in the countries where the surveys are implemented, a series of rapid-response, high-frequency phone surveys. These surveys are intended to be representative of most groups in the society and to be deployed in several rounds over time. The surveys have the advantage of rapidly tracking the effects of the pandemic as they transpire but may have the shortcoming of failing to capture populations without phone service.

These rapid surveys can help understanding the policy response to the pandemic. For instance, surveys collected in several countries of the Latin American and Caribbean region in May and June show there is wide variation in abiding by lockdown measures mandated across countries. In Bolivia, El Salvador, Honduras, and Peru, over 90 percent of the population report that they respect and follow the lockdown. In other countries, such as Chile, Costa Rica, and Paraguay, the share is much lower, 50 percent to 70 percent (World Bank 2020c).

The surveys also track the differential impact on children's education and health. Early evidence from phone surveys suggests that human capital losses due to school closures may likely affect poor and rural children disproportionately, notably because they are often unable to engage in distance learning. In Nigeria, the richest 20 percent of households were much more likely than the rest of the population to report that their children were pursuing learning activities, including remote learning, following school closures (Siwatu et al. 2020). In Zambia, 52 percent of learners in Lusaka who previously attended school and are now engaged in learning activities, whereas only 44 percent do so in rural areas of the country (Finn and Zadel 2020).

The coping strategies families have to adopt may also include more drastic measures such as reducing food consumption. Emerging data from COVID-19 phone surveys suggest that this strategy is being widely used. In Nigeria and Indonesia, for example, 50 and 68 percent of households, respectively, reported reducing their food consumption (Siwatu et al. 2020; World Bank 2020d). Depending on duration and severity, the impact of reduced food intake on children's health, cognitive development, and future human capital accumulation, as well as on future adult health and productivity, may be substantial.

The earliest results of these surveys (still in its first rounds) are also indicative of the heterogeneous results that the pandemic has on labor markets. In Ethiopia, surveyed respondents who experienced job loss or stopped working cited COVID-19 as the primary reason (62.8 percent). Figure B2.2.1 shows that this impact was similar across households in the bottom 40 (62.3 percent) and in the top 60 percent of the income distribution (63.0 percent). In Indonesia, a higher rate of wage workers in top 60 households stopped working than in bottom 40 households. Papua New Guinea also shows the bottom 40 reporting a lower job loss rate than the top 60, that is, 17 and 28 percent, respectively. In contrast, the survey in Cambodia reports the bottom 40 suffering higher job losses associated with COVID-19 than the top 60: 14 and 9 percent, respectively.

These examples of high-frequency surveys from Ethiopia, Indonesia, and Papua New Guinea seem to indicate that households in the middle and at the high end of the distribution may actually face similar or even higher rates of job loss than those at the bottom of the distribution. This outcome may occur because those at the bottom tend to be involved in agriculture, self-employment, or in essential service occupations and keep working, whereas those in the middle of the distribution may be employed in transport, hospitality, and retail services, which are more affected by job closures as a result of the pandemic, together with a lower national share of jobs that are tele-workable.

The differences can also be seen across the urban/rural divide. A survey in Mongolia, for example, found that 14 percent of urban respondents reported having lost employment, compared to only 9 percent of rural households (World Bank 2020e). In Uzbekistan, median per capita income combined from all sources fell by 38 percent in April compared to the previous month but declines were larger in urban areas, falling 46 percent in a single month (World Bank 2020f).

These early comparisons are preliminary and should be taken with caution. The outbreak is sweeping across countries according to differing timelines. In addition, differences in the timing of school openings and agricultural seasons may also influence the human capital accumulation and labor market effects captured by these surveys, adding to the complexity of comparing impacts across countries. The Papua New Guinea and Zambia surveys were conducted in June; the surveys in

(continued)

Mongolia, Indonesia, and Cambodia were fielded in mid-May; the Nigerian survey was conducted between May and April, and the Ethiopian and Uzbekistan surveys refer to mid-April.

High-frequency phone surveys conducted by the World Bank, partnering with national institutions, are providing rapid insights into which households are being affected by COVID-19 and how. Because of the nature of the data collection, which requires phone usage and service, some hard-to-reach households may be excluded. But as additional rounds of surveys are collected, adjustments in questionnaires, sample frame, and general design may allow for better capturing the evolution of the pandemic, its effects, and the policy responses to be implemented by authorities. These surveys will provide a wealth of data critical for combating the pandemic.

FIGURE B2.2.1 Share of Survey Respondents Who Stopped Working or Experienced Job Losses

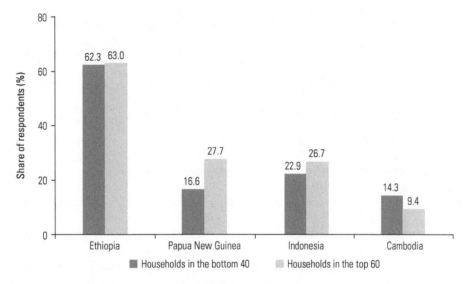

Source: Preliminary microdata from the first round of the high-frequency phone surveys.
Note: Each respondent from Indonesia is the head of the household or the main breadwinner, and the survey includes only those who are working wage jobs. If all workers (wage, and nonwage in farm and nonfarm activities) were included, the rates would drop to 22.7 and 25.0 for households in the bottom 40 and top 60, respectively. There is only one respondent in each household for Cambodia, Ethiopia, and Papua New Guinea.

Source: Personal communication with Kristen Himelein, Ririn Salwa Purnamasari, Kimsun Tong, and Christina Wieser for information about the rapid-response, high-frequency phone surveys in their countries of engagement.
Note: In Ethiopia, the first round (out of seven) was fielded between April 22 and May 13, 2020, with 3,249 households, and was jointly collected by the World Bank and the Central Statistical Authority. In Papua New Guinea, the World Bank and the local telecom company fielded a survey of 3,115 respondents in a first round (out of five) between June 18 and July 3, 2020. In Indonesia, the first of five rounds was collected May 1–17, 2020, from 4,338 households, with national and urban and rural representation. In Cambodia, a survey of 700 respondents was fielded between May 11 and May 26, 2020. It is representative at national and urban and rural levels, and was jointly collected by the World Bank, the National Institute of Statistics, and Nuppun Research and Consulting.

and reliable data are more important than ever for tracking the effects of the pandemic and designing appropriate policy measures (box 2.2).

The effects of job losses and reduced earnings spill across borders through lower remittances. Current estimates indicate that remittances have fallen by 20 percent, which disproportionately affects low-income households and developing economies. For instance, international remittances account for a significant share of GDP in many low-income economies such as Nepal (25 percent) and Ethiopia (7 percent), as well as in lower-middle- and upper-middle-income economies such as Guatemala (12 percent), Moldova (10 percent), Sri Lanka (8 percent), and Tunisia (5 percent). Although a large share of international remittances tends to go to the nonpoor, a sharp fall in remittances can increase the likelihood of families falling into poverty and, in some cases, reduce investments in human capital development that remittances often finance. Domestic remittances are an important income source for rural households as well, particularly in low- and lower-middle-income economies. For example, nearly 40 percent of poor households in Nigeria receive either domestic or international remittances. Because domestic remittances are often sent by urban informal-sector workers, including seasonal migrants in economies such as Bangladesh and India, to their families in rural areas, a substantial shock to the urban informal sector is likely to directly reduce income from remittances in rural areas (World Bank 2020g).

In addition to the disproportionate effect on labor market outcomes among low-income deciles, a study conducted across 54 economies finds that 90 percent of households have inadequate home environments to protect against the virus. Among those in the bottom 40, the figure is 94 percent (Brown, Ravallion, and van de Walle 2020). The same study also finds that 40 percent of households do not have formal health care facilities within five kilometers. In developing economies, limited access to health care is particularly prevalent among the rural poor, as well as among the urban poor who live in congested informal settlements with low-quality health services (World Bank 2020h). This inadequate access to health care points to strong, direct wealth effects on the capacity of households to protect themselves against the virus. Poorer households will have less ability to follow the World Health Organization's preventive health recommendations and will be less likely to receive adequate treatment if they contract COVID-19. This vulnerability is also reflected in data from high-income economies, such as the United States, which indicates higher mortality rates in areas with high levels of economic segregation and concentrations of poverty, people of color, and crowded housing (Chetty et al. 2020).

Even when the immediate impacts of COVID-19 are felt by households across the entire income distribution, the poorest may be hit harder because they have fewer coping mechanisms. The bottom 40 and top 60 cope in different ways. In Ethiopia and Indonesia, high-frequency surveys recently collected to trace the impact of the pandemic show that the employment effects seem to be quite even across the entire distribution; people are losing their jobs at a similar rate across quintiles. But in Ethiopia, 24.7 percent of households in the top 60 could rely on savings as a coping strategy during the pandemic, while only 12 percent of the bottom 40 could do so. Absence of savings has real effects: 30 percent of households in the bottom quintile reported running out of food, while only 15 percent of those in the top quintile did so (Adebe, Bundervoet, and Wieser 2020).

In developing economies, inadequate social security systems fail to compensate for the differential impact of the pandemic. Informal workers are particularly vulnerable to economic setbacks from COVID-19, given that they are less likely to benefit from social security systems that cover those in the formal sector. The International Labour Organization estimates that 1.6 billion workers in the informal economy, or nearly half the global workforce, face substantial threats to their livelihoods. For example, in the first month of the COVID-19 pandemic, the income of informal workers dropped by about 60 percent globally, representing a drop of 81 percent in Africa and the Americas, 21.6 percent in Asia and Pacific, and 70 percent in Europe and Central Asia (ILO 2020). Although governments have been adopting emergency economic measures to provide households with some form of a safety net, low-income and middle-income economies share characteristics that may impede the reach of social protection responses (Baldwin and di Mauro 2020; Gerard, Imbert, and Orkin 2020).

Shared prosperity and its connection to other welfare indicators

Growth of mean income is a commonly used measure of how most of the population fares during periods of economic growth or decline. It is also one of the components of the shared prosperity measure, and the two are highly correlated, as shown in figure 2.2. However, rapid growth in average incomes could be driven by rapid increases among the rich. An alternative distribution-sensitive measure of well-being is growth of median income or consumption, given that it reflects improvements in the welfare of people in the middle of the income distribution. The median also has the advantage of not being affected by underreporting of incomes by those at the top of the distribution (which would bias the mean downward). Several recent academic papers advocate use of the median, arguing that as a measure of income-related well-being, the median is superior to the commonly used GDP per capita and to survey-based measures at the mean.[10]

Growth in median income and shared prosperity are both distribution-sensitive measures of growth that are higher when growth in average incomes is high and when inequality is decreasing. It is therefore not surprising that the two are highly correlated (figure 2.6).[11]

However, the median may fail to capture information about the economic performance of those at the bottom of the distribution. Similarly, it may also not describe what happens to groups above or below the median, which is of special interest when economic gains are very different across different groups. If economic growth has been faster at the bottom than in the rest of the distribution, growth at the median would understate how inclusive growth has been. Conversely, if growth has been faster at the top, then the median could overstate progress at the bottom. These deficiencies make shared prosperity a better measure of progress at the bottom of the distribution.

One reason shared prosperity focuses on the bottom 40 is simply that their share in total income is much less than 40 percent. In the majority of economies, the share of income accruing to the bottom 40 is between 10 and 25 percent. Namibia and Zimbabwe are particularly unequal, with the bottom 40 accruing less than 10 percent of total income (figure 2.7). Across the world, the share of income earned by the top 10 percent is often larger, sometimes much larger, than the share earned by the bottom 40.

The ratio of the share of income between the top 10 percent and bottom 40 percent is known as the Palma ratio. Palma (2011) calls attention to evidence from the developed world that shows that changes in income shares tend to take place between the bottom 40 and the top 10, with the middle (fifth to ninth) deciles having fairly stable and consistent shares over time. Among the 91 economies represented in this round of data, the share of the five middle quintiles looks quite stable. The striking fact is that the Palma ratio varies widely across economies, ranging, in this sample of economies,

FIGURE 2.6 Shared Prosperity and Growth of the Median

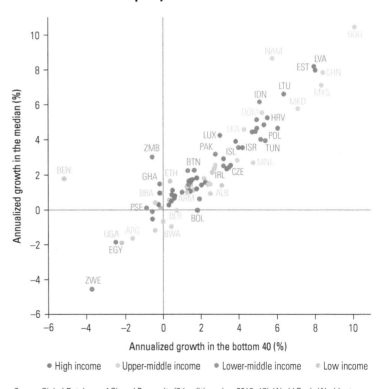

Source: Global Database of Shared Prosperity (7th edition, circa 2012–17), World Bank, Washington, DC, https://www.worldbank.org/en/topic/poverty/brief/global-database-of-shared-prosperity.

FIGURE 2.7 Share of Income, by Decile

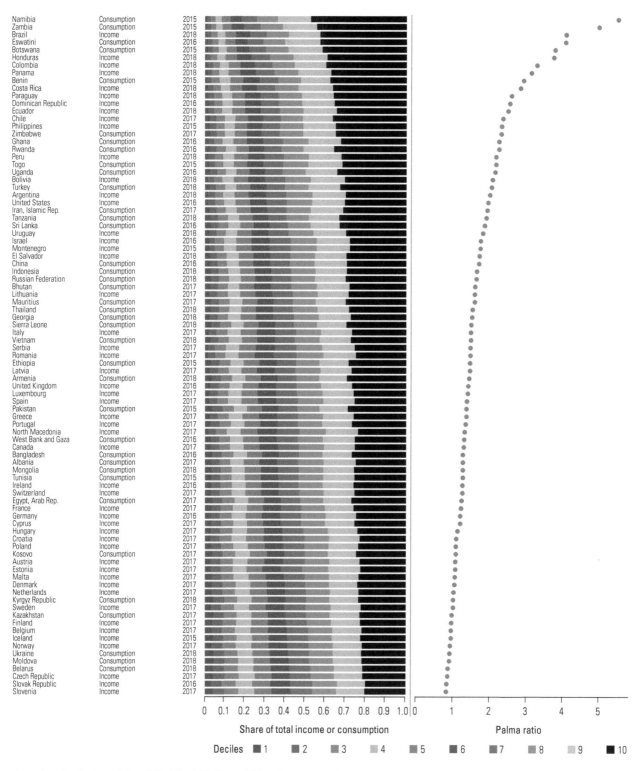

Source: PovcalNet (online analysis tool), World Bank, Washington, DC, http://iresearch.worldbank.org/PovcalNet/.
Note: The income shares and the Palma ratio are from the last year of the shared prosperity period for each economy. For example, if the shared prosperity period is 2010–15, then the income shares and the Palma ratio reflect data from 2015.

between 0.8 and 6.0. In other words, the share of the top 10 is in most cases larger than the share of the bottom 40. As a measure of inequality, the Palma ratio shows important differences in inequality across the economies in the sample.

The welfare benefits of promoting shared prosperity are clear. Evidence from the current sample of 91 economies shows that shared prosperity is correlated with faster poverty reduction (panel a of figure 2.8). This is not surprising: poverty tends to fall as average incomes increase, and even more so when growth occurs at the bottom of the distribution, which is exactly what shared prosperity measures. Moreover, a positive shared prosperity premium is associated with a reduction in inequality, as measured by the Gini coefficient (figure 2.8, panel b).[12] This association is also not surprising, given that both are measures of inequality change.

The connection between inclusive growth, poverty, and inequality is well known in the

FIGURE 2.8 **Correlation of Shared Prosperity and the Shared Prosperity Premium with Poverty and Inequality**

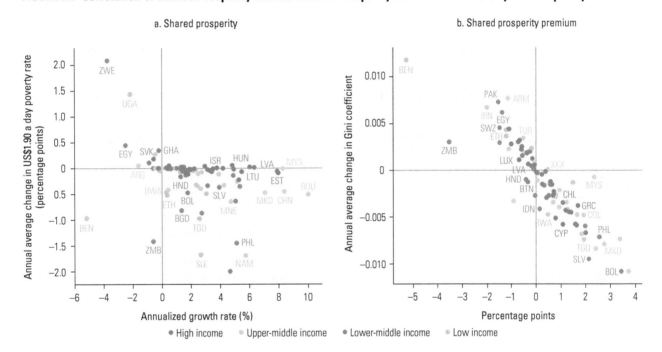

Sources: Global Database of Shared Prosperity (7th edition, circa 2012–17), World Bank, Washington, DC, https://www.worldbank.org/en/topic/poverty/brief/global-database-of-shared-prosperity; PovcalNet (online analysis tool), World Bank, Washington, DC, http://iresearch.worldbank.org/PovcalNet/.
Note: The 91 economies in the figure are based on availability of the shared prosperity indicator. Changes in poverty and the Gini coefficient are calculated over the same period for which shared prosperity is calculated, which varies by economy.

BOX 2.3 **The Importance of Equity for Poverty Reduction**

It has long been established that an arithmetic identity links a reduction in absolute poverty to growth in mean incomes and changes in the distribution of income (Bourguignon 2003, 2004; Datt and Ravallion 1992; Ferreira 2012). Generally speaking, poverty reduction in an economy can be driven by either higher average growth, or a reduction in inequality of incomes, or a combination of the two. Thus, to achieve the same poverty reduction during a slowdown in growth, a more equal distribution in incomes is required. It is also well established that economies with lower income inequality today will typically experience a greater reduction in future poverty for a given level of future growth.[a] In other words, economies with lower levels of initial income inequality will observe a higher (absolute) growth elasticity of poverty reduction. The literature refers to this as the double-dividend effect of reducing inequality today: a reduction in inequality today leads

(continued)

BOX 2.3 **The Importance of Equity for Poverty Reduction** *(continued)*

to a reduction in poverty today and accelerates poverty reduction in the future (Alvaredo and Gasparini 2015; Bourguignon 2004).

Empirical evidence suggests that the magnitude of this double-dividend effect on poverty reduction may be substantial. Using data from 135 economies for the period 1974–2018, Bergstrom (2020) finds that a 1 percent reduction in inequality (as measured by the standard deviation of log-income) leads, on average, to a larger reduction in poverty than a 1 percent increase in mean incomes.[b] Moreover, several papers find that the growth elasticity of poverty reduction is notably decreasing in initial inequality (Bergstrom 2020; Bourguignon 2003; Kraay 2006; Ravallion 1997, 2001; World Bank 2005). For example, based on a sample of 65 economies during 1981–2005 and using

the US$1.00 poverty line, it was found that growth elasticity was highest among low-inequality economies, with an absolute value of approximately 4.0 in economies with a Gini index in the mid-20s, and lowest among high-inequality economies, with an absolute value close to 1.0 for economies with a Gini index of about 60 (World Bank 2005). These findings suggest that reducing inequality can have substantial effects on poverty reduction. Importantly, this result is not inconsistent with the finding that most of the reduction in poverty over the past few decades can be attributed to growth in average incomes.[c] Rather, this simply implies that distributive changes have not been the main drivers of poverty reduction. For example, recent research commissioned for this report highlights that, despite

the sizable effect that inequality reduction can have on poverty reduction, the majority of changes in poverty over the past 40 years can largely be explained by growth in mean incomes, attributing this finding to the fact that changes in mean incomes have been an order of magnitude larger than changes in inequality (Bergstrom 2020).

Most developing economies have low average income and hence low growth elasticity of poverty. Figure B2.3.1 shows the distribution of economies by their average income or consumption and their respective growth elasticities of poverty. In addition, the figure includes lines representing the connection between these two variables for a given distribution of income (as measured by the standard deviation of income or consumption). Most economies in Sub-Saharan Africa have low levels of income and of growth

FIGURE B2.3.1 Growth's Impact on Poverty Reduction Depends on the Mean and Distribution of Income

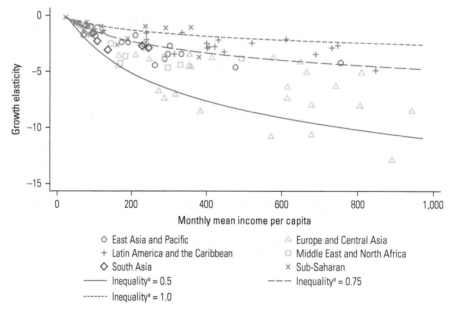

Source: Bergstrom 2020.
a. As per standard deviation.

(continued)

BOX 2.3 **The Importance of Equity for Poverty Reduction** *(continued)*

elasticity of income. Therefore, they need to grow to make their growth more effective in poverty reduction. Moreover, changes in inequality render little change in growth elasticity of poverty when average income is low. In contrast, Latin American economies and some East Asian economies, despite being at middle-income levels, have low growth elasticity of poverty because their inequality levels are high. These economies could gain more poverty reduction per unit of economic growth if they were able to reduce inequality. Economies in Europe and Central Asia experience the most efficient growth elasticity of poverty because of their high levels of income or consumption and lower inequality. Of course, the fastest route to increasing poverty reduction would be a combination of economic growth and inequality reduction.

Although poverty decompositions are a useful tool for determining how growth and changes in inequality translate into changes in poverty, such decompositions shed no light on how changes in inequality and growth came about, nor how they are related. Thus, such analysis ignores the possibility that inequality can have additional impacts on poverty through the impact it has on growth. Theoretically, the effect of inequality on growth is ambiguous. The conventional view is that higher inequality promotes stronger incentives, generates greater savings and

investment, and endows the rich with the minimum capital needed to start economic activity, thereby stimulating growth (Aghion, Caroli, and Garcia-Penalosa 1999; Barro 2000; Kaldor 1957; Okun 2015). Conversely, it has been argued that inequality hurts growth because it leads to redistributive pressures, either through the median voter who enacts redistributive taxes (Persson and Tabellini 1994), or by generating social conflict, expropriation, and rent-seeking behavior (Alesina 1994; Alesina and Rodrik 1994; Benabou 1996; Benhabib and Rustichini 1996; Glaeser, Scheinkman, and Shleifer 2003; Perotti 1996). A further view is that inequality, coupled with borrowing constraints and financial market imperfections, prevents the talented poor from undertaking profitable investments in physical and human capital, thereby limiting the full growth potential of the economy (Banerjee and Newman 1993; Galor and Zeira 1993). In an attempt to reconcile some of these conflicting theories, one paper proposes a model in which increases in inequality in a context of low levels of inequality provide incentives to be more productive, hence spurring growth, whereas increases from higher levels of inequality lead to rent-seeking behaviors, thereby depressing growth (Benhabib 2003).

On the empirical side, the effect of inequality on growth, despite numerous studies,

remains inconclusive. The earliest papers, using a cross-section of economies, typically found negative effects (Alesina and Rodrik 1994; Persson and Tabellini 1994). However, with the introduction of a new data set (Deininger and Squire 1996), the empirical literature evolved to using panel data estimation techniques; such studies typically found positive effects of inequality on growth (Forbes 2000; Li and Zou 1998). More recently, however, several papers find again a negative effect (Castelló-Climent 2010; Dabla-Norris et al. 2015; Halter, Oechslin, and Zweimüller 2014; Ostry, Berg, and Tsangarides 2014), although the validity of their estimation technique has been questioned because of the presence of weak instruments (Kraay 2015). It has been suggested that the inconsistencies of these empirical findings reflect a gap between the intricacy of the relationship, as expressed in the theoretical literature, and the simple relationships that are commonly estimated (Voitchovsky 2009). In support of a more complex relationship, several papers provide empirical evidence of a nonlinear, context-specific relationship between inequality and growth (Banerjee and Duflo 2003; Grigoli, Paredes, and Di Bella 2016; Grigoli and Robles 2017).

Source: Bergstrom 2020.
a. To be precise, the effect that initial inequality has on growth elasticity is theoretically ambiguous (Ravallion 2007). However, under certain assumptions it can be shown that growth elasticity is unambiguously decreasing with inequality (Bourguignon 2003; Ferreira 2012). Moreover, empirical evidence highlights a negative relationship between growth elasticity and the level of initial inequality.
b. Moreover, Fosu (2017), using different data and a different empirical specification than Bergstrom (2020), also finds that inequality elasticity tends to be larger, on average, relative to (absolute) growth elasticity.
c. Studies that find that changes in poverty are primarily driven by changes in mean incomes include Alvaredo and Gasparini (2015); Dollar and Kraay (2002); Fosu (2017); and Kraay (2006).

academic literature and confirms the importance of promoting inclusive growth that involves shared prosperity (box 2.3).

Comparing 2000–05 and the very recent post-2015 period, inequality has been decreasing in many economies (figure 2.9). The selection of economies is limited to only those that have comparable data, or where methodologies and measurement remained constant. Over this comparison period and under these conditions, the majority of economies in Europe and Central Asia, Latin America and the Caribbean, and Sub-Saharan Africa experienced a decline in inequality. High-income economies were more likely to experience an increase in the Gini coefficient for the period, although from usually lower levels than other economies.

While previous patterns of change in inequality vary across economies, the negative longer-term consequences of COVID-19 for income inequality are clear. Hill and Narayan

(2020) argue that "while the short-run implications of COVID-19 for income distribution per se are uncertain and varying across economies, the longer-term risks the crisis poses to inequality and social mobility are less ambiguous." The authors argue that the pandemic will have stronger effects in more unequal societies, because in those societies, the poorer groups of the population are more vulnerable to risks due to the poor working in activities more likely to be affected by the pandemic and by weak social protection systems. These then amplify into long-term impacts due to the "scarring" effects of employment losses, closing of small and medium enterprises, and reduced investments in health and education, all of which lead to more vulnerability and less resilience and higher inequality in the future.

Consequently, without strong interventions, the crisis may trigger cycles of higher income inequality, lower social mobility among the vulnerable, and lower resilience to future shocks. Some populations, such as children, women, and less-skilled workers in rural and urban informal labor markets, are particularly fragile and hence require special attention.

Who is in the bottom 40?

Figure 2.10 provides a profile of the bottom 40 in each economy for 124 economies with data from at least 2012. The figure does so by reporting the share of individuals with a particular characteristic, involving demographics or geographic location, who are in the bottom 40. If having such a characteristic is not correlated with people's positions along the distribution, then 40 percent of a given group would be in the bottom 40 of the population, and 60 percent would be in the top 60.

An example of a characteristic uncorrelated with income is gender. Across all 124 economies shown, about 40 percent of females and males are in the bottom 40, and 60 percent are in the top 60, meaning that the gender distribution is fairly even. This even distribution occurs because gender is an individual-level characteristic, and poverty is a household-level indicator. For gender groups, shares would vary greatly only if there were large shares of single-gender households (including single-person households) that differed between the rich and the poor.

FIGURE 2.9 Changes in the Gini Coefficient

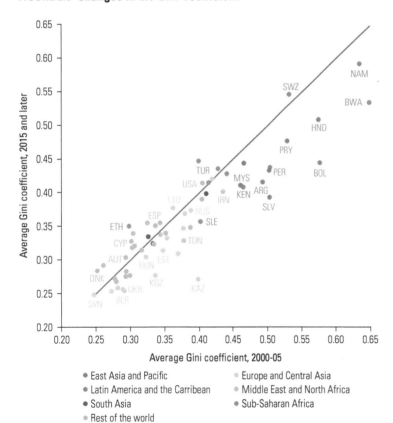

Source: PovcalNet (online analysis tool), World Bank, Washington, DC, http://iresearch.worldbank.org /PovcalNet/.
Note: The figure includes 62 economies with Gini coefficients in the period 2000–05 and 2015 and after, and over comparable data series.

FIGURE 2.10 Representation of Different Groups in the Bottom 40, by Economy

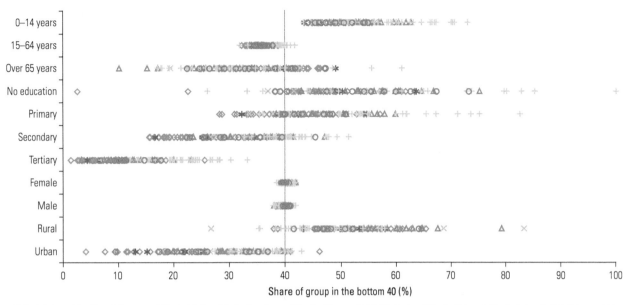

Source: Poverty and Equity Briefs (database), April 2020, World Bank, Washington, DC, https://www.worldbank.org/en/topic/poverty/publication/poverty-and-equity-briefs.
Note: All characteristics are at the individual level. Education subgroups are limited to people age 15 and older. There are 124 economies with data from 2012 and later.

Some characteristics are much more likely to be found among the bottom 40 than the top 60, and some groups are disproportionately represented in the bottom 40 in almost every economy. For example, in every economy with available data, more than 40 percent of children ages 0–14 are in the bottom 40, meaning they are overrepresented in the bottom of the distribution. Conversely, those with tertiary education are disproportionately likely to be in the top 60. In low-income economies, the education profiles of the bottom 40 and top 60 are more disparate than in higher-income economies. This difference may reflect more disparate access to education, differences in compulsory education policies, and returns to education. For example, on average, in low-income economies, 8 percent of those with tertiary education are in the bottom 40, compared with 21 percent in high-income economies. The share of individuals with tertiary education in the bottom 40 ranges from 1 percent in Zambia to 37 percent in Maldives. In wealthier economies, a larger share of the population that has completed tertiary education is in the bottom 40. Although this may seem counterintuitive, it reflects the fact that higher educational attainment is more common in wealthier economies.

The geographic distribution of those in the bottom 40 also shows an important disparity across economies. Larger shares of the bottom 40 live in urban areas in high-income economies than in low-income economies. In low-income economies, about 18 percent of urban residents belong to the bottom 40, compared with 37 percent of urban residents in high-income economies. Interestingly, all regions share these characteristics. From Sub-Saharan Africa to Europe and Central Asia, children, adults with less schooling, and the rural population are more likely to be in the bottom 40, indicating that these patterns are robust relative to geographic conditions and economy-specific income levels (there may be differences, however, in how rural areas are defined across economies; see box 3.1 in chapter 3 of this report).

As explained in more detail in chapter 3, these are the same leading demographic characteristics seen among the poor. Whether the international poverty line of US$1.90 a day is used or the lower-middle-income poverty line of US$3.20 a day, a disproportionate share of the poor are children, rural, and have only primary or less schooling. These similarities underline the vulnerability of these groups, given that they are more likely to be at the bottom of the distribution.[13]

Annex 2A

Shared prosperity estimates, by economy

The mean of the bottom 40 within each economy refers to the average household per capita consumption or income among this segment of the population. The choice of income or consumption depends on the data available for each economy and, in most cases, is consistent with the welfare aggregate used to measure poverty.

For China, shared prosperity is estimated by PovcalNet using grouped data. Because grouped data are provided separately for urban and rural populations, the national bottom 40 must be estimated. The bottom 40 is identified using the national poverty gap and choosing a poverty line that corresponds to the threshold consumption level of the national bottom 40. PovcalNet uses a parametric Lorenz curve fitted on grouped data, an adjustment for differences in price levels between urban and rural areas, and urban–rural population shares from the World Development Indicators database. Because shared prosperity is estimated using grouped data, the measure is approximate and may differ from the results based on official microdata (see PovcalNet What's New technical notes for details).[14]

For economies in Europe and Central Asia and Organisation for Economic Co-operation and Development–Europe using European Union Statistics on Income and Living Conditions data and household income per capita as the welfare aggregate, the estimates for shared prosperity include negative incomes.

Economies are included in the fall 2020 edition of the GDSP if the following requirements have been met:

- Two relevant household surveys have been conducted and have yielded comparable data.

- Among comparable surveys, one must be conducted within two years of 2012, and the other within two years of 2017.

- The period between the selected initial and end years should range between three and seven years.

- In cases where multiple surveys can fulfill these criteria, the most recent survey years are typically chosen.

Table 2A.1 indicates the economies included in this edition of the GDSP, reference period, welfare aggregate, and indicators of growth among the bottom 40, the median, and the mean in baseline and final years.

TABLE 2A.1 Data on Shared Prosperity, by Economy

| Economy | Period[c] | Type[d] | Annualized growth in mean consumption or income per capita[a,b] | | | Mean consumption or income per capita[a] | | | | | |
| | | | | | | Baseline (US$ a day, 2011 PPP) | | | Most recent year (US$ a day, PPP) | | |
			Bottom 40 (%)	Median (%)	Total population (%)	Bottom 40%	Median	Total population	Bottom 40 %	Median	Total population
East Asia and Pacific											
China[e]	2013–16	C	8.38	7.86	7.12	3.92	7.05	9.47	4.99	8.84	11.64
Indonesia	2014–18	c	5.06	6.18	4.93	2.50	4.09	5.66	3.05	5.20	6.87
Mongolia	2011–18	c	0.99	1.01	0.66	4.40	7.15	8.92	4.72	7.67	9.34
Malaysia	2012–16	i	8.30	7.14	5.95	7.88	15.27	21.76	11.13	20.58	27.95
Philippines	2012–15	i	5.12	4.03	2.56	2.42	4.46	6.96	2.81	5.02	7.50
Thailand	2014–18	c	1.45	1.40	1.15	6.73	11.29	14.84	7.13	11.93	15.54
Vietnam	2012–18	c	4.91	5.16	5.01	3.70	6.38	7.93	4.93	8.63	10.63
Europe and Central Asia											
Albania	2014–17	c	2.46	0.93	0.81	3.90	6.87	8.40	4.19	7.07	8.61
Armenia	2013–18	c	1.26	1.00	2.40	3.68	5.78	6.84	3.91	6.07	7.70
Belarus	2013–18	c	0.71	–0.02	–0.02	11.89	17.84	20.18	12.32	17.83	20.16
Czech Republic	2012–17	i	3.53	2.55	2.82	16.33	24.27	27.14	19.42	27.52	31.19
Estonia	2012–17	i	7.98	8.00	7.20	12.12	19.83	24.21	17.79	29.14	34.27
Georgia	2013–18	c	2.65	2.35	1.42	3.04	5.55	7.19	3.47	6.23	7.71
Croatia	2012–17	i	5.47	5.27	4.28	8.71	15.25	17.79	11.37	19.72	21.93
Hungary	2012–17	i	4.84	4.49	4.60	9.82	16.61	18.83	12.44	20.68	23.58
Kazakhstan	2012–17	c	–0.02	–0.67	–0.56	6.91	10.37	12.16	6.90	10.03	11.82
Kyrgyz Republic	2013–18	c	3.15	2.52	2.44	3.07	4.58	5.43	3.58	5.19	6.12
Lithuania	2012–17	i	6.33	6.63	7.43	9.39	16.43	20.04	12.77	22.65	28.68
Latvia	2012–17	i	7.91	8.21	8.23	8.28	14.69	17.88	12.11	21.80	26.56
Moldova	2013–18	c	1.90	0.62	0.32	5.45	8.32	9.68	5.98	8.59	9.84
Montenegro	2012–15	i	4.72	2.70	1.35	4.84	10.61	13.48	5.55	11.49	14.03
North Macedonia	2012–17	i	7.06	5.79	4.31	3.74	7.96	9.49	5.26	10.55	11.72
Poland	2012–17	i	6.01	4.67	4.02	11.22	19.36	22.83	15.03	24.33	27.80
Romania	2012–17	i	10.02	10.48	9.96	4.24	8.65	10.11	6.83	14.23	16.26
Russian Federation	2013–18	c	–0.44	–1.17	–2.27	9.30	15.99	22.35	9.10	15.08	19.93
Serbia	2013–17	i	3.89	2.83	1.48	4.31	9.45	11.38	5.02	10.57	12.07
Slovak Republic	2011–16	i	–0.58	–0.52	–1.08	14.03	22.45	24.28	13.63	21.88	22.99
Slovenia	2012–17	i	2.20	1.57	1.52	19.91	30.11	33.17	22.20	32.54	35.77
Turkey	2013–18	c	2.14	1.79	2.67	7.13	13.17	17.45	7.92	14.39	19.91
Ukraine	2013–18	c	–0.59	–0.10	0.14	8.45	12.21	13.63	8.21	12.15	13.73
Kosovo	2012–17	c	2.36	1.53	1.89	4.43	6.90	7.97	4.98	7.44	8.75
Latin America and the Caribbean											
Argentina[f]	2013–18	i	–1.62	–1.62	–1.55	7.70	15.81	20.55	7.09	14.57	19.00
Bolivia	2013–18	i	1.78	–0.02	–1.65	4.40	9.96	14.25	4.80	9.95	13.12
Brazil	2013–18	i	–0.43	0.42	0.66	5.58	12.23	20.29	5.46	12.49	20.97
Chile	2013–17	i	4.92	4.67	3.83	8.12	14.37	21.93	9.84	17.24	25.49
Colombia	2013–18	i	2.34	1.45	0.41	3.83	8.31	13.96	4.30	8.93	14.25
Costa Rica	2013–18	i	1.40	1.58	0.60	6.90	13.83	22.44	7.39	14.95	23.12
Dominican Republic	2011–16	i	5.19	5.56	4.25	4.18	8.08	12.58	5.39	10.59	15.49
Ecuador	2013–18	i	1.25	1.33	0.47	4.48	9.04	13.51	4.77	9.66	13.83
Honduras	2013–18	i	1.30	2.25	1.72	2.08	4.80	7.82	2.22	5.37	8.52
Panama	2013–18	i	5.29	4.87	3.87	5.92	13.51	21.42	7.66	17.13	25.90

(continued)

Economy	Period[c]	Type[d]	Annualized growth in mean consumption or income per capita[a,b]			Mean consumption or income per capita[a]					
						Baseline (US$ a day, 2011 PPP)			Most recent year (US$ a day, PPP)		
			Bottom 40 (%)	Median (%)	Total population (%)	Bottom 40%	Median	Total population	Bottom 40 %	Median	Total population
Peru	2013–18	i	2.45	1.46	1.49	4.47	9.37	12.67	5.05	10.08	13.64
Paraguay	2013–18	i	1.57	1.12	0.34	5.59	11.23	17.17	6.04	11.87	17.46
El Salvador	2013–18	i	3.95	3.57	1.82	3.84	7.12	9.99	4.66	8.48	10.93
Uruguay	2013–18	i	2.00	1.42	1.43	10.00	19.23	25.24	11.05	20.64	27.09
Middle East and North Africa											
Egypt, Arab Rep.	2012–17	c	−2.51	−1.85	−1.14	3.15	4.49	5.37	2.76	4.07	5.06
Iran, Islamic Rep.	2014–17	c	−0.13	0.95	1.89	6.59	11.61	15.35	6.57	11.95	16.23
West Bank and Gaza	2011–16	c	−0.89	0.11	−0.55	5.48	8.92	11.21	5.21	8.97	10.86
Tunisia	2010–15	c	5.36	3.96	3.38	4.33	7.59	9.45	5.62	9.22	11.17
South Asia											
Bangladesh	2010–16	c	1.35	1.65	1.54	1.88	2.81	3.54	2.04	3.10	3.88
Bhutan	2012–17	c	1.63	2.27	1.67	3.52	5.99	8.04	3.81	6.70	8.74
Sri Lanka	2012–16	c	4.24	4.60	4.72	3.31	5.33	7.37	3.83	6.24	8.66
Pakistan	2010–15	c	2.72	3.19	4.25	2.27	3.28	4.00	2.60	3.83	4.93
Sub-Saharan Africa											
Benin	2011–15	c	−5.20	1.78	0.06	1.06	1.80	2.70	0.87	1.92	2.71
Botswana	2009–15	c	0.42	−0.95	−3.30	2.12	4.66	9.94	2.18	4.37	7.97
Eswatini	2009–16	c	4.67	4.46	6.14	1.09	2.22	3.80	1.50	3.01	5.73
Ethiopia	2010–15	c	0.35	1.64	1.56	1.45	2.29	2.81	1.47	2.49	3.03
Ghana	2012–16	c	−0.20	1.48	1.27	2.39	4.60	6.32	2.37	4.88	6.64
Mauritius	2012–17	c	2.71	2.56	2.02	5.60	9.26	12.32	6.40	10.50	13.62
Malawi	2010–16	c	3.05	1.40	1.57	0.68	1.22	1.83	0.81	1.33	2.01
Namibia	2009–15	c	5.73	8.67	6.64	1.72	3.34	7.63	2.36	5.38	11.02
Rwanda	2013–16	c	0.31	0.56	−0.17	0.99	1.68	2.55	1.00	1.70	2.54
Sierra Leone	2011–18	c	2.67	2.38	2.86	1.12	1.78	2.26	1.35	2.10	2.75
Togo	2011–15	c	2.55	2.14	0.62	0.87	1.72	2.58	0.96	1.87	2.64
Tanzania	2011–18	c	−0.15	0.11	0.92	1.19	1.91	2.57	1.18	1.92	2.72
Uganda	2012–16	c	−2.20	−1.89	−1.01	1.40	2.38	3.33	1.28	2.20	3.20
Zambia	2010–15	c	−0.59	3.03	2.93	0.66	1.29	2.48	0.64	1.49	2.87
Zimbabwe	2011–17	C/c	−3.75	−4.54	−3.50	1.86	3.37	4.85	1.48	2.55	3.92
High income											
Austria	2012–17	i	1.44	1.59	1.20	28.18	46.60	53.49	30.27	50.43	56.76
Belgium	2012–17	i	0.43	0.51	0.42	27.33	43.10	47.99	27.92	44.22	49.01
Canada	2012–17	l	1.43	1.06	1.17	27.41	48.48	56.97	29.44	51.10	60.39
Switzerland	2012–17	i	−0.26	0.31	0.34	36.03	57.95	69.38	35.57	58.85	70.55
Germany	2011–16	l	−0.20	0.96	0.80	27.89	44.01	51.95	27.62	46.15	54.06
Denmark	2012–17	i	1.34	1.46	1.68	28.98	44.36	50.84	30.98	47.69	55.26
Spain	2012–17	i	1.75	1.20	1.12	15.81	30.38	35.73	17.25	32.25	37.77
Finland	2012–17	i	0.58	0.67	0.65	29.08	43.27	49.72	29.93	44.75	51.35
France	2012–17	i	0.61	0.80	0.19	26.73	43.09	52.47	27.56	44.83	52.97
United Kingdom	2011–16	i	1.76	1.82	2.42	21.18	36.91	43.84	23.11	40.40	49.40
Ireland	2011–16	i	3.43	2.43	3.05	21.24	35.29	42.29	25.15	39.78	49.15
Iceland	2010–15	i	3.15	2.93	3.31	26.68	40.35	44.89	31.16	46.62	52.82
Israel	2010–16	l	4.18	3.56	2.56	11.21	24.14	31.25	14.33	29.77	36.36

(continued)

TABLE 2A.1 Data on Shared Prosperity, by Economy *(continued)*

Economy	Period[c]	Type[d]	Annualized growth in mean consumption or income per capita[a,b]			Mean consumption or income per capita[a]					
						Baseline (US$ a day, 2011 PPP)			Most recent year (US$ a day, PPP)		
			Bottom 40 (%)	Median (%)	Total population (%)	Bottom 40%	Median	Total population	Bottom 40%	Median	Total population
Italy	2012–17	i	0.48	1.12	1.04	18.56	34.07	40.38	19.02	36.03	42.53
Luxembourg	2012–17	i	2.96	4.26	3.66	33.77	58.53	71.55	39.07	72.10	85.63
Malta	2012–17	i	3.80	3.92	3.74	20.58	32.87	37.65	24.79	39.84	45.23
Netherlands	2012–17	i	1.53	1.73	1.89	27.87	43.07	48.90	30.06	46.94	53.70
Norway	2012–17	i	0.44	0.87	1.02	38.93	59.46	65.65	39.79	62.09	69.07
Portugal	2012–17	i	3.32	2.35	2.00	11.88	20.59	25.61	13.99	23.12	28.26
Sweden	2012–17	i	1.39	1.67	1.98	20.22	44.38	49.97	30.23	48.20	55.11
United States	2010–16	I	1.31	1.23	1.66	24.51	49.02	62.62	26.50	52.74	69.13

Sources: Global Database of Shared Prosperity (7th edition, circa 2012–17), World Bank, Washington, DC, http://www.worldbank.org/en/topic/poverty/brief/global-database-of-shared-prosperity; PovcalNet (online analysis tool), World Bank, Washington, DC, http://iresearch.worldbank.org/PovcalNet/; WDI (World Development Indicators) (database), World Bank, Washington, DC, http://data.worldbank.org/products/wdi. Data as of May 21, 2020.

Note: PPP = purchasing power parity.

a. Based on real mean per capita consumption or income measured at 2011 PPP using PovcalNet data. For some economies, means are not reported due to grouped or confidential data.

b. The annualized growth rate is computed as (Mean in year 2/Mean in year 1)^(1/(Reference Year 2 – Reference Year 1)) – 1.

c. Refers to the year in which the underlying household survey data were collected and, in cases in which the data collection period bridged two calendar years, the first year in which data were collected is reported. The initial year refers to the nearest survey collected five years before the most recent survey available; only surveys collected between three and five years before the most recent survey are considered. The final year refers to the most recent survey available between 2015 and 2019.

d. Denotes whether the data reported are based on consumption (c) or income (i) data. Capital letters indicate that grouped data were used.

e. See Atamanov et al. (2020).

f. Covers urban areas only.

Annex 2B

Data for shared prosperity over different periods

This chapter analyzes the World Bank's shared prosperity indicator based on data from the seventh edition of the Global Database of Shared Prosperity (GDSP), which presents income growth for the bottom 40 percent of the population in 91 economies circa 2012–17. The definition allows for the calculation of shared prosperity with two data points that are within two years of the benchmark years, 2012 and 2017.

The exact period for which shared prosperity is measured varies by economy, based on survey availability. Economies in Sub-Saharan Africa have the most variation in the period over which shared prosperity is measured because of the varied and infrequent collection of household surveys. Survey availability in Europe and Central Asia, Latin America and the Caribbean, and the rest of the world is the most consistent. As a result, shared prosperity is measured over the same periods for almost all economies in these regions (figure 2B.1).

But comparisons across regions should be made with caution. In many cases, there is little overlap between periods measured by the circa 2012–17 shared prosperity indicators; the periods range from 2009–15 for Botswana and Namibia to 2014–18 for Indonesia and Thailand.

The number of economies that can be included depends on the availability of household surveys. Although 166 economies have poverty rates in PovcalNet, fewer economies have shared prosperity indicators, given that calculation of this indicator requires more data. Whereas one household survey is needed to compute poverty, two comparable household surveys are needed to compute shared prosperity. Moreover, these surveys must also be conducted circa 2012–17 to ensure comparability of the shared prosperity indicator across economies.

Over time, the coverage of economies in the GDSP has varied (table 2B.1). The largest number of economies covered was in the fourth edition in 2017, with 93 economies. The current GDSP covers 91 economies. There are 78 economies represented in both the sixth and seventh editions of the GDSP, thanks to regular data collection in these economies. For example, in Latin America and the Caribbean, 14 economies have shared prosperity estimates in both editions; and in 13 of these, shared prosperity indicators have been updated with newer surveys.

Less frequent data collection means that some economies are only sporadically represented in the GDSP and have

FIGURE 2B.1 Varying Periods of Measurement for Shared Prosperity, Global Database of Shared Prosperity, Seventh Edition, 2012–17

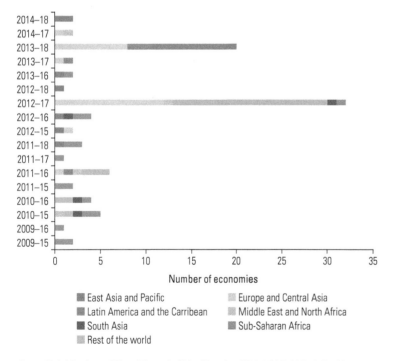

Source: Global Database of Shared Prosperity (7th edition, circa 2012–17), World Bank, Washington, DC, https://www.worldbank.org/en/topic/poverty/brief/global-database-of-shared-prosperity.

infrequent monitoring of shared prosperity. For example, although increased data collection efforts have boosted the representation of Sub-Saharan Africa from 12 economies in the previous edition of the GDSP to 15 in the current edition (table 2B.2), only 6 of the region's 48 economies are in both. Moreover, only one of these has a shared prosperity indicator that has been updated with new household survey data; the other five economies are using the same household surveys as in the previous edition of the GDSP, because the coverage still fits within the definition of the time period and no new surveys have been conducted. If efforts at better data collection continue, however, it will be possible to have more information about shared prosperity in the region in the future.

In South Asia, shared prosperity indicators for the four available economies are the same in both the sixth and seventh editions, meaning that no new data have become available to update shared prosperity periods.

Shared prosperity has not been calculated recently for some of the economies included in the last seven rounds of the GDSP. For example, 11 economies represented in earlier rounds of the GDSP have not been included recently because of a lack of newer survey data,[15] highlighting that data collection needs to be continuous and regular. Although the agenda for reducing data deprivation is actively progressing, collecting frequent

TABLE 2B.1 **Number of Economies in the Global Database of Shared Prosperity, by Edition**

Edition	Release	Shared prosperity circa	Number of economies
1st	AM 2014	2006–11	65
2nd	AM 2015	2007–12	85
3rd	AM 2016	2008–13	82
4th	AM 2017	2009–14	93
5th	SM 2018	2010–15	88
6th	AM 2018	2010–15	91
7th	SM 2020	2012–17	91

Source: World Bank compilation based on data from the Global Database of Shared Prosperity, World Bank, Washington, DC, http://www
.worldbank.org/en/topic/poverty/brief/global-database-of-shared-prosperity.
Note: Data used must be within two years of the designated period measuring shared prosperity. AM = annual meetings in October;
SM = spring meetings in April.

TABLE 2B.2 **Changing Economy Coverage in the Global Database of Shared Prosperity, Sixth and Seventh Editions**

Region	Number of economies				
	Total	GDSP, 6th edition (PSPR 2018)	GDSP, 7th edition (PSPR 2020)	GDSP, 6th and 7th editions	With updated SP
East Asia and Pacific	25	8	7	7	6
Europe and Central Asia	30	26	24	22	22
Latin America and the Caribbean	31	16	14	14	13
Middle East and North Africa	14	3	4	3	2
South Asia	8	4	4	4	0
Sub-Saharan Africa	48	12	15	6	1
Rest of the world	62	22	23	22	21
World	**218**	**91**	**91**	**78**	**65**

Sources: Global Database of Shared Prosperity World Bank, Washington, DC, https://www.worldbank.org/en/topic/poverty/brief
/global-database-of-shared-prosperity.; PovcalNet (online analysis tool), World Bank, Washington, DC, http://iresearch.worldbank.org
/PovcalNet/; World Bank 2018a.
Note: The number of economies is based on the set used to calculate global poverty in the 2018 lineup. GDSP = Global Database of
Shared Prosperity; PSPR = Poverty and Shared Prosperity report; SP = shared prosperity indicator.

MAP 2B.1 Shared Prosperity Indicator, Economy Coverage

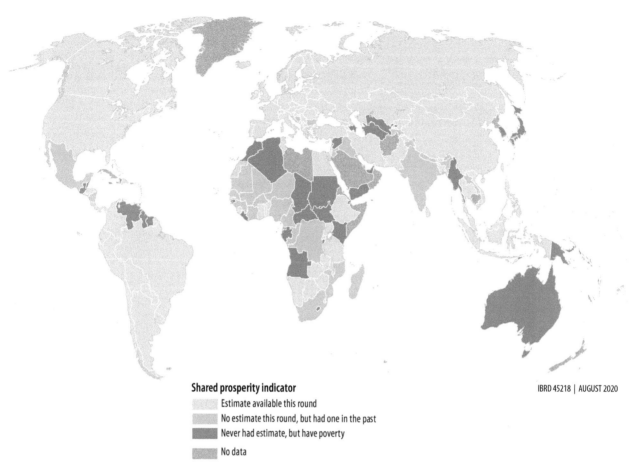

Shared prosperity indicator

- Estimate available this round
- No estimate this round, but had one in the past
- Never had estimate, but have poverty
- No data

IBRD 45218 | AUGUST 2020

Sources: Global Database of Shared Prosperity World Bank (7th edition), circa 2012-17, Washington, DC, https://www.worldbank.org/en/topic/poverty/brief/global
-database-of-shared-prosperity; PovcalNet (online analysis tool), World Bank, Washington, DC, http://iresearch.worldbank.org/PovcalNet/
Notes: The 166 economies shown in this map have direct poverty estimates in PovcalNet. "This round" refers to the seventh edition of the Global Database of Shared Prosperity, circa 2012–17.

surveys for shared prosperity is a longer-term task.

Data collection continues to present a significant challenge in some regions. Shared prosperity cannot be calculated for the majority of economies in some regions and groups (map 2B.1). Only 91 of 166 economies with a poverty estimate also have shared prosperity estimates in this round. In addition, there are 50 economies for which a poverty rate can be calculated, yet shared prosperity has never been calculated (figure 2B.2). For example, 25 developing economies in the East Asia and Pacific region are included in the global poverty count. For 19 of these 25 economies, the

FIGURE 2B.2 Data Coverage for Shared Prosperity and Poverty Indicators

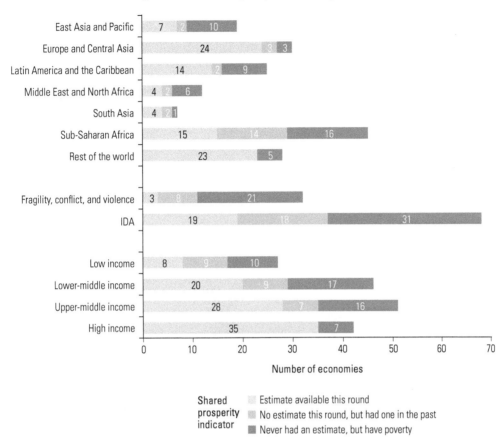

Number of economies

Shared
prosperity
indicator

⬜ Estimate available this round
▨ No estimate this round, but had one in the past
⬛ Never had an estimate, but have poverty

Sources: Global Database of Shared Prosperity (7th edition), circa 2012-17. World Bank, Washington, DC, http://www.worldbank.org/en /topic/poverty/brief/global-database-of-shared-prosperity; PovcalNet (online analysis tool), World Bank, Washington, DC, http://iresearch .worldbank.org/PovcalNet/.
Notes: The figure is based on the 166 economies with direct poverty estimates in PovcalNet. FCV = fragility, conflict, and violence; IDA = International Development Association; SP = shared prosperity. "This round" refers to the seventh edition of the Global Database of Shared Prosperity, circa 2012–17.

World Bank has access to household survey data for estimating poverty in at least one year, but shared prosperity indicators are available for only 7 economies in this round. The data gap is driven mainly by infrequent surveys in small Pacific Island economies. In Latin America and the Caribbean, the economies for which a shared prosperity indicator has never been calculated are mostly small economies of Central America and the Caribbean (figure 2B.2). Europe and Central Asia is the only region that has consistently collected household surveys such that all economies have at least one survey used for global poverty monitoring (figure 2B.3).

FIGURE 2B.3 Shared Prosperity Indicator, Population Coverage

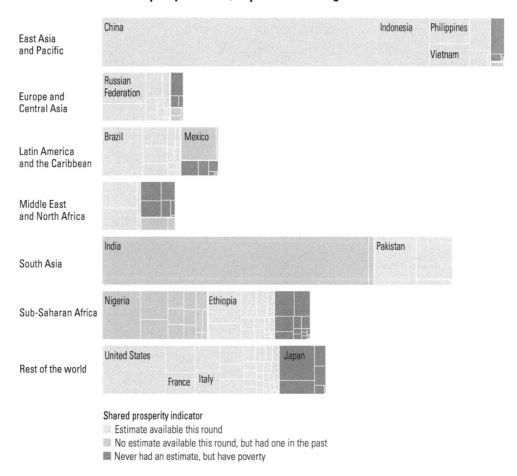

Shared prosperity indicator

- Estimate available this round
- No estimate available this round, but had one in the past
- Never had an estimate, but have poverty

Sources: Global Database of Shared Prosperity World Bank, Washington, DC, https://www.worldbank.org/en/topic/poverty/brief/global
-database-of-shared-prosperity; PovcalNet (online analysis tool), World Bank, Washington, DC, http://iresearch.worldbank.org/PovcalNet/.
Notes: The figure includes 166 economies with a direct estimate of poverty available in PovcalNet. The size of the rectangle is proportional to the population in 2018. "This round" refers to the seventh edition of the Global Database of Shared Prosperity, circa 2012–17.

Annex 2C

Comparison of two shared prosperity rounds

At least two rounds (or "editions") of the Global Database of Shared Prosperity (GDSP) are needed to compare trends in shared prosperity. To focus on recent changes, the fifth (circa 2010–15) and seventh (circa 2012–17) editions of the GDSP were chosen. There are 75 economies that are represented in both editions. Of these, 68 had different periods for shared prosperity represented across the two editions. Shared prosperity can be the same across different editions of the GDSP if no new data were collected, and the period of measurement still fulfills the date parameters in both editions, because survey data can be within two years of the benchmark years. For example, a shared prosperity measurement period of 2011–15 is applicable to both periods circa 2010–15 and 2012–17.

Tables 2C.1 and 2C.2 provide summaries of the changes in shared prosperity and the shared prosperity premium. Summary statistics at region or income-level groupings should be analyzed with caution, because the number of economies represented is extremely low in some cases. For example, only two FCV economies have shared prosperity figures in both the fifth and seventh editions of the GDSP. More detailed comparisons and economy-level trends are shown in table 2C.3.

More than half of the economies—35 out of 68—had higher shared prosperity in the more recent round than in the previous round. However, in some regions and groups, shared prosperity is, on average, lower in the more recent period (Latin America and the Caribbean; the Middle East and North Africa; South Asia; Sub-Saharan Africa; economies affected by fragility, conflict, and violence; IDA economies; low-income economies; lower-middle-income economies; and upper-middle-income economies).

By income group, only economies in the high-income category had higher average shared prosperity circa 2012–17 than circa 2010–15. By region, only East Asia and Pacific, Europe and Central Asia, and Rest of the World had average increases in shared prosperity over the two rounds of data considered.

Changes in the shared prosperity premium show a more consistent decline across regions and groups. In all regions except Europe and Central Asia and other high-income economies, the premium is lower in the more recent period. Among income groups, only the high-income group has a higher premium in the more recent round of data.

TABLE 2C.1 Comparing the Changes in Shared Prosperity across Two Editions of the Global Database of Shared Prosperity

	Economies (number)			Average shared prosperity (%)		Average change in SP, unweighted (percentage points)
	Total	Higher SP	Lower SP	Circa 2010–15	Circa 2012–17	
East Asia and Pacific	5	4	1	3.36	3.50	0.14
Europe and Central Asia	24	15	9	2.17	3.54	1.37
Latin America and the Caribbean	13	3	10	3.11	2.01	−1.10
Middle East and North Africa	3	0	3	1.35	−1.18	−2.53
South Asia	1	0	1	2.82	2.72	−0.11
Sub-Saharan Africa	2	0	2	4.45	−0.95	−5.40
Rest of the world	20	13	7	−0.23	1.50	1.74
Fragile and conflict-affected states	2	0	2	1.86	0.73	−1.13
International Development Association	8	3	5	2.56	1.32	−1.24
Low income	2	0	2	4.45	−0.95	−5.40
Lower-middle income	13	8	5	2.08	2.07	−0.01
Upper-middle income	21	5	16	2.45	2.15	-0.31
High income	32	22	10	1.03	2.69	1.66
All	**68**	**35**	**33**	**1.77**	**2.29**	**0.52**

Sources: Global Database of Shared Prosperity (5th edition, circa 2010–15 ; 7th edition, circa 2012–17), World Bank, Washington, DC, https://www.worldbank.org/en/topic /poverty/brief/global-database-of-shared-prosperity.
Note: Among the economies in the fifth and seventh editions of the GDSP, 68 economies were included in both and had shared prosperity that was updated in the seventh edition. Higher SP = shared prosperity is higher in the seventh edition (circa 2012–17) than in the fifth edition (circa 2010–15). See table 2C.3 for a complete list of the 68 economies.

TABLE 2C.2 Comparing the Changes in the Shared Prosperity Premium across Two Editions of the Global Database of Shared Prosperity

	Economies (number)			Average shared prosperity premium (%)		Average change in SPP, unweighted (percentage points)
	Total	Higher SPP	Lower SPP	Circa 2010–15	Circa 2012–17	
East Asia and Pacific	5	1	4	1.21	0.64	-0.56
Europe and Central Asia	24	17	7	0.33	0.82	0.49
Latin America and the Caribbean	13	6	7	1.22	0.98	-0.24
Middle East and North Africa	3	0	3	1.40	-1.24	-2.64
South Asia	1	0	1	0.21	-1.53	-1.74
Sub-Saharan Africa	2	0	2	2.14	-0.36	-2.49
Rest of the world	20	8	12	-0.05	0.01	0.06
Fragile and conflict-affected states	2	0	2	0.90	0.06	-0.84
International Development Association	8	1	7	1.66	0.05	-1.61
Low income	2	0	2	2.14	-0.36	-2.49
Lower-middle income	13	4	9	1.10	0.49	-0.61
Upper-middle income	21	10	11	0.86	0.77	-0.09
High income	32	18	14	0.02	0.25	0.23
All	**68**	**32**	**36**	**0.55**	**0.44**	**-0.11**

Source: Global Database of Shared Prosperity (5th edition, circa 2010–15 ; 7th edition, circa 2012–17), World Bank, Washington, DC, https://www.worldbank.org/en/topic /poverty/brief/global-database-of-shared-prosperity.
Note: Among the economies in the fifth and seventh editions of the Global Database of Shared Prosperity, 68 economies were included in both and had shared prosperity premiums that were updated in the seventh edition. Higher SPP = shared prosperity premium is higher in the seventh edition (circa 2012–17) than in the fifth edition (circa 2010–15). See table 2C.3 for a complete list of the 68 economies.

TABLE 2C.3 **Comparing the Changes in the Fifth and Seventh Editions of the Global Database of Shared Prosperity, 68 Economies**

	5th Edition, Circa 2010–15			7th Edition, Circa 2012–17		
	Period	Shared prosperity (%)	Shared prosperity premium (percentage points)	Period	Shared prosperity (%)	Shared prosperity premium (percentage points)
East Asia and Pacific						
Indonesia	2011–14	4.05	0.43	2014–18	5.06	0.13
Mongolia	2011–16	0.69	0.71	2011–18	0.99	0.33
Philippines	2009–15	2.43	1.05	2012–15	5.12	2.56
Thailand	2009–13	4.81	1.32	2014–18	1.45	0.30
Vietnam	2010–14	4.82	2.52	2012–18	4.91	−0.11
Europe and Central Asia						
Albania	2008–12	−1.22	0.09	2014–17	2.46	1.65
Armenia	2011–16	2.25	−2.33	2013–18	1.26	−1.14
Belarus	2011–16	4.06	0.61	2013–18	0.71	0.72
Croatia	2010–15	0.47	0.58	2012–17	5.47	1.19
Czech Republic	2010–15	1.42	0.39	2012–17	3.53	0.70
Estonia	2010–15	6.15	−0.48	2012–17	7.98	0.78
Georgia	2011–16	6.44	2.12	2013–18	2.65	1.23
Hungary	2010–15	1.19	−0.54	2012–17	4.84	0.24
Kazakhstan	2010–15	4.09	0.61	2012–17	−0.02	0.55
Kosovo	2012–15	3.50	1.93	2012–17	2.36	0.47
Kyrgyz Republic	2011–16	0.59	0.62	2013–18	3.15	0.71
Latvia	2010–15	7.52	1.04	2012–17	7.91	−0.33
Lithuania	2010–15	6.65	−1.45	2012–17	6.33	−1.10
Moldova	2011–16	2.79	2.40	2013–18	1.90	1.57
Montenegro	2009–14	−2.73	−0.46	2012–15	4.72	3.37
North Macedonia	2009–14	6.20	4.30	2012–17	7.06	2.75
Poland	2010–15	2.52	0.44	2012–17	6.01	2.00
Romania	2010–15	0.06	−1.08	2012–17	10.02	0.05
Russian Federation	2010–15	1.62	1.15	2013–18	−0.44	1.83
Serbia	2012–15	−1.70	−0.83	2013–17	3.89	2.41
Slovak Republic	2010–15	−0.62	−0.01	2011–16	−0.58	0.51
Slovenia	2010–15	−0.78	−0.22	2012–17	2.20	0.68
Turkey	2011–16	2.53	−0.94	2013–18	2.14	−0.53
Ukraine	2011–16	−0.85	−0.16	2013–18	−0.59	−0.73
Latin America and the Caribbean						
Argentina	2011–16	0.15	0.15	2013–18	−1.62	−0.07
Bolivia	2011–16	1.67	0.61	2013–18	1.78	3.43
Brazil	2011–15	3.80	1.61	2013–18	−0.43	−1.09
Chile	2009–15	5.97	0.48	2013–17	4.92	1.09
Colombia	2011–16	3.49	2.01	2013–18	2.34	1.93
Costa Rica	2011–16	2.00	0.05	2013–18	1.40	0.80
Ecuador	2011–16	2.95	1.03	2013–18	1.25	0.79
El Salvador	2011–16	4.08	1.15	2013–18	3.95	2.13
Honduras	2011–16	1.17	3.12	2013–18	1.30	−0.42
Panama	2011–16	4.00	0.11	2013–18	5.29	1.42
Paraguay	2011–16	4.90	3.25	2013–18	1.57	1.23
Peru	2011–16	3.08	0.90	2013–18	2.45	0.96
Uruguay	2011–16	3.18	1.41	2013–18	2.00	0.57

(continued)

TABLE 2C.3 Comparing the Changes Shared Prosperity in the Fifth and Seventh Editions of the Global Database of Shared Prosperity, 68 economies *(continued)*

	5th Edition, Circa 2010–15			7th Edition, Circa 2012–17		
	Period	Shared prosperity (%)	Shared prosperity premium (percentage points)	Period	Shared prosperity (%)	Shared prosperity premium (percentage points)
Middle East and North Africa						
Egypt, Arab Rep.	2010–12	2.58	1.81	2012–17	−2.51	−1.37
Iran, Islamic Rep.	2009–14	1.25	2.52	2014–17	−0.13	−2.01
West Bank and Gaza	2009–11	0.21	−0.14	2011–16	−0.89	−0.34
South Asia						
Pakistan	2007–13	2.82	0.21	2010–15	2.72	−1.53
Sub-Saharan Africa						
Rwanda	2010–13	4.82	2.04	2013–16	0.31	0.48
Uganda	2009–12	4.09	2.24	2012–16	−2.20	−1.19
Other high income						
Austria	2010–15	−0.47	−0.19	2012–17	1.44	0.24
Belgium	2010–15	0.57	0.09	2012–17	0.43	0.01
Cyprus	2010–15	−4.34	−1.30	2012–17	0.29	1.07
Denmark	2010–15	0.57	0.11	2012–17	1.34	−0.34
Finland	2010–15	0.53	0.36	2012–17	0.58	−0.07
France	2010–15	0.74	0.53	2012–17	0.61	0.42
Germany	2007–11	0.82	1.11	2011–16	−0.20	−1.00
Greece	2010–15	−8.35	−1.37	2012–17	1.80	1.69
Iceland	2009–14	−0.13	0.34	2010–15	3.15	−0.16
Ireland	2009–14	0.24	0.47	2011–16	3.43	0.38
Italy	2009–14	−2.60	−0.70	2012–17	0.48	−0.56
Luxembourg	2009–14	−0.09	0.19	2012–17	2.96	−0.70
Malta	2009–14	4.52	0.85	2012–17	3.80	0.06
Netherlands	2010–15	0.95	0.29	2012–17	1.53	−0.37
Norway	2010–15	2.11	−0.84	2012–17	0.44	−0.58
Portugal	2010–15	−0.87	−0.13	2012–17	3.32	1.33
Spain	2010–15	−2.16	−0.63	2012–17	1.75	0.64
Sweden	2010–15	1.80	−0.60	2012–17	1.39	−0.59
Switzerland	2009–14	1.22	0.23	2012–17	−0.26	−0.59
United Kingdom	2010–15	0.26	0.15	2011–16	1.76	−0.66

Sources: Global Database of Shared Prosperity (5th edition, circa 2010–15 ; 7th edition, circa 2012–17), World Bank, Washington, DC, https://www.worldbank.org/en/topic /poverty/brief/global-database-of-shared-prosperity.
Note: The table covers the 68 economies included in both the fifth and seventh editions of the GDSP that also had updated shared prosperity.

Notes

1. Formally, the shared prosperity index can be decomposed as follows: $g_{40} = g_{mean} + g_{shareB40}$, where g_{40} is the growth of income (or consumption) among the bottom 40 percent of the population; g_{mean} is the growth in the mean; and $g_{shareB40}$ is the *growth* in the income *share* of the bottom 40. Rearranging this equation yields the shared prosperity premium, formally the difference between the income (or consumption) growth of the bottom 40 and the mean of the population: $g_{shareB40} = g_{40} - g_{mean} \equiv$ *shared prosperity premium.* For antecedents and technical discussions on measuring shared prosperity, see Ferreira, Galasso, and Negre (2018); Rosenblatt and McGavock (2013); and World Bank (2015).

2. Growth rates are always expressed in per year averages over the time period in question. In the case of Benin, mean household consumption of the bottom 40 declined on average 5.3 percent per year over the shared prosperity monitoring period of 2011–15. The mean household consumption of the bottom 40 in Romania grew an average of 10.2 percent per year over the period 2012–17.

3. For economy-specific estimates, see annex 2A.

4. The correlation coefficient between mean income growth and shared prosperity is +0.856 for this sample of economies.

5. There are 75 recurring economies in the fifth and seventh editions of the GDSP, but 7 economies use the same shared prosperity periods and are excluded from the comparison.

6. Detailed data on shared prosperity and the shared prosperity premium by region and economy over the two editions of the GDSP are in annex 2C.

7. These 10 economies are: Argentina, Brazil, Egypt, Germany, the Islamic Republic of Iran, Kazakhstan, the Russian Federation, Switzerland, Uganda, and West Bank and Gaza.

8. Shared prosperity in Argentina and Brazil is measured during the 2013–18 period, and the region's financial crisis occurred during 2014–16.

9. Projections of global poverty in chapter 1, both for 2020 and 2021 and toward 2030, assume no changes in relative inequality within and between economies. But as indicated in annex 1C, relaxing these assumptions with some experimental methods to incorporate changes in measures of inequality would render different results, in some cases leading to higher poverty rates in 2030 than under the neutral-distribution assumptions. Something similar would happen with shared prosperity projections if shared prosperity premiums were projected to be negative in the coming years. A further discussion of the connection between poverty and inequality is included in box 2.3.

10. Birdsall and Meyer (2015) advocate using the survey-based median household consumption (or income) per capita as a standard development measure because it is "a simple, robust and durable indicator of typical individual material well-being in a country" (Birdsall and Meyer 2015, 343). Pritchett (2020) makes repeated use of median income (or consumption) from surveys instead of any other measure of well-being to assess progress in poverty reduction.

11. The correlation coefficient between growth in the median and the shared prosperity index is +0.8999 for this sample of economies.

12. The correlation coefficient between changes in the Gini coefficient and the shared prosperity premium is −0.92. If one uses changes in the Palma index as a measure of inequality, the scatterplot has a similar negative slope and the correlation coefficient is lower but still quite high, at −0.81, confirming the close connection between the shared prosperity premium and changes in inequality.

13. Chapter 3 shows that women are slightly more likely to be among the poor (regardless of which poverty line is used), although with noticeable variations across regions. The presence of women in households with children may explain the likelihood that women are more likely than men to be poor, but not necessarily to be in the bottom 40.

14. See PovcalNet: Publications, World Bank, Washington, DC, http://iresearch.worldbank.org/PovcalNet/publications.aspx.

15. The 11 economies that do not have shared prosperity in the fifth through seventh editions of the GDSP but do have shared prosperity in the first through fourth editions are Cameroon, Democratic Republic of Congo, Republic of Congo, Guinea, India, Iraq, Lao People's Democratic Republic, Mali, Nepal, Nigeria, and Senegal.

References

Abebe, Girum, Tom Bundervoet, and Christina Wieser. 2020. "Monitoring COVID-19 Impacts on Firms in Ethiopia: Results from a High-Frequency Phone Survey of Firms." World Bank, Washington, DC.

Aghion, Philippe, Eve Caroli, and Cecilia Garcia-Penalosa. 1999. "Inequality and Economic Growth: The Perspective of the New Growth Theories." *Journal of Economic Literature* 37 (4): 1615–60.

Alesina, Alberto Francesco. 1994. "Political Models of Macroeconomic Policy and Fiscal Reforms." In *Voting for Reform: Democracy, Political Liberalization, and Economic Adjustment*, edited by Stephan Haggard and Steven Benjamin Webb, 37–60. Washington, DC: World Bank; New York: Oxford University Press.

Alesina, Alberto Francesco, and Dani Rodrik. 1994. "Distributive Politics and Economic Growth." *Quarterly Journal of Economics* 109 (2): 465–90.

Alvaredo, Facundo, and Leonardo Gasparini. 2015. "Recent Trends in Inequality and Poverty in Developing Countries." In *Handbook of Income Distribution*, vol. 2A, edited by Anthony B. Atkinson and François J. Bourguignon, 697–805. Handbooks in Economics Series. Amsterdam: North-Holland.

Atamanov, Aziz, Raul Andres Castaneda Aguilar, Tony Henri Mathias Jany Fujs, Reno Dewina, Carolina Diaz-Bonilla, Daniel Gerszon Mahler, Dean Mitchell Jolliffe, et al. 2020. "March 2020 PovcalNet Update: What's New." Global Poverty Monitoring Technical Note 11 (March), World Bank, Washington, DC.

Avdiu, Besart, and Gaurav Nayyar. 2020. "When Face-to-Face Interactions Become an Occupational Hazard: Jobs in the Time of COVID-19." *Future Development* (blog), March 30. https://www.brookings.edu/blog/future-development/2020/03/30/when-face-to-face-interactions-become-an-occupational-hazard-jobs-in-the-time-of-covid-19/.

Baldwin, Richard, and Beatrice Weder di Mauro, eds. 2020. *Mitigating the COVID Economic Crisis: Act Fast and Do Whatever It Takes*. London: CEPR Press.

Banerjee, Abhijit Vinayak, and Esther Duflo. 2003. "Inequality and Growth: What Can the Data Say?" *Journal of Economic Growth* 8 (3): 267–99.

Banerjee, Abhijit Vinayak, and Andrew F. Newman. 1993. "Occupational Choice and the Process of Development." *Journal of Political Economy* 101 (2): 274–98.

Barro, Robert J. 2000. "Inequality and Growth in a Panel of Countries." *Journal of Economic Growth* 5 (1): 5–32.

Basu, Kaushik. 2001. "On the Goals of Development." In *Frontiers of Development Economics: The Future in Perspective*, edited by Gerald Marvin Meier and Joseph E. Stiglitz, 61–86. Washington, DC: World Bank; New York: Oxford University Press.

Basu, Kaushik. 2006. "Globalization, Poverty, and Inequality: What Is the Relationship? What Can Be Done?" *World Development* 34 (8): 1361–73.

Beegle, Kathleen, and Luc Christiaensen, eds. 2019. *Accelerating Poverty Reduction in Africa*. Washington, DC: World Bank.

Benabou, Roland. 1996. "Inequality and Growth." NBER Working Paper 5658 (July), National Bureau of Economic Research, Cambridge, MA.

Benhabib, Jess. 2003. "The Tradeoff between Inequality and Growth." *Annals of Economics and Finance* 4 (2): 491–507.

Benhabib, Jess, and Aldo Rustichini. 1996. "Social Conflict and Growth." *Journal of Economic Growth* 1 (1): 125–42.

Bergstrom, Katy 2020. "The Role of Inequality for Poverty Reduction." Policy Research Working Paper; no. WPS 9409 Washington, D.C. : World Bank Group.

Birdsall, Nancy, and Christian J. Meyer. 2015. "The Median Is the Message: A Good Enough Measure of Material Wellbeing and Shared Development Progress." *Global Policy* 6 (4): 343–57.

Bourguignon, François J. 2003. "The Growth Elasticity of Poverty Reduction: Explaining Heterogeneity across Countries and Time Periods." Working Paper 28104, World Bank, Washington, DC.

Bourguignon, François J. 2004. "The Poverty-Growth-Inequality Triangle." Working Paper 125, Indian Council for Research on International Economic Relations, New Delhi.

Brown, Caitlin S., Martin Ravallion, and Dominique van de Walle. 2020. "Can the World's Poor Protect Themselves from the New Coronavirus?" NBER Working Paper 27200 (May), National Bureau of Economic Research, Cambridge, MA.

Castelló-Climent, Amparo. 2010. "Inequality and Growth in Advanced Economies: An Empirical Investigation." *Journal of Economic Inequality* 8 (3): 293–321.

Chetty, Raj, John N. Friedman, Nathaniel Hendren, Michael Stepner, and the Opportunity Insights Team. 2020. "How Did COVID-19 and Stabilization Policies Affect Spending and Employment? A New Real-Time Economic Tracker Based on Private Sector Data." NBER Working Paper 27431 (June), National Bureau of Economic Research, Cambridge, MA.

Ciaschi, Matias, Rita Damasceno Costa, Rafael Macedo, Anna Luisa Paffhausen, and Liliana D. Sousa. 2020. "A Reversal in Shared Prosperity in Brazil." Report 1 (July), World Bank, Washington, DC.

Dabla-Norris, Era, Kalpana Kochhar, Frantisek Ricka, Nujin Suphaphiphat, and Evridiki Tsounta. 2015. "Causes and Consequences of Income Inequality: A Global Perspective." With contributions by Preya Sharma and Veronique Salins. IMF Staff Discussion Note SDN/15/13 (June), International Monetary Fund, Washington, DC.

Datt, Guarav, and Martin Ravallion. 1992. "Growth and Redistribution Components of Changes in Poverty Measures: A Decomposition with Applications to Brazil and India in the 1980s." *Journal of Development Economics* 38 (2): 275–95.

Deininger, Klaus W., and Lyn Squire. 1996. "A New Data Set Measuring Income Inequality." *World Bank Economic Review* 10 (3): 565–91.

Dingel, Jonathan I., and Brent Neiman. 2020. "How Many Jobs Can Be Done at Home?" NBER Working Paper 26948 (April), National Bureau of Economic Research, Cambridge, MA.

Dollar, David, and Aart C. Kraay. 2002. "Growth Is Good for the Poor." *Journal of Economic Growth* 7 (3): 195–225.

Dutz, Mark A. 2018. *Jobs and Growth: Brazil's Productivity Agenda*. International Development in Focus Series. Washington, DC: World Bank.

Ferreira, Francisco H. G. 2012. "Distributions in Motion: Economic Growth, Inequality, and Poverty Dynamics." In *The Oxford Handbook of the Economics of Poverty*, edited by Philip N. Jefferson, 427–62. New York: Oxford University Press.

Ferreira, Francisco H. G., Emanuela Galasso, and Mario Negre. 2018. "Shared Prosperity: Concepts, Data, and Some Policy Examples."

Policy Research Working Paper 8451, World Bank, Washington, DC.

Finn, Arden, and Andrew Zadel. 2020. "Monitoring COVID-19 Impacts on Households in Zambia." Report 1 (July), World Bank, Washington, DC.

Forbes, Kristin. 2000. "A Reassessment of the Relationship between Inequality and Growth." *American Economic Review* 90 (4): 869–87.

Fosu, Augustin Kwasi. 2017. "Growth, Inequality, and Poverty Reduction in Developing Countries: Recent Global Evidence." *Research in Economics* 71 (2): 306–36,

Furceri, Davide, Prakash Loungani, Jonathan D. Ostry, and Pietro Pizzuto. 2020. "Will COVID-19 Affect Inequality? Evidence from Past Pandemics." *COVID Economics* 12 (May 1): 138–57.

Galor, Oded, and Joseph Zeira. 1993. "Income Distribution and Macroeconomics." *Review of Economic Studies* 60 (1): 35–52.

Gerard, François, Clément Imbert, and Kate Orkin. 2020. "Social Protection Response to COVID-19 Crisis: Options for Developing Countries." COVID-19 Brief (April), Economics for Inclusive Prosperity. https://econfip.org/policy-brief/social-protection-response-to-the-covid-19-crisis-options-for-developing-countries/.

Glaeser, Edward L., José A. Scheinkman, and Andrei Shleifer. 2003. "The Injustice of Inequality." *Journal of Monetary Economics* 50 (1): 199–222.

Gottlieb, Charles, Jan Grobovsek, and Markus Poschke. 2020. "Working from Home across Countries." Cahiers de recherche 07-2020, Center for Interuniversity Research in Quantitative Economics, Université de Montréal, Montréal.

Grigoli, Francesco, Evelio Paredes, and C. Gabriel Di Bella. 2016. "Inequality and Growth: A Heterogeneous Approach." IMF Working Paper WP/16/244, International Monetary Fund, Washington, DC.

Grigoli, Francesco, and Adrian Robles. 2017. "Inequality Overhang." IMF Working Paper WP/17/76 (March 28), International Monetary Fund, Washington, DC.

Halter, Daniel, Manuel Oechslin, and Josef Zweimüller. 2014. "Inequality and Growth: The Neglected Time Dimension." *Journal of Economic Growth* 19 (1): 81–104.

Hatayama, Maho, Mariana Viollaz, and Hernan Winkler. 2020. "Jobs' Amenability to Working from Home: Evidence from Skills Surveys for 53 Countries." Policy Research Working Paper 9241, World Bank, Washington, DC.

Hill, Ruth, and Ambar Narayan. 2020. "How Is COVID-19 Likely to Affect Inequality? A Discussion Note." Unpublished report, World Bank, Washington, DC.

ILO (International Labour Organization). 2020. "COVID-19 Crisis and the Informal Economy: Immediate Responses and Policy Challenges." ILO Brief (May), ILO, Geneva.

Kaldor, Nicholas. 1957. "A Model of Economic Growth." *Economic Journal* 67 (268): 591–624.

Kraay, Aart C. 2006. "When Is Growth Pro-poor? Evidence from a Panel of Countries." *Journal of Development Economics* 80 (1): 198–227.

Kraay, Aart C. 2015. "Weak Instruments in Growth Regressions: Implications for Recent Cross-Country Evidence on Inequality and Growth." Policy Research Working Paper 7494, World Bank, Washington, DC.

Li, Hongyi, and Heng-Fu Zou. 1998. "Income Inequality Is Not Harmful for Growth: Theory and Evidence." *Review of Development Economics* 2 (3): 318–34.

McNamara, Robert S. 1972. "Annual Address by Robert S. McNamara, President of the World Bank and Its Affiliates." *Summary Proceedings, 1972 Annual Meetings of the Boards of Governors*, Report 53408, 16–31. Washington, DC: World Bank.

Merotto, Dino Leonardo. 2019. "Uganda: Jobs Strategy for Inclusive Growth." Jobs Series 19, World Bank, Washington, DC.

Okun, Arthur M. 2015. *Equality and Efficiency: The Big Tradeoff*. Brookings Classic Series. Washington, DC: Brookings Institution Press.

Ostry, Jonathan D., Andrew Berg, and Charalambos G. Tsangarides. 2014. "Redistribution, Inequality, and Growth." IMF Staff Discussion Note SDN/14/02 (April), International Monetary Fund, Washington, DC.

Palma, José Gabriel. 2011. "Homogeneous Middles vs. Heterogeneous Tails and the End of the 'Inverted-U': The Share of the Rich Is What Its All About." Cambridge Working Papers in Economics CWPE 1111 (January), Faculty of Economics, University of Cambridge, Cambridge, UK.

Papageorge, Nicholas W., Matthew V. Zahn, Michèle Belot, Eline van den Broek-Altenburg,

Syngjoo Choi, Julian C. Jamison, and Egon Tripodi. 2020. "Socio-Demographic Factors Associated with Self-Protecting Behavior during the COVID-19 Pandemic." NBER Working Paper 27378 (June), National Bureau of Economic Research, Cambridge, MA.

Perotti, Roberto. 1996. "Growth, Income Distribution, and Democracy: What the Data Say." *Journal of Economic Growth* 1 (2): 149–87.

Persson, Torsten, and Guido Enrico Tabellini. 1994. "Is Inequality Harmful for Growth?" *American Economic Review* 84 (3): 600–21.

Pritchett, Lant. 2020. "Randomizing Development: Method or Madness?" In *Randomized Control Trials in the Field of Development: A Critical Perspective*, edited by Florent Bédécarrats, Isabelle Guérin, and François Roubaud, chapter 2. Oxford, UK: Oxford University Press.

Ravallion, Martin. 1997. "Can High-Inequality Developing Countries Escape Absolute Poverty?" *Economics Letters* 56 (1): 51–57.

Ravallion, Martin. 2001. "Growth, Inequality, and Poverty: Looking beyond Averages." *World Development* 29 (11): 1803–15.

Ravallion, Martin. 2007. "Economic Growth and Poverty Reduction: Do Poor Countries Need to Worry about Inequality?" 2020 Vision Briefs BB08 (Special Edition), International Food Policy Research Institute, Washington, DC.

Rawls, John A. 1971. *A Theory of Justice*. Cambridge, MA: Belknap Press of Harvard University Press.

Roosevelt, Franklin Delano. 1937. "Inaugural Address: Address by Franklin D. Roosevelt, 1937." January 20, Joint Congressional Committee on Inaugural Ceremonies, Washington, DC. https://www.inaugural.senate.gov/about/past-inaugural-ceremonies/38th-inaugural-ceremonies/.

Rosenblatt, David, and Tamara J. McGavock. 2013. "A Note on the Simple Algebra of the Shared Prosperity Indicator." Policy Research Working Paper 6645, World Bank, Washington, DC.

Schmitt-Grohé, Stephanie, Ken Teoh, and Martín Uribe. 2020. "COVID-19: Testing Inequality in New York City." *COVID Economics* 8 (April 22): 27–43.

Siwatu, G., A. Palacios-Lopez, K. Mcgee, A. Amankwah, T. Vishwanath, and M. Azad. 2020. "Impact of COVID-19 on Nigerian Households: Baseline Results." World Bank, Washington, DC.

Voitchovsky, Sarah. 2009. "Inequality and Economic Growth." In *The Oxford Handbook of Economic Inequality*, edited by Wiemer Salverda, Brian Nolan, and Timothy M. Smeeding, 549–74. New York: Oxford University Press.

World Bank. 2005. *World Development Report 2006: Equity and Development.* Washington, DC: World Bank; New York: Oxford University Press.

World Bank. 2015. *A Measured Approach to Ending Poverty and Boosting Shared Prosperity: Concepts, Data, and the Twin Goals.* Policy Research Report. Washington, DC: World Bank.

World Bank. 2018a. *Poverty and Shared Prosperity 2018: Piecing Together the Poverty Puzzle.* Washington, DC: World Bank.

World Bank. 2018b. "Seizing a Brighter Future for All: Former Yugoslav Republic of Macedonia Systematic Country Diagnostic." Report 121840-MK (November), World Bank, Washington, DC.

World Bank. 2018c. *Argentina: Escaping Crises, Sustaining Growth, Sharing Prosperity.* Washington, DC: World Bank.

World Bank. 2019a. "Systematic Country Diagnostic of the Philippines: Realizing the Filipino Dream for 2040." Report 143419-PH, World Bank, Washington, DC.

World Bank. 2019b. "Understanding Poverty and Inequality in Egypt." Background paper for this report, World Bank, Washington, DC.

World Bank. 2020a. "The Socio Economic Impacts of COVID-19 in Cambodia: Results from a High Frequency Phone Survey of Households." Unpublished report, July 8, Poverty and Equity Global Practice, World Bank, Washington, DC.

World Bank. 2020b. "Poverty and Distributional Impact of COVID-19 Shock in Indonesia." Unpublished report, Poverty and Equity Global Practice, World Bank, Washington, DC.

World Bank. 2020c. "COVID-19 in Latin America and the Caribbean: High-Frequency Phone Surveys, Results First Round." May–June, World Bank, Washington, DC.

World Bank. 2020d. "Indonesia High-Frequency Monitoring of COVID-19 Impacts." Round 1, May 1–17, unpublished manuscript, World Bank, Washington, DC.

World Bank. 2020e. "Results of Mongolia COVID-19 Household Response Phone Survey." World Bank, Washington, DC.

World Bank. 2020f. "Economic and Social Impacts of COVID-19: May 2020 update from Listening to the Citizens of Uzbekistan." World Bank, Washington, DC.

World Bank. 2020g. "World Bank Predicts Sharpest Decline of Remittances in Recent History." Press Release 2020/175/SPJ, April 22, World Bank, Washington, DC.

World Bank. 2020h. "Poverty and Distributional Impacts of COVID-19: Potential Channels of Impact and Mitigating Policies." Unpublished report, April 16, Poverty and Equity Global Practice, World Bank, Washington, DC.

Key Socioeconomic Characteristics of the Global Poor: Vulnerability to Conflict, Climate Risks, and COVID-19

3

Four out of five people below the international poverty line still live in rural areas, and half of the poor are children. Women also represent a majority of the poor in most regions and among some age groups. Of the global poor age 15 and older, about 70 percent have no schooling or only some basic education. In addition to these well-known demographic characteristics, this chapter introduces profiles of the global poor by conflict and catastrophic flood risk at the subnational level. More than 40 percent of the global poor live in economies affected by conflict and violence, and, in some economies, most of the poor are concentrated in specific subnational areas. About 132 million of the global poor live in areas with high flood risk. Moreover, many of the poor face exposure to multiple risks. In a number of countries, a large share of the poor live in areas that are affected by conflict and that face high exposure to floods. Facing the COVID-19 (coronavirus) pandemic, many of the new poor are likely to live in congested urban settings and to work in the sectors most affected by lockdowns and mobility restrictions; many are engaged in informal services and not reached by existing social safety nets. Conflict, climate change, and COVID-19 are having a clear impact on the global poor, in many cases having joint incidence upon those living in poverty. The profiles presented in this chapter underscore that poverty reduction policies need to have a clear demographic focus by promoting inclusive growth and helping the poor gain access to education, health, employment, and business opportunities. It is now clear that this does not suffice and that mechanisms to cope with conflict, climate change, and the pandemic—through management and prevention of these risks—are also crucial antipoverty policies.

Introduction

Chapter 1 of this report traces the evolution of the number of people whose incomes fall below the international poverty line of US$1.90 a day (in purchasing power parity terms) in countries around the world. This chapter describes the key socioeconomic characteristics of this population group, marshaling the latest available data and comparing it with the profile of the global poor presented in The 2018 *Poverty and Shared Prosperity* report (World Bank 2018a).

Now as then, the stringent data requirements for the profile of the global poor limit the ability to go beyond core sociodemographic characteristics such as age, gender, education, and type of residence; these variables can be constructed, in a comparable fashion, for the majority of countries for which micro data are available. The innovation of this chapter is that it expands the profile of the global poor across two dimensions to include the extent to which, within countries, the global poor may be concentrated in areas that are more exposed to conflict and to climate risks (as measured by the likelihood of experiencing catastrophic floods).

This profile of the poor is based on harmonized household surveys from 142 countries in the Global Monitoring Database (GMD).[1] It updates the previous profile, which was based on the harmonized data for 91 countries for 2015 (World Bank 2018a). The micro data sample used for the current profile covers about 85 percent of the world's population and 95 percent of the extreme poor in 2018, without India. Overall, the coverage of the micro data is good across most regions.[2]

This chapter first describes the demographic characteristics of the global poor and how these characteristics have changed in recent years. Then the chapter describes how the poor in economies and areas within economies are affected by past conflict or are exposed to likely climate change effects, such as catastrophic floods, in the coming decade. It discusses how the majority of the poor live in conflict-affected economies and how they are sometimes, but not always, concentrated in specific areas within each country, making the correlation between poverty and conflict more nuanced and complex. Using an overlay of poverty and conflict maps, the chapter produces a more detailed description of the global poor by exposure to conflict. Next, a similar procedure is adopted to identify the share of the global poor who are exposed to the catastrophic risk of floods. The chapter then continues with a profile of the poor under the lower-middle-income poverty line of US$3.20 a day. As the population group with incomes not far above the international poverty line of US$1.90 a day, this group is the most vulnerable to falling into poverty because of the impact of COVID-19 and is therefore an approximation of the likely characteristics of the new poor caused by the pandemic. A discussion of the contrast between the new poor because of the pandemic and the other groups described closes the chapter.

Key socioeconomic characteristics of the global poor

The latest survey data highlight the fact that the global poor remain overwhelmingly rural. Four out of every five individuals below the international poverty line live in rural areas,

FIGURE 3.1 Share of Rural Poor and Rural Population, by Region

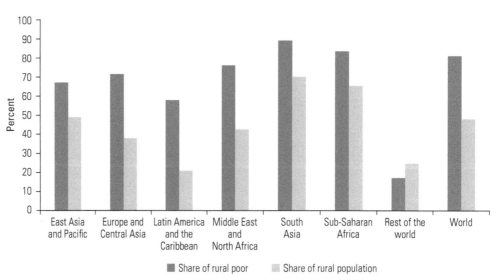

Source: World Bank estimates based on Global Monitoring Database data.

although the rural population accounts for only 48 percent of the global population. In fact, poverty is becoming more rural over time. Between 2015 and 2018, the share of rural poor in the total population of poor people increased by more than 2 percentage points. Consistent with the overall lower levels of urbanization in Sub-Saharan Africa and South Asia, the share of the rural population among the poor is especially high in those regions (83 percent and 89 percent, respectively), whereas the rural poor account for two-thirds of the total poor in East Asia and Pacific and for less than 60 percent in Latin America (figure 3.1). Overall, the incidence of rural poverty is more than four times higher than the incidence of urban poverty according to latest data. Rural poverty continues to be strongly associated with employment in the agricultural sector; the incidence of extreme poverty is much higher among those employed in agriculture compared with those employed in other sectors. The characteristics of rural areas may differ, however, from one country to another, making poverty comparisons across urban and rural areas challenging (box 3.1).

Sustained increases in educational attainment have been a key contributor to economic growth and poverty reduction in many developed and developing countries, and, at a time of rapid technological change, returns to education can be especially high. The educational profile of the global poor highlights the difficulties of eliminating extreme poverty by 2030. In 2018, 35 percent of the global poor adults in the 15 and older age group had no schooling (compared with 9 percent of the nonpoor), and a further 35 percent of global poor adults have only some or completed primary education. Lower levels of educational attainment are more common among both poor and nonpoor individuals in rural areas as compared with urban areas. This fact highlights the multidimensional character of rural poverty—among poor adults residing in rural areas, 39 percent report having no education, more than double the share with no education in urban areas.

BOX 3.1 The Rural and Urban Poor

Global poverty is estimated in a way that makes comparisons across countries and time possible. However, making such comparisons for urban areas, or for rural areas, across countries is fraught with a number of challenges. A key methodological challenge is the inconsistent definition of urban areas across countries. Urban-rural classifications used in household income and expenditure surveys typically follow administrative urban definitions, which vary widely across countries. For example, population thresholds in urban definitions range from 2,000 in Ethiopia to 5,000 in India and 100,000 in China. Thus, simply adopting each country's urban definition in the comparison of urban poverty across countries could be misleading.

To address this challenge, a group of international organizations has developed a globally consistent urban definition: the Degree of Urbanization. It is based on a simple approach, requiring only a population grid as an input. Given this grid, urban areas are defined as consisting of both cities and towns and semi-dense areas, which are defined as follows:

- Cities: areas with a population of at least 50,000 inhabitants in contiguous dense grid cells (more than 1,500 inhabitants per square kilometer)
- Towns and semi-dense areas: areas with a population of at least 5,000 inhabitants in contiguous grid cells with a density of at least 300 inhabitants per square kilometer

Ongoing work at the World Bank aims to provide in future studies and reports a better understanding of urban poverty at the global scale by taking advantage of the globally consistent measures of urban areas (the Degree of Urbanization approach) and poverty (global poverty). This line of research also investigates alternative approaches to defining urban areas as well as other key methodological issues, such as the methodology of spatial cost-of-living adjustment.

Sources: Dijkstra et al. 2020. Definitions of rural and urban areas: Shohei Nakamura, personal communication.

The prevalence of low educational attainment among the poor varies considerably across regions, mirroring broader regional differences in levels of education. In Sub-Saharan Africa and the Middle East and North Africa, the share of poor adults with no education exceeds 35 percent. By contrast, only 12 percent of poor adults have no education in East Asia and Pacific, and less than 3 percent in Europe and Central Asia. Overall, the poor in these two regions and in Latin America and the Caribbean have higher educational attainment than the nonpoor in the Middle East and North Africa, South Asia, and Sub-Saharan Africa (figures 3.2 and 3.3).

Educational attainment continues to improve overall, in both high- and low-income countries. Estimates for birth

FIGURE 3.2 Educational Attainment among the Poor, by Region (age 15 and older)

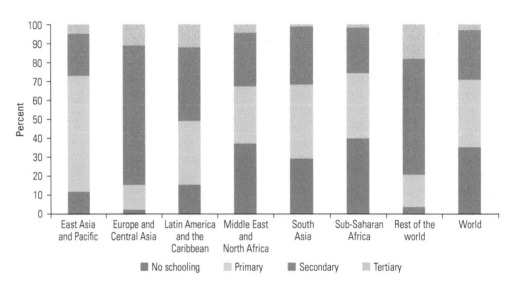

Source: World Bank estimates based on Global Monitoring Database data.

FIGURE 3.3 Educational Attainment of the Population, by Region (age 15 and older)

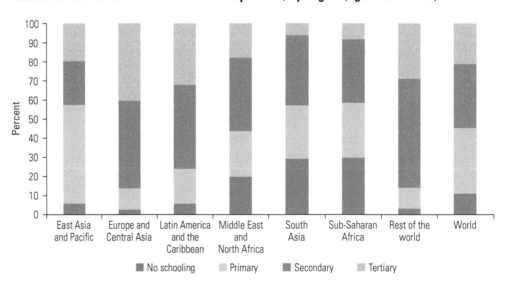

Source: World Bank estimates based on Global Monitoring Database data.

cohorts spanning the 1940s to the 1980s show children having higher levels of educational attainment compared with their parents (Narayan et al. 2018). Comparing the current profile of the global poor with the profile from about 2015 shows that the share of the poor with no education decreased slightly (−0.5 percentage point), while the share of the poor with primary education fell by 3.1 percentage points. The share of the poor with secondary education increased by 3.3 percentage points and those with tertiary education increased by 0.3 percentage point during the same period (figure 3.4). The share of the latter remains low overall, at 2.7 percent in 2018 compared with 21.3 percent among the total population (table 3B.3).[3]

A proper profile of the poor by age and gender would require the ability to measure poverty at the individual level. The survey data used in this chapter, and in this report more generally, measure poverty based on household-level estimates of expenditure or income, abstracting from existing inequalities in the distribution of resources and consumption within households.[4] With these caveats in mind, the profile of the global poor is very young. Half of the global poor in 2018 are children younger than age 15, even though this age group accounts for only a quarter of the world's population (figures 3.5 and 3.6). Children and youth (those ages 15–24) together account for two-thirds of the global poor, much higher than the 40 percent cumulative population share of the 0–24 age group globally. The high share of children and youth in the profile of the global poor is most prominent in Sub-Saharan Africa, but it can be observed across most regions, though to a lesser degree in Europe and Central Asia. A different profile of the poor is observed only in high-income economies, where the poor are skewed toward the elderly. However, in high-income countries the incidence of people living below the international poverty line is less than 1 percent in each of the age categories. By contrast, the poverty rate exceeds 40 percent in Sub-Saharan Africa, reaching 47 percent for the region's 0–14 age group.

Along the gender dimension, figure 3.7 displays the ratio of the share of women among the poor to the share of

FIGURE 3.4 Changes in the Share of Global Poor and of the Global Population, by Educational Attainment, 2015–18

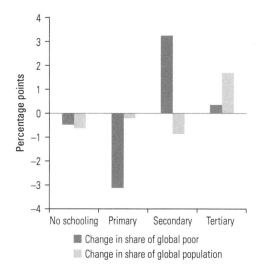

Source: World Bank estimates based on Global Monitoring Database data.

women in the population of each region, as well as globally. For this index, values in excess of 100 should be interpreted as women being overrepresented among the poor compared with the overall population. The data reveal that this overrepresentation is the case globally, but also across most regions of the world, except in Europe and Central Asia, Latin America and the Caribbean, and other high-income countries. Women's overrepresentation is primarily driven by South Asia and Sub-Saharan Africa, with the widest gaps being among children. Girls are more likely than boys to be overrepresented among the poor, as are women in their main reproductive years (25–34) across most world regions (Muñoz-Boudet et al. 2020; World Bank 2018a).

The 2018 *Poverty and Shared Prosperity* report (World Bank 2018a) notes a greater concentration of children in the 0–14 age group among the global poor in 2015 as compared with an earlier profile circa 2013. This increasing concentration of children among the poor can again be observed by comparing the 2018 profile to 2015 (figure 3.8). Between 2015 and 2018, the share of children among the global poor increased by 1.4 percentage points, even though the share of

FIGURE 3.5 **Age Profile of the Global Poor in 2018, by Region**

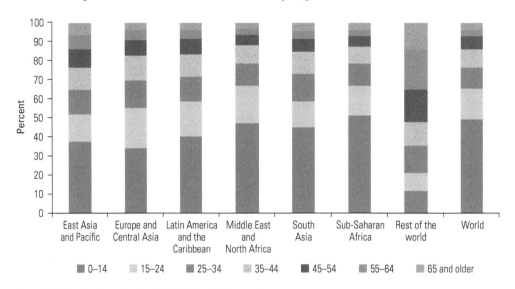

Source: World Bank estimates based on Global Monitoring Database data.

FIGURE 3.6 **Age Profile of the Population in 2018, by Region**

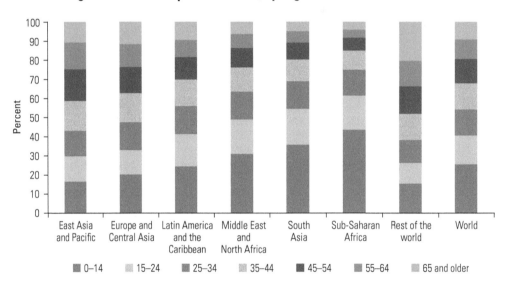

Source: World Bank estimates based on Global Monitoring Database data.

children in the global population declined by 1.5 percentage points during the same period. Although the population profile overall has registered a decrease in the share of the population between ages 0 and 34, and an increase in the share of the population older than 34, the poor do not show similar dynamics. Among the poor, while the share of youth ages 15–24 and of those ages 25–34 declined, older age groups have not increased

in relative terms. The decrease in the share of those ages 15–34 has been largely counterbalanced by the increase in the share of children up to age 14. The concentration of children—primarily rural—in the global profile of the poor is an amalgamation of similar patterns at the country level. If the poor population of each country is grouped into 15-year age cohorts (0–14, 15–29, and so on), in more than three-quarters of countries represented

FIGURE 3.7 Ratio of Poor Women to Women in the Overall Population, by Region

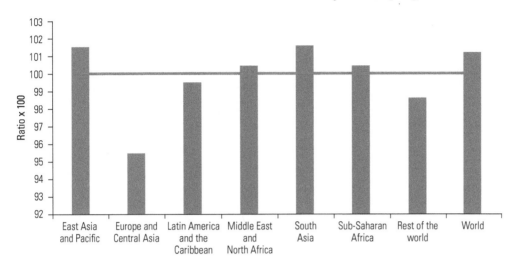

Source: World Bank estimates based on Global Monitoring Database data.

in the data, children in the 0–14 age cohort account for a larger share of the country's poor than any other age cohort.[5]

The core sociodemographic profile of the global poor presented in this chapter highlights that global poverty continues to be increasingly concentrated in rural areas and that a large share of the global poor have low educational attainment and rely on subsistence agriculture for their livelihoods. Global poverty is also heavily concentrated among children, who account for a quarter of the global population but for half of the global poor. Although due in part to countries with high poverty rates having larger household sizes, both for poor and nonpoor households, it is also the case that among the poor, and in Sub-Saharan Africa more broadly, there are more dependents for every working-age adult, and these dependency ratios have not decreased in recent years (World Bank 2018a). Characteristics such as low educational attainment, remote locations away from economic opportunities, precarious connections to the labor market, and employment in low-productivity sectors make it challenging to escape poverty.

Finally, the global profile described in this chapter and the poverty estimates presented

FIGURE 3.8 Comparing Changes in the Share of Poor and Global Population Share, by Age Group, 2015 and 2018

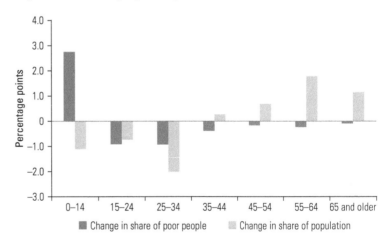

Source: World Bank estimates based on Global Monitoring Database data.

in this report more broadly do not present a full picture of the demographic characteristics of global poverty because of incomplete data coverage. Global poverty figures are generally based on nationally representative household surveys (or, occasionally, population census data). Despite recent improvements in the quality and availability of these data, a number of groups remain undercounted—or even omitted—from survey

BOX 3.2 Data Limitations to Profiling the Global Poor

The most prominent group of the undercounted poor consists of individuals living in countries that have weak or nonexistent national-level poverty data. Overall, 54 countries suffer from moderate to severe data deprivation—defined as having one or no data points—over the period 2009 to 2019. Survey-related data deprivation can be caused by lack of necessary technical or financial resources, difficulties in conducting fieldwork (such as enumerator safety due to existing conflict), or one-off events such as the COVID-19 (coronavirus) pandemic. Data deprivation is particularly severe in fragile and conflict-affected situations (FCS), where multiple constraints may be at play and where there are also difficulties in accessing the auxiliary data needed to compile internationally comparable poverty statistics. Pre-COVID-19 studies estimated that the majority of the world's poor would be living in FCS by the end of 2030, making it likely that the share of the poor represented by those missing from FCS statistics will only increase (Corral et al. 2020).[a]

Many other populations in countries with regular household surveys are also likely to be undercounted. Various nonhousehold groups are typically excluded from the sampling frame of household surveys. These disparate groups include those living in urban slums, illegal immigrants, refugees, the internally displaced, and some ethnic minorities. In many cases, these missing populations have a higher probability of living in poverty than the country or economy as a whole, which makes it particularly important

that attention be paid to the best way of ensuring their inclusion in government statistics.

The size of some of these population groups is difficult to estimate precisely, but it can be significant. Carr-Hill (2013) estimates the cumulative size of pastoralist, slum, and institutionalized populations that may be missing from sampling frames to be between 171 million and 322 million, equivalent to about 4.5–5.0 percent of the world's population. Together, these groups may represent up to a quarter of the poorest wealth quintile, given that poverty rates tend to be higher among them. Moreover, estimates of homelessness, defined as not having a roof over one's head, put the global number in 2003 at about 100 million, and possibly as high as 1 billion if those living in informal squatter settlements are included (UNHCS 2003). Many, if not most, of the homeless in the developing world are likely to fall close to or below the threshold for extreme poverty.

The number of displaced people, both refugees and the internally displaced, around the world has increased substantially over the past few decades. In 2019, the United Nations High Commissioner for Refugees estimates that there were more than 70 million forcibly displaced people worldwide, of whom about 40 million were internally displaced, 26 million were refugees, and 4 million were asylum seekers (UNHCR 2019). Estimating poverty among the displaced is made difficult by the fact that these populations may be excluded from sampling frames more generally, but even in specialized surveys they may

be hard to locate, contact, and interview because of constraints related to security, accessibility, or technical capacity. This shortcoming is important, because poverty rates among displaced populations tend to be high as a result of the paucity of labor market opportunities, lack of basic infrastructure and services, and the effects of trauma or distress (Beegle and Christiaensen 2019). Even these estimates may not fully capture the extent of poverty because internally displaced persons who are registered, or otherwise easy to contact, are likely to be those living in comparatively easier circumstances.

Some immigrant, religious, and ethnic groups may be deliberately undercounted or prevented from participating in censuses. For instance, in the 2014 Population Census in Myanmar, members of the country's Muslim Rohingya minority were not given a choice to self-identify in the census questionnaire, and in northern Rakhine State a considerable segment of the population was left out of the census exercise because of ongoing communal tensions.

Lack of better poverty data makes it difficult to make progress in eliminating extreme poverty; having full information about the extent and location of extreme poverty is vital for effective, data-informed policy making. Closing data gaps will require tackling (1) the lack of institutional willingness, capacity, or resources to design and implement surveys; and (2) the inability to reach parts of a country's territory because of conflict or infrastructure, or, now, mobility restrictions during the pandemic. Innovative

(continued)

BOX 3.2 **Data Limitations to Profiling the Global Poor** *(continued)*

use of technology and big data (for example, geospatial data, mobile records, social media), in combination with statistical tools, can help tackle data deprivations. So can efforts to adopt consistent and transparent definitions and procedures for enumerating both fixed and mobile institutional populations and the homeless, as well as national and international efforts, such as the United Nations High Commissioner for Refugees–World Bank Joint Data Center for Forced Displacement, to remedy data gaps around refugees, undocumented migrants, and the internally displaced.[b]

Source: Parry 2020.
a. Of the additional 88 million poor due to the pandemic, under the baseline scenario in chapter 1 of this report, figure 1.4, 18 million are in FCS economies. This represents only 20 percent of the new poor, which hints at a smaller share of FCS poor among the global poor in coming years. This is only indicative and not fully comparable because the methods adopted in (Corral et al. 2020) aim to overcome data limitations in FCS economies and are not strictly comparable with the projection methods adopted in chapter 1. Further research is needed to recalibrate projections of the share of the FCS poor in the world in the next decade.
b. See "Brief: World Bank-UNHCR Joint Data Center on Forced Displacement Fact Sheet," World Bank, Washington, DC, May 2020, https://www.worldbank.org/en/programs/forceddisplacement/brief/unhcr-world-bank-group-joint-data-center-on-forced -displacement-fact-sheet.

and census data collection efforts and thus are also absent in national poverty statistics (box 3.2).[6]

Efforts aimed at eradicating global poverty by 2030 should thus include tackling constraints to ensure the greatest possible coverage of the global poor in the data as the baseline against which progress in poverty eradication is measured. One of the recommendations of the Atkinson Report (World Bank 2017) on improving poverty measurement advocated an investigation into the extent to which there are missing people in the global poverty estimates, and for proposals with respect to adjustments for survey underrepresentation and noncoverage, as well as an investigation into the accuracy of baseline population data for each country (World Bank 2017). The Atkinson Report notes that these steps are particularly important because, as global poverty falls over time, the missing population will become proportionally more significant.

Poverty and conflict: A global and subnational perspective

One of the increasingly salient features of global poverty, and one that makes eradicating extreme poverty considerably more challenging, is the growing association between poverty and fragility and conflict.

A recent World Bank report notes that the 43 economies with the highest poverty rates are all either part of the group of fragile and conflict-affected situations (FCS) or in Sub-Saharan Africa (Corral et al. 2020). During the period 2000–19, poverty rates fell sharply in countries that were never fragile or conflict-affected, or that briefly experienced fragility or conflict but then escaped them. In contrast, poverty rates in recurrent or chronic FCS countries fell only marginally, or even increased during

FIGURE 3.9 Share of the Global Poor and of the Global Population, by FCS 2020 Typology

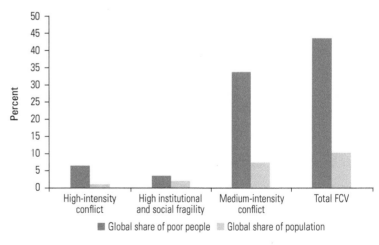

Source: World Bank estimates based on Global Monitoring Database data.
Note: FCS = fragile and conflict-affected situations; FCV = fragility, conflict, and violence.

the period. This was also the case for countries that entered the FCS group during the period and did not subsequently escape FCS status.

The World Bank lists 37 countries as being affected by fragility, conflict, and violence in its 2020 FCS list.[7] Together these countries are home to about 10 percent of the world's population; however, they account for more than 40 percent of the global poor according to the latest data (figure 3.9). Most of the FCS poor are in medium-intensity conflict countries; this result is driven by Nigeria being part of that country grouping, accounting for 40 percent of the total poor in the medium-intensity

conflict group. But more than 6 percent of the poor are in countries with high-intensity conflict, even though these countries account for less than 1 percent of the world's population.

In the context of poverty reduction, the effects of conflict can linger in its aftermath. Conflict imposes a poverty burden on affected countries that accumulates as a conflict debt that must then be paid down once violent conflict comes to an end (box 3.3). The World Bank's Human Capital Project highlights the fact that significant gaps in human capital, manifested in poor educational and health outcomes, affect the future productivity of workers and the future competitiveness of economies (World Bank 2018b). Conflict contributes directly to these gaps by affecting long-term workforce productivity through reduced access to education and increases in deaths and injuries, stunting, and mental disorders (Akresh, Verwimp, and Bundervoet 2011; Akresh et al. 2012; Bundervoet, Verwimp, and Akresh 2009; Ghobarah, Huth, and Russett 2003; Singhal 2019). Furthermore, expectations of further outbreaks of violence will inhibit capital inflows and further reduce productivity, while fear of the spread of violence can amplify its impact beyond the directly affected individuals, firms, and regions. Finally, while conflict is a symptom of weak state capacity, it also perpetuates weak capacity, with repercussions for the state's ability to

FIGURE 3.10 Educational Attainment, by FCS Grouping

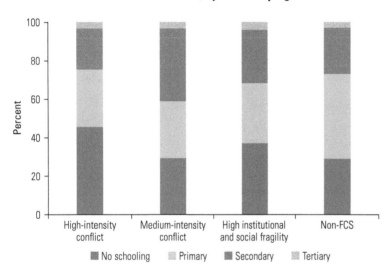

Source: World Bank estimates based on Global Monitoring Database data.
Note: FCS = fragile and conflict-affected situations.

BOX 3.3 **Poverty and Conflict: A Vicious Circle?**

There is a well-established link between armed conflict and economic welfare; conflict is associated with a notable cotemporaneous reduction of gross domestic product per capita, both through the destruction of resources that could be used in production and through the higher production and transport costs and increased uncertainty associated with conflict (Abadie and Gardeazabal 2003; Collier

1999; Mueller and Tobias 2016). In many poor countries, postconflict economic recovery and poverty reduction are stymied by the fact that peace does not last long enough for recovery to take place before some level of violence recurs. Nor does the recovery of human and physical capital take place instantaneously with the onset of peace. Indeed, the empirical relationship between poverty and conflict (measured here

by fatalities), both at the country level and the subnational level, appears to be stronger for cumulative conflict than for contemporaneous conflict in the year for which poverty is estimated (figure B3.3.1).

Mueller and Techasunthornwat (2020) propose a framework for analyzing this dynamic relationship between conflict and poverty through the concept of conflict debt, with cumulative

(continued)

BOX 3.3 **Poverty and Conflict: A Vicious Circle?** *(continued)*

FIGURE B3.3.1 Relationship between Contemporaneous and Past Cumulative Conflict and Poverty

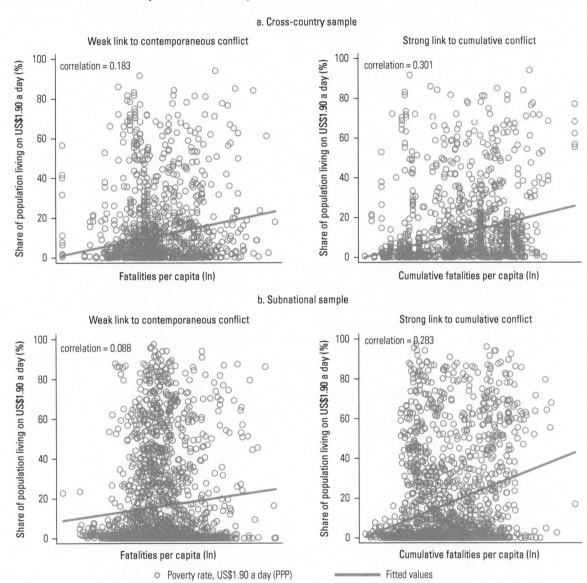

a. Cross-country sample

Weak link to contemporaneous conflict

correlation = 0.183

Strong link to cumulative conflict

correlation = 0.301

Y-axis: Share of population living on US$1.90 a day (%)
X-axis (left): Fatalities per capita (ln)
X-axis (right): Cumulative fatalities per capita (ln)

b. Subnational sample

Weak link to contemporaneous conflict

correlation = 0.088

Strong link to cumulative conflict

correlation = 0.283

Y-axis: Share of population living on US$1.90 a day (%)
X-axis (left): Fatalities per capita (ln)
X-axis (right): Cumulative fatalities per capita (ln)

○ Poverty rate, US$1.90 a day (PPP)   ▬▬▬ Fitted values

Sources: ACLED (Armed Conflict Location and Event Data Project) (database), Robert S. Strauss Center for International Security and Law, Austin, TX, http://www .acleddata.com/; Fatalities View, UCDP (Uppsala Conflict Data Program) (database), Department of Peace and Conflict Research, Uppsala University, Uppsala, Sweden, http://ucdp.uu.se/?id=1.
Notes: ln=logarithm. PPP = purchasing power parity.

history of past conflict, not just contemporaneous conflict, being an impediment to a country's ability to address poverty or inclusive growth. In this framework ongoing conflict contributes to the buildup of a stock of conflict over time, but past conflict affects poverty less and less over time. In other words, after a period of peace, countries are able to repay past conflict debt; that is, the effect of past conflict on poverty today will slowly dissipate.

Empirical models based on the above framework suggest a statistically robust relationship between conflict debt and poverty, and the differences in conflict and poverty between countries are a key driver of

(continued)

BOX 3.3 **Poverty and Conflict: A Vicious Circle?** *(continued)*

this relationship. With regard to magnitude, an increase by 1 in conflict debt is associated with an increase in the poverty rate of 1.767 percentage points.[a] Similar models, estimated at the subnational level, confirm the relationship between conflict debt and higher subnational poverty rates, although the positive correlation between subnational conflict debt and subnational poverty rates disappears once countrywide conflict debt is accounted for. In other words, important regional spillovers in the way conflict affects poverty may occur, an obvious pathway being internal displacement.[b]

A key concern is the possibility of reverse causality, in the sense of poverty causing conflict and not the other way around. Yet when the relationship between poverty

and conflict debt is estimated conditional on contemporaneous conflict, the association between conflict debt and the poverty rate is robust to controlling for contemporaneous conflict, but the reverse is not true. Countries with large conflict debts suffer from poverty but, controlling for this debt, there is no association between poverty and armed conflict. Furthermore, the relationship between poverty and contemporaneous conflict is not fully robust to account for the effects of unobserved variables common across countries within a particular continent or time period, suggesting that poverty rates have a stronger statistical relationship with past conflict than with present conflict, such that reverse causality cannot be the main driver of these correlations.

Using the model estimates, it is possible to simulate the conflict debt for a conflict of a given type to gain an understanding of how economically significant the relationship is between a history of conflict and poverty. Figure B3.3.2 shows the implied increase of the poverty rate for two different conflict histories. Panel a shows a single conflict episode of five years' duration, and panel b simulates the effect of a repeated cycle of peace and violence. With a single conflict episode, it can be seen that the poverty rate increases dramatically with the start of the conflict and subsequently rises to almost 7 percentage points after five years of conflict. It then falls gradually as the conflict debt falls but is still about 1 percentage point higher 10 years after the end of the

FIGURE B3.3.2 **Simulating Poverty Dynamics with a Single Conflict Episode and Recurrent Conflict**

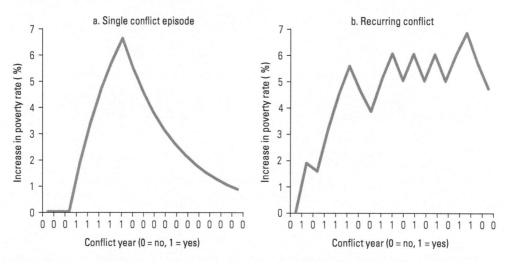

Sources: ACLED (Armed Conflict Location and Event Data Project) (database), Robert S. Strauss Center for International Security and Law, Austin, TX, http://www.acleddata.com/; Fatalities View, Uppsala Conflict Data Program (database), Department of Peace and Conflict Research, Uppsala University, Uppsala, Sweden, http://ucdp.uu.se/?id=1.

BOX 3.3 **Poverty and Conflict: A Vicious Circle?** *(continued)*

conflict. Dynamics of this type are consistent with poverty reduction catching up in countries escaping from conflict. However, a recurrent cycle of peace and violence does not allow countries to repay the conflict debt before the onset of new violence, leading to persistently high poverty rates. This trend can also be seen using subnational poverty data—in years preceding the year for which poverty is measured, a higher absolute incidence of violent years tends to be associated with higher poverty rates, on average, which is consistent with the difficulty of reducing poverty when faced with a recurrent cycle of violence (figure B3.3.3).

FIGURE B3.3.3 Subnational Poverty Rates and Cumulative Number of Past Conflict Years

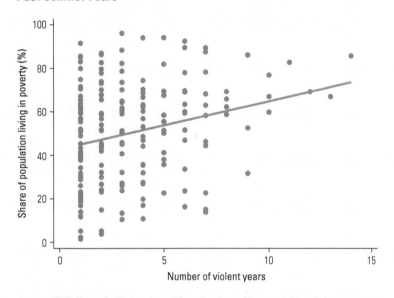

Sources: ACLED (Armed Conflict Location and Event Data Project) (database), Robert S. Strauss Center for International Security and Law, Austin, TX, http://www.acleddata.com/; Global Monitoring Database; Mueller and Techasunthornwat 2020.

Source: Largely based on Mueller and Techasunthornwat 2020.
a. The variable conflict debt captures the buildup of a stock of conflict debt from ongoing conflict over numerous years. Every year in which the rate of violent conflict fatalities is above 8 per 100,000 population increases by 1 the number of conflict years and by δ the past conflict debt. The parameter δ is a decay parameter that is smaller than 1 if conflict in the past affects current poverty less and less over time. It can be interpreted as the (mental) health and skills of the affected population recovering in the years following conflict or as investors regarding a region or country as increasingly stable with lasting peace.
b. At the end of 2018, some 41.3 million people worldwide were internally displaced because of armed conflict (UNHCR 2019).

FIGURE 3.11 **Share of Global Population, by Age Group**

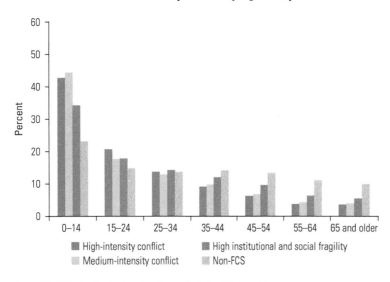

Source: World Bank estimates based on Global Monitoring Database data.
Note: FCS = fragile and conflict-affected situations.

FIGURE 3.12 **Share of Global Poor, by Age Group**

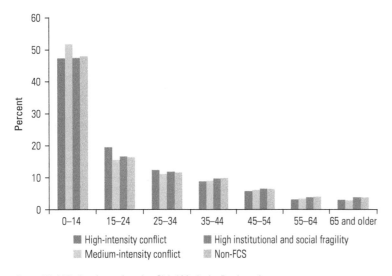

Source: World Bank estimates based on Global Monitoring Database data.
Note: FCS = fragile and conflict-affected situations.

pursue effective poverty alleviation strategies and policy interventions.

The recent *World Bank Group Strategy for Fragility, Conflict, and Violence 2020–2025* (World Bank 2020a) documents the stark differences in human capital between FCS and non-FCS economies; countries in the former group, especially economies characterized by high-intensity conflict, lag behind non-FCS economies on all six of the indicators underlying the World Bank's Human Capital Index.[8] Broader measures of multidimensional poverty encompassing monetary, education, and infrastructure dimensions similarly show that households in FCS countries are multidimensionally poor more often than those in non-FCS countries (World Bank 2020a). A comparison of educational attainment across the various FCS categories of economies based on the World Bank's classification into high-intensity conflict countries, medium-intensity conflict countries, and countries with high institutional and social fragility shows that the poor include a larger share of adults without schooling in high-intensity conflict economies (46 percent) than in non-FCS economies (29 percent) (figure 3.10).

Countries affected by conflict and fragility, many of which are in Sub-Saharan Africa, tend to have a younger demographic profile and a much higher share of children in the overall population compared with non-FCS countries (figure 3.11). However, these overall demographic patterns do not appear to account for the concentration of children in the global profile of the poor. The conflict-affected countries, as well as those affected by institutional fragility, have similar rates of children in the total population of the poor as non-FCS countries (figure 3.12).

A subnational perspective on conflict and poverty

Conflict and poverty are generally not uniformly distributed within country borders (Simler 2016). As noted in box 3.3, the incidence of poverty and conflict history at the subnational level are positively correlated; in other words, poverty rates tend to be higher, on average, in areas with higher levels of conflict debt, although this correlation is not strong. Map 3.1, which plots the joint distribution of subnational poverty and conflict using data from the Armed Conflict Location and Event Data Project database of geolocated conflict events around the world, demonstrates the same phenomenon. In map 3.1 conflict history (or conflict debt) is defined as cumulative discounted years with violence, where a violent year is one with more than 0.08 fatalities per 1,000 population, a common threshold in the conflict literature (Mueller 2016).[9] Map 3.1 shows that many territories within economies in Central and Eastern Africa may have high poverty rates but are not affected by conflict recent or past (defined here as conflict debt of less than 0.19), and conversely there are areas in countries such as Chad, Mauritania, Niger, and Sudan where levels of conflict debt are high but poverty rates are relatively lower. However, a number of subnational regions in countries such as Central African Republic, Chad, the Democratic Republic of Congo, Nigeria, South Sudan, and Uganda are afflicted by both high poverty rates and high levels of conflict debt.

Conflict is often localized and varies in how much it directly affects the poor of a given country, regional spillovers notwithstanding. Overall, for 76 countries in the sample of 116 countries for which subnational poverty estimates are available for the period 2009–18, there is no recent history of conflict, such that none of the poor resides in conflict-affected areas, whereas in 40 countries at least some of the poor reside in areas with a history of conflict.[10] The share of the poor residing in areas with conflict history varies widely across economies, as shown in figure 3.13, from a very small proportion in countries such as Ethiopia, Mali, and Mauritania to more than 80 percent in economies including South Sudan and West Bank and Gaza. On average, a higher share of the poor live in areas with conflict history in the Middle East and North Africa, South Asia, and Sub-Saharan Africa than in other developing regions.[11]

MAP 3.1 Joint Distribution of Subnational Poverty (at the US$1.90-a-Day Poverty Line) and Conflict in Sub-Saharan Africa

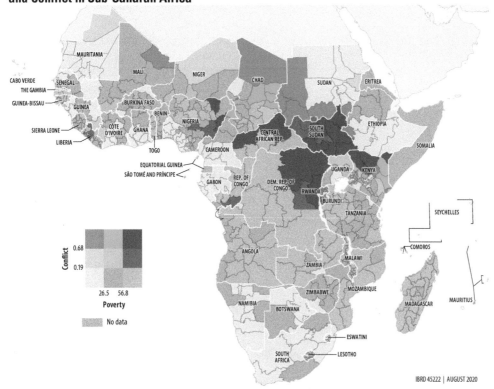

Sources: Mueller and Techasunthornwat 2020, based on data from ACLED (Armed Conflict Location and Event Data Project) (database), Robert S. Strauss Center for International Security and Law, Austin, TX, http://www.acleddata.com/; Global Subnational Atlas of Poverty; and Global Monitoring Database data.
Note: The year for which poverty is measured differs across countries, but in all cases, the most recent year for which data is available is used (between 2009 and 2018). Poverty refers to the percentage of the population living at the US$1.90-a-day poverty line. Conflict data cover the period 1989–2018. Average distance from the last year of conflict to the survey year of the poverty estimate is 13 years. Conflict debt index equals the sum total of violent years, where a current violent year equals 1 if the number of deaths per 1,000 population exceeds 0.08. Earlier conflict years, similarly defined, are discounted by a decay parameter δ (see box 3.3). The conflict scale is divided into three categories: no conflict debt (conflict debt ≤ 0.19), some conflict debt (0.19 < conflict debt ≤ 0.68), and heavy conflict debt burden (conflict debt > 0.68).

FIGURE 3.13 Share of Poor Residing in Areas with at Least Some Conflict History

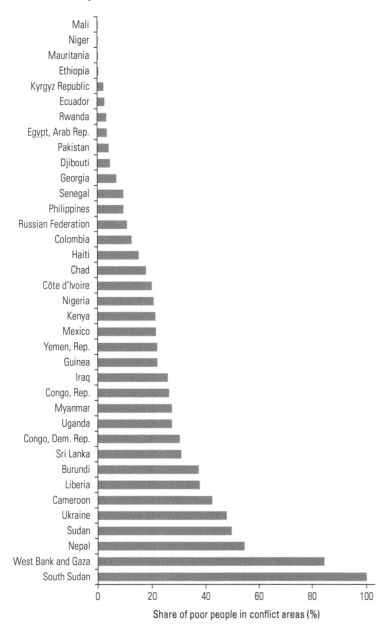

Share of poor people in conflict areas (%)

Sources: World Bank estimates based on data from ACLED (Armed Conflict Location and Event Data Project) (database), Robert S. Strauss Center for International Security and Law, Austin, TX, http://www.acleddata.com/; Global Subnational Atlas of Poverty; and Global Monitoring Database.
Note: Areas with at least some conflict history have a conflict debt index greater than 0.19. See box 3.3 for the definition of the conflict debt index.

These varying shares of concentration of the poor in areas with a history of conflict are the consequence of multiple factors, including territorial and population size of the country, proximity to international borders, and age of the conflict, all of which affect the possibility of population displacement. Further research is needed to assess the connections between

the size of the country, proximity to international borders, and age of the conflict, and the concentration of large groups of the population in given areas or their displacement from high-conflict areas to low-conflict areas within or outside the country.

Recurrent conflict, including in the recent past, may prevent a country from repaying its conflict debt, thus perpetuating weak state institutions, retarding human capital accumulation, and obstructing poverty reduction. In contrast, past conflict, even if prolonged, can still be associated with a higher incidence of poverty, but, dynamically, with falling poverty, given a sufficiently long window of sustained peace for poverty reduction to recover after conflict. As the total number of poor and the conflict history for each subnational unit in the data are observed, it is possible to get a sense of the share of the poor in each country who are affected by conflict, particularly by residing in areas with conflict history. Results can be obtained both in the aggregate and separately for different types of conflict history at the subnational level, such as no conflict history; a history of recent conflict, defined as at least one violent year during the past five; and a history of past conflict, defined as having had conflict in the past (with a starting point of 1992), but not in the five years before the year for which poverty data are available.

In a number of countries, different groups of poor people may be affected by recent and older conflict history. For instance, in South Sudan, slightly more than 40 percent of the country's poor are in areas with recent conflict, whereas the rest are in areas with conflict debt from earlier conflict situations. In Sudan, half of the poor are in areas with a history of conflict. This half represents 40 percent who are in areas of recent conflict and 10 percent who are in areas of older conflict. In Colombia, where about 10 percent of the poor reside in areas with a conflict history, the majority are in areas with nonrecent conflict. Globally, about 10 percent of the population lives in areas with a conflict history, primarily recent conflict, but also older conflict. Almost a quarter of the poor live in subnational areas with a conflict history. In Sub-Saharan Africa, which accounts for the bulk of the poor in conflict-affected areas, 30 percent of the population and 35 percent of the poor live in areas with either ongoing or past (primarily recent) conflict. As illustrated in figure 3.14, the impact of conflict on poverty depends on the nature of the conflict history: most of the poor living in conflict areas are living in areas of recent conflict. Addressing poverty in areas that have ongoing or recent conflict may require a different set of interventions than in areas with conflict debt from earlier years. For instance, in cases of active conflict, programs aimed at disarmament, demobilization, and reintegration, as well as supporting security and stability and protecting core state and community-based institutions, may be of immediate importance, whereas in countries that are moving out of fragility a broader range of interventions, including those focusing on resource mobilization, service delivery, and macro-fiscal stability, may be warranted (World Bank 2020a).

Policy implications

In summary, the connection between conflict and poverty is complex and nuanced. Nearly half the global poor live in conflict-affected countries. In many cases, however, only a small share of the poor live in specific areas of conflict whereas in others most of the poor are living in areas directly struck by recent conflict. This confluence of poverty and conflict underscores the importance of having policies that differentiate between those who live in areas of high conflict and those who escaped from the area but are still affected by the lingering effects of the conflict. It also calls for policy differentiation across regions, particularly to prevent those localities affected by conflict, recent or past, from suffering from systematic underinvestment and neglect.

These distinctions may be important from a policy point of view because poverty in conflict and nonconflict areas may exhibit different trajectories and may be driven by different factors. The World Bank (2020a) shows that, in countries classified as FCS at the beginning of the 2000s but that have fully escaped FCS status sometime in the past two decades, poverty rates in or near 2000 were similar to poverty rates in chronic FCS countries (classified

FIGURE 3.14 **Distribution of the Poor and of the Population, by Conflict Type, Globally and in Sub-Saharan Africa**

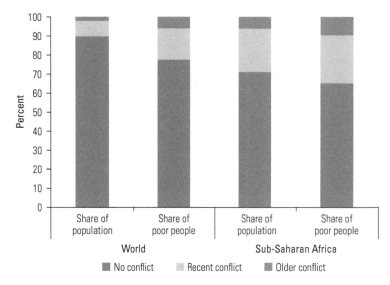

Sources: World Bank estimates based on data from ACLED (Armed Conflict Location and Event Data Project) (database), Robert S. Strauss Center for International Security and Law, Austin, TX, http://www.acleddata.com/; and Global Monitoring Database.
Note: "Recent conflict" refers to the five-year period ending in the year of the survey providing poverty data, which varies across countries. "Older conflict" includes conflicts that have occurred since 1992 but not in the five years preceding the year for which poverty data are available.

as FCS in every year during 2000–19); however, whereas the former saw rapid poverty reduction trends similar to non-FCS countries, poverty largely stagnated in chronic FCS countries. In contrast, in FCS countries that move in and out of FCS status, poverty reduction over the same period was modest (World Bank 2020a). This is compatible with the idea of conflict debt explained in box 3.3 and the need for policies toward sustained peace and, better still, conflict prevention for poverty reduction.

Given that countries in the recurrent FCS group are likely to still account for a large share of the world's poor by 2030, focusing on prevention and monitoring markers of fragility to prevent countries from falling into fragility and conflict, or from cycling in and out of conflict, should be among key policy concerns (Corral et al. 2020; World Bank 2020a). The fact that the conflict debt effect lingers for years, hindering all sources of development—from human capital to infrastructure, from psychological health to institution building—highlights the importance of prevention to avoid the large and persisting costs of conflict in terms of poverty. Ending current conflicts, avoiding recurrence of past conflicts, and preventing future conflicts are all necessary policies for global poverty reduction.

Poverty and climate risks

Continued conflict is a key impediment to reaching the World Bank Group's goals on poverty reduction and shared prosperity, but it is not the only major obstacle. A recent World Bank report argues that climate change is another acute threat to poverty reduction, particularly in the economies of Sub-Saharan Africa and South Asia—the regions where most of the global poor are concentrated (Hallegatte et al. 2016). As chapter 1 notes, an update of the methods and data in this report estimates that between 68 million and 132 million people (depending on different scenarios) could be pushed into poverty by 2030 through various channels of climate change impact (Jafino et al. 2020).[12]

Ample evidence indicates that those living in poverty or near the poverty line are particularly vulnerable to shocks such as natural disasters; greater vulnerability means that they lose more when such shocks occur. This peril is due to a number of factors, including (1) lower-quality assets, such as lower-quality housing stock or savings through investments in their homes or cattle, which are more vulnerable to damage and loss from floods and droughts; (2) greater reliance on fragile infrastructure, such as unpaved roads, with lower ability to protect against disruptions to infrastructure services; (3) greater dependence on livelihoods derived from agricultural and ecosystems incomes, which are more vulnerable to natural disasters; (4) greater vulnerability to rising food prices in the aftermath of disaster-related supply shocks; and (5) long-term human capital impacts through compromised health and education, including greater susceptibility to climate-related diseases such as diarrhea and malaria (Hallegatte et al. 2016).

Winsemius et al. (2015) find that, in addition to being more vulnerable, poor people are also generally more exposed to natural disasters, although not universally so. Their analysis, based on 52 countries, shows that, in about half of the countries where the exposure of poor and nonpoor people differs significantly (a third of the overall sample), poor people are overexposed (compared with the nonpoor) to floods at the national level. Similar patterns are also found with respect to exposure to drought.[13] Where flood maps are available at a higher resolution, overexposure of poor households to floods is much more pronounced in urban areas: 73 percent of analyzed populations live in countries with a positive poor-exposure bias to fluvial floods, notably in countries in West and Southern Africa (for example, Angola, Cameroon, the Democratic Republic of Congo, Nigeria, and Zambia). The relationship between poverty and flood exposure can be complex; at the national level, richer areas (such as economically active coastal towns) are often more exposed, but at the local scale, especially within cities, poor people are much more likely to live in unsafe neighborhoods, often as a result of land market frictions.

This report builds on earlier work for the *Shock Waves* report (Hallegatte et al. 2016) and presents new estimates of exposure to flooding at principal subnational administrative divisions (for example, provinces or states) (see box 3.4) for a larger set of countries (184 in total). The present analysis overlays the exposure to flooding on subnational estimates of international poverty for these divisions. Flooding is only one of several types of climate risks and thus does not take into account the impact of droughts, high temperatures, or other natural disasters such as earthquakes or cyclones. The focus on flooding in this section primarily reflects the fact that floods are one of the most common and severe hazards, especially in lower-income countries where infrastructure systems, including drainage and flood protection, tend to be least developed; and there is more local-level variability in the exposure to flooding, in comparison with subnational variation in temperature, which makes the joint exposure to flood risk and poverty at the subnational level more amenable to examination.

The focus on flooding does, however, bring to the fore certain countries and regions while not capturing the full extent of disaster risks elsewhere. For instance, river and urban flood risks in countries such as Rwanda are high, whereas the earthquake risk (not related to climate) is medium, and the risk of extreme heat (related to climate) is low.[14] However, in India—which is at high risk not just of river, urban, and coastal floods, but also of earthquakes, landslides, and extreme heat, the overall level of climate and nonclimate risks discussed in this chapter would be intensified with a broader

BOX 3.4 Estimating the Number of Poor Affected by Flood Risk on a Global Scale

To estimate the number of people who are exposed to intense flood risk, a combined flood hazard map is generated. For each country and each subnational administrative unit, a single flood hazard layer is created by combining different flood types. The resulting flood map has a 90-square-meter resolution. Each pixel shows estimated inundation depths in meters. For pixels in which different flood types overlap, the higher inundation depth estimate is used. Examples of such locations include coastal areas near rivers that are exposed to both coastal and fluvial flooding. The flood hazard map is then resampled to match the spatial resolution of the Global Human Settlement Layer population density map.[a]

Once the flood map is constructed, it is possible to define flood risk categories by aggregating flood hazards computed on a continuous scale into risk categories (0 meter = no risk; 0–0.15 meter = low risk; 0.15–0.5 meter = moderate risk; 0.5–1.5 meters = high risk; over 1.5 meters = very high risk) and assigning each grid cell in a country to one of the five risk categories. For example, a pixel that has an estimated inundation depth of 5 centimeters is classified as low risk, whereas a pixel with a depth of 4.3 meters is classified as very high risk.

Then flood risk categories are assigned to population headcounts at the pixel level and aggregated to the administrative unit (for

example, province or district level), which enables the calculation of population headcounts for each flood risk category and for each subnational administrative unit. This process yields an estimate of the number and share of people exposed to no, low, moderate, high, and very high flood risk during an intense flood event. Finally, given estimates of poverty at the administrative unit level from the Global Monitoring Database, it is possible to compute the number of poor people in each administrative unit exposed to flood risk by multiplying poverty shares by the population numbers estimated to be exposed to flooding.

Source: Rentschler and Salhab 2020.
a. Global Human Settlement Layer (database), Joint Research Centre, European Commission, Brussels, http://ghslsys.jrc.ec.europa.eu/.

---

measure of disaster risks. In Central and West Africa, the poor in many countries are more exposed to floods relative to the overall population and are also more exposed to higher temperatures (Hallegate et al. 2016). In other words, the discussion in this chapter presents, in some sense, a lower bound of the magnitude of challenges the countries with high poverty incidence face from exposure to climate risks. The set of countries highlighted here would not have changed substantially with more comprehensive coverage of climate risks.

This study takes a once-a-century flood to represent a relatively rare and intense disaster. A flood of 100-year magnitude has, on average, a 1 percent probability of occurrence in any given year, which translates to 10 percent probability in a decade, or 50 percent probability in a lifetime (68 years). These are significant probabilities that lie well within reasonable planning horizons of governments. For comparison, the Dutch flood protection system protects against events up to 1 in 10,000 years. In addition, it should be noted that these probabilities apply independently to a given

river basin or microclimate. This study considers hundreds of thousands of such locations, meaning that, globally, hundreds of once-a-century flood events happen every year.

Globally, some 1.47 billion people are estimated to be living in areas with high flood risk, including about 132 million poor people (as defined by the international poverty line of US$1.90 a day). Globally, exposure among the poor, measured as the share of global poor with high risk of flooding (16.4 percent of total) is close to that of the overall population (18.6 percent). In some regions, such as East Asia and Pacific, the Middle East and North Africa, and South Asia, the exposure of the poor is lower, on average (figure 3.15). Differences in exposure, however, may not imply the same ability to adapt or mitigate the impact of floods. The poor may need special attention because of their vulnerabilities, even when they are not more exposed (Hallegatte and Rentschler 2015; Rentschler 2013).

However, if the joint occurrence of poverty and flood exposure is considered, Sub-Saharan Africa stands out, as can be seen by comparing

FIGURE 3.15 Share of Population and of the Poor with High Flood Exposure, by Region

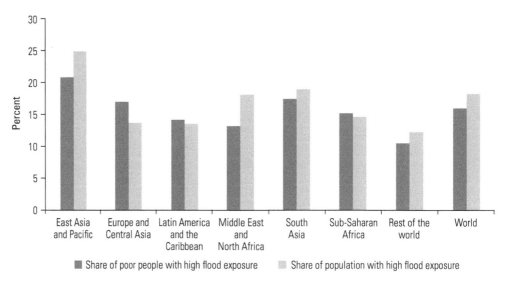

Legend: ■ Share of poor people with high flood exposure ■ Share of population with high flood exposure

Source: World Bank estimates based on data from Rentschler and Salhab 2020.

MAP 3.2 Share of Global Population with High Flood Exposure

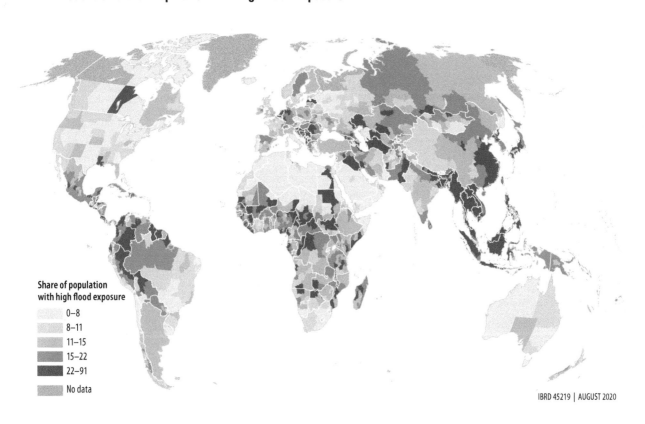

Share of population with high flood exposure
- 0–8
- 8–11
- 11–15
- 15–22
- 22–91
- No data

IBRD 45219 | AUGUST 2020

Source: Rentschler and Salhab 2020.
Note: Share corresponds to the percentage of population in a given territory by grouping territories or principal administrative divisions representing 20 percent of all territories or divisions shown.

MAP 3.3 Share of Population That Lives below the US$1.90-a-Day Poverty Line and Has High Flood Exposure

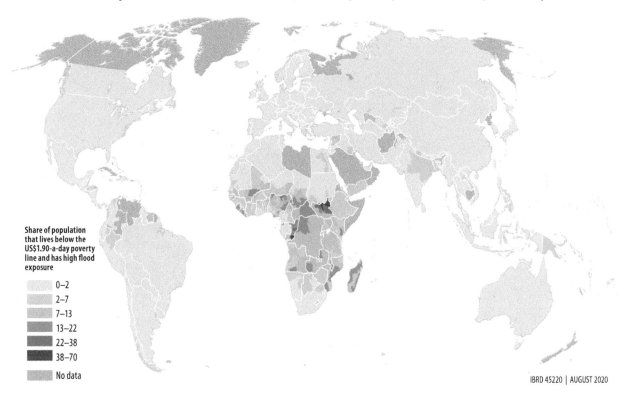

Share of population
that lives below the
US$1.90-a-day poverty
line and has high flood
exposure

- 0–2
- 2–7
- 7–13
- 13–22
- 22–38
- 38–70
- No data

IBRD 45220 | AUGUST 2020

Sources: Global Monitoring Database; Rentschler and Salhab 2020.
Note: Share corresponds to the percentage of population in a given territory by grouping territories or principal administrative divisions that represent 20 percent of all territories shown.

the global map of total population exposure (map 3.2) with the map of the share of population with high flood exposure who are also below the international poverty line (map 3.3). Globally, the region accounts for slightly more than 10 percent of the total population with high flood risks, but for more than half of the global poor who face high flood risks. East Asia and Pacific, in contrast, accounts for more than a third of the total population exposed to flood risks, but for less than 10 percent of the global poor who are at risk of flooding. In Sub-Saharan Africa, some 6 percent of the population is both poor and facing high risks of flooding, as compared with 2 percent in South Asia and fewer than 1 percent in East Asia and Pacific. This picture reinforces the multidimensional character of poverty highlighted in chapter 1 of this report—not only does Sub-Saharan Africa lag behind other regions on measures of monetary poverty, educational attainment, and access to basic services, but the poor in Sub-Saharan Africa also suffer from greater exposure (and vulnerability) to climate change risks such as flooding and to other

dimensions of climate risks such as droughts and higher temperatures (Hallegate et al. 2016).

Considering the joint distribution of subnational poverty rates and the share of the poor in subnational areas who are exposed to flood risk, the two populations do not fully overlap. There are areas in the Republic of Congo, Ethiopia, Gabon, and South Africa where a relatively high share of the poor are exposed to flood risks, but poverty rates are relatively low. However, a number of subnational regions in Central and West Africa, as well as in Madagascar and Mozambique, can be characterized as having both high incidence of poverty and considerable exposure among poor people to flood risks associated with climate change (map 3.4). Globally, four out of the top ten subnational regions by the absolute number of $1.90/day poor with high flood exposure (and all top ten subnational regions in terms of the proportion of the $1.90/day poor with high flood exposure) are located in Sub-Saharan Africa (Rentschler and Salhab 2020).

MAP 3.4 Joint Distribution of Poverty and Flood Risk in Sub-Saharan Africa

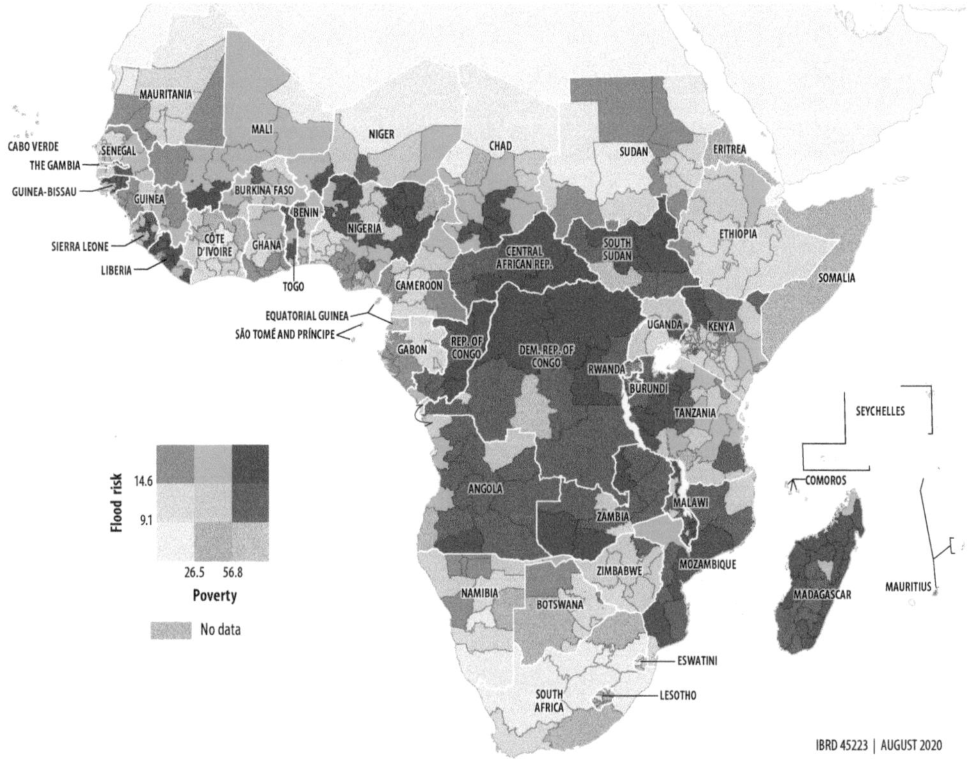

Sources: World Bank estimates based on data from the Global Subnational Atlas of Poverty, Global Monitoring Database, and Rentschler and Salhab 2020.
Note: Scale thresholds for poverty and climate risk are based on terciles. Both axes represent the percentage of the population. Those who live with a flood risk face inundation depths of over 0.15 meters in the event of a 1-to-100-year flood. Those in poverty live below the US$1.90-a-day poverty line.

Vulnerability and multiple risks: Poverty in the face of COVID-19, conflict, and climate risks

Paragraphs above highlight the challenges to global poverty posed by conflict and certain dimensions of climate change, such as flooding. A pre-COVID-19 study by Corral et al. (2020) estimates that the share of the global poor in FCS countries will rise from less than 50 percent today to become a majority of the poor by 2030, with Sub-Saharan Africa contributing a large share of the total. Likewise, as many as 132 million people are expected to be living in poverty by 2030 on account of the multiple impacts of climate change (see box 1.3 in chapter 1 of this report), and many of them will be in Sub-Saharan Africa (Jafino et al. 2020). There does not appear to be a systematic relationship between the share of the poor in areas

with a history of conflict and those with high exposure to flooding in countries with high degrees of exposure to both, as can be seen in figure 3.16, which plots the data for countries with poverty rates higher than the 2030 goal of 3 percent. However, figure 3.16 highlights the multifaceted challenges in Sub-Saharan Africa; many of the countries in the figure, particularly those such as Cameroon, Liberia, and South Sudan, that have a relatively large share of the poor living in areas both affected by a history of conflict and facing high exposure to floods, are in Sub-Saharan Africa.[15] In these specific cases, future efforts to reduce poverty may be hampered by exposure to multiple risks.

Further research is needed to assess the connections between poverty, conflict, and other likely impacts of climate change, including changes in food prices, the occurrence of other natural disasters, and extreme temperature and associated health issues. For instance, Winsemius et al. (2015), in assessing future changes in the exposure of poor people to floods and droughts, find that the number of poor exposed could increase rapidly in some parts of West Africa. Furthermore, rapid urbanization in many countries in Africa could have a notable impact on flood exposure patterns in the coming decades independently of climate change (Winsemius et al. 2015). Figure 3.16 is an illustration of potential joint impacts of conflict and floods on poverty. The joint incidence of conflict and other climate risks, or among several climate or nonclimate risks, is likely; therefore, antipoverty policies need to take into consideration measures to address these multiple challenges. Simple targeting based on demographics will not suffice. Prevention and mitigation policies that take into account conflict history and the prospect of climate change impacts are also fundamentally needed.

An approximation of those vulnerable to extreme poverty

Many households are vulnerable to falling into extreme poverty because of shocks such as loss of employment, underemployment, or illness, and many of the new poor will likely come from households that were living just above the US$1.90-a-day poverty line. The deleterious effects of conflict and of climate change on poverty are also likely to be concentrated among those whose incomes are not far above the poverty threshold. And, as chapter 1 notes, many of the global poor live in middle-income countries, such as India and Nigeria, where the income requirement for being nonpoor is higher than the international poverty line; for lower-middle-income countries this threshold is US$3.20 a day. To get a better sense of the global poverty profile that accounts for higher income standards in lower-middle-income countries and for households that may fall below the international poverty line because of the COVID-19 pandemic or other negative income shocks, this section presents a profile of the population below the US$3.20-a-day threshold, with a focus on the key

FIGURE 3.16 Joint Exposure to Conflict and Floods and Share of the Total Population below the International Poverty Line

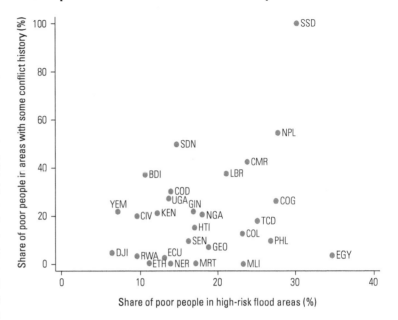

Source: World Bank estimates based on data from Mueller and Techasunthornwat 2020; Rentschler and Salhab 2020.
Note: The figure includes a sample of countries with poverty rates higher than 3 percent and some history of conflict. Countries with a zero share of poor in conflict areas, as well as countries with poverty rates of less than 3 percent, are not displayed.

differences between the population below US$3.20 a day and those below the international poverty line of US$1.90 a day.

The core sociodemographic characteristics of the population below the US$3.20-a-day threshold more closely resemble those of the overall population (rather than the global extreme poor), which is not surprising given that using the higher threshold expands the size of the left tail of the welfare distribution under consideration. Nonetheless, some differences remain. More than three-quarters of those below the US$3.20-a-day line live in rural areas, compared with less than half of the population overall (figure 3.17). The disproportionate representation of rural residents among the US$3.20-a-day poor is still most pronounced in Europe and Central Asia, Latin America and the Caribbean, and the Middle East and North Africa. In these regions, the share of those below the poverty threshold in rural areas is at least 25 percentage points greater than their share in the overall population.

A comparison of educational attainment among US$3.20-a-day poor adults (figure 3.18)

FIGURE 3.17 Share of Rural Population among US$3.20-a-Day Poor and in the Overall Population

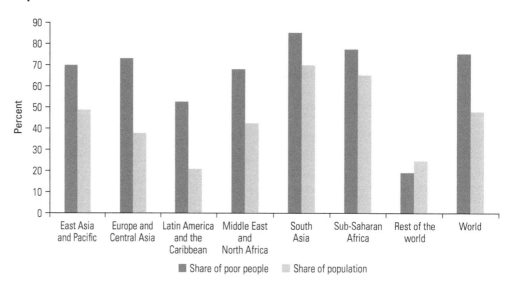

Source: World Bank estimates based on Global Monitoring Database data.

FIGURE 3.18 Profile of US$3.20-a-Day Poor, by Educational Attainment (age 15 and older)

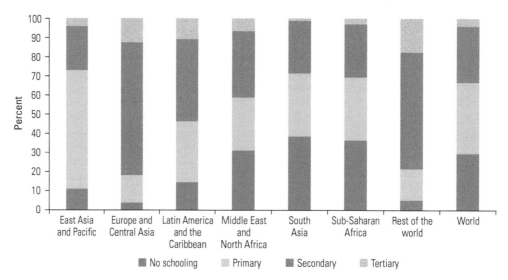

Source: World Bank estimates based on Global Monitoring Database data.

with that of the global extreme poor (figure 3.2) and with the general adult population (figure 3.3) shows that the share of US$3.20-a-day adults with no education is 6 percentage points lower, and the share of those with at least secondary education is 4 percentage points higher, when compared with the global extreme poor adults. Still, the educational profile of the US$3.20-a-day poor is much closer to the profile of the US$1.90-a-day poor than it is to the overall educational distribution among adults, of whom more than half (or 20 percentage points more than the US$3.20-a-day poor) have at least secondary education. In other words, even at this higher income standard, the education gap between the poor and the nonpoor remains pronounced.

FIGURE 3.19 Age Distribution among the US$3.20-a-Day Poor, by Region

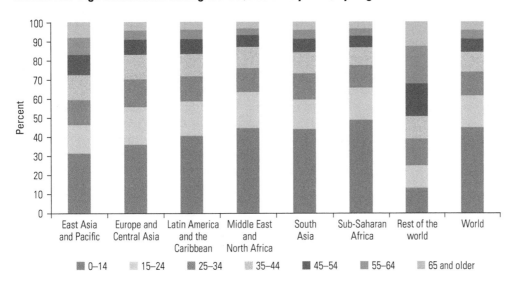

Source: World Bank estimates based on Global Monitoring Database data.

FIGURE 3.20 Ratio of Poor Women (Living on US$3.20 a Day) to Women in the Overall Population, by Region

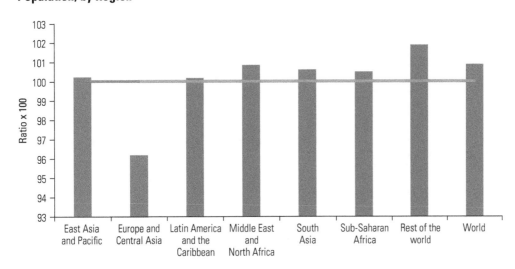

Source: World Bank estimates based on Global Monitoring Database data.

Children are disproportionately represented in the profile of the US$3.20-a-day poor (figure 3.19), as they are among the global extreme poor, but to a somewhat smaller degree. Still, as with education, the profile of the US$3.20-a-day poor is much closer to the profile of the international poverty line poor than it is to the overall age distribution of the population: 45 percent of the US$3.20-a-day poor are children ages 0–14, even though overall children account for only a quarter

of the population globally. Women are also overrepresented among the US$3.20-a-day poor (figure 3.20), but by smaller margins compared with the international poverty line poor. Europe and Central Asia continues to be the region with fewer women among the poor than in the population overall.

Another similarity between the profiles of the global extreme poor and the US$3.20-a-day poor is the overrepresentation of FCS countries in both groups. Those with incomes greater than US$1.90 a day and less than US$3.20 a day, like the extreme poor, are more heavily concentrated in FCS countries: 20 percent of the population in this income range is in FCS countries, even though this group accounts for 10 percent of the population globally (figure 3.21). Thus, eradicating global poverty in conflict-affected countries is especially challenging because, in addition to poverty being endemic in many of those countries, there is a high concentration of households with incomes not far above the international poverty line that are vulnerable to falling below the international poverty threshold as a result of recurrent violence.

Similarly, a significant proportion of the population exposed to high flood risks is also vulnerable to poverty. Rentschler and Salhab (2020) estimate, for this report, that approximately 1.47 billion people are exposed to moderate to very high risk of floods. Of these, 132 million are poor under the US$1.90 poverty line, 344 million under the US$3.20 line, and 588 million under the US$5.50 line (figure 3.22). This underlines that mitigation and adaptation policies to cope with catastrophic floods must also pay special attention to the fact that a large proportion of those exposed to these risks are also poor and hence more vulnerable and less able to cope with these shocks. Moreover, this exercise accounts for only one potential impact of climate change. In another background paper for this report, Jafino et al. (2020) indicate that natural disasters are only one of the main impacts of climate change. Effects on food prices and health are

FIGURE 3.21 Share of Population Living on US$1.90-a-Day to US$3.20-a-Day and of the Total Population, by Country Conflict Category

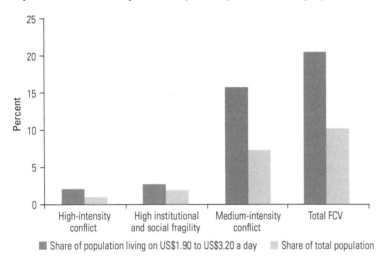

Source: World Bank estimates based on Global Monitoring Database data.
Note: FCV = fragility, conflict, and violence.

FIGURE 3.22 Number of Poor Living at the Three Poverty Lines Who Are Also Exposed to Catastrophic Floods

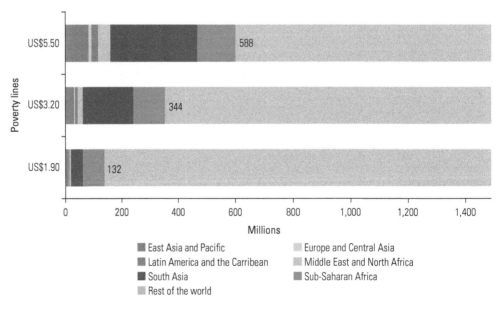

Source: Rentschler and Salhab 2020.

FIGURE 3.23 **Comparative Regional Profile of US$1.90-a-Day and US$3.20-a-Day Poverty Lines, without India**

Share of poor people living on US$3.20 a day

Share of poor people living on US$1.90 a day

- ■ East Asia and Pacific
- ▨ Europe and Central Asia
- ■ Latin America and the Caribbean
- ▨ Middle East and North Africa
- ■ South Asia, excluding India
- ▨ Sub-Saharan Africa
- ▨ Rest of the world

Source: World Bank estimates based on Global Monitoring database data.
Note: Both populations are exclusive of India.

potentially larger than the effects of disasters when considering poverty generation. Again, the poor are either more exposed or more vulnerable to the potential impacts of climate change risks and therefore antipoverty policies need to include mechanisms to prevent or lessen these shocks.

Raising the threshold from US$1.90 a day to US$3.20 a day introduces noticeable changes into the regional distribution of the population below the poverty line (figure 3.23). Sub-Saharan Africa accounts for three-quarters of those below the US$1.90-a-day threshold (excluding India), but for only 62 percent of those below the US$3.20-a-day threshold. The relative prominence of the East Asia and Pacific and South Asia regions increases considerably as the poverty line is raised, underscoring that, although certain regions and countries may have few people living below the international poverty line, they may have large numbers of households living on incomes that are not far above it, who are thus potentially vulnerable to

falling into poverty in the event of exogenous negative shocks.[16]

The challenges of tackling endemic poverty more broadly, and of reducing poverty amid conflict and climate risks, will be further exacerbated by the COVID-19 pandemic, which, according to the latest data, may push some 88 million to 115 million people into extreme poverty during 2020 (see chapter 1 of this report). Existing data do not allow a detailed description to be given of the characteristics of those being made poor by the pandemic, in part because it is still unfolding. However, potentially relevant evidence is emerging based on simulations of COVID-19 impacts and newly collected data from high-frequency surveys (see box 2.2 in chapter 2 of this report). These findings suggest that the new poor may differ from those who were already poor before the pandemic, with significant implications for policy.

COVID-19 and poverty: Who are the new poor?

The impact of COVID-19 on poverty in various countries and regions will depend on a combination of factors, the most important of which are the magnitude of the pandemic's economic effects and the number of people living near the international poverty line in hard-hit areas.[17] For instance, although the economic decline in Sub-Saharan Africa is projected to be more modest than in advanced economies, it will likely spur one of the largest increases in extreme poverty: some 27 million to 40 million new poor, reflecting the large number of people who were living on the edge of poverty. In South Asia, some 49 million to 57 million people may be newly impoverished (see chapter 1, figure 1.5).

A large share of the new poor will be concentrated in countries that are already struggling with high poverty rates, but middle-income countries will also be significantly affected. Overall, some 72 million of the projected new poor will be in middle-income countries—more than four-fifths of the total new poor. When applying the higher regional poverty thresholds appropriate for lower-middle-income countries (US$3.20 a day) and upper-middle-income countries (US$5.50 a day), the poverty impact of COVID-19 will be much greater.

The world's new poor may differ from those who were already poor in more than just the income-level composition of their countries of residence. Within countries, a large share of the global poor are rural, whereas many of the new poor are likely to be found in congested urban settings, which can serve as a conduit for the spread of the pandemic. Many of the new poor are likely to be engaged in informal services, construction, and manufacturing, rather than agriculture. These are sectors in which economic activity is most affected by lockdowns and other mobility restrictions as well as continued social distancing. Recent simulations of profiles of the new poor based on population-weighted estimates from a sample of 110 countries show that the new poor are projected to be more likely to live in urban areas, live in dwellings with better access to infrastructure, and own slightly more basic assets than those who are poor in both 2019 and 2020. The new poor who are age 15 years and older are also more likely to be paid employees and work more in nonagriculture (manufacturing, service, commerce sectors) than the chronic poor. The new poor tend to be more educated than the chronic poor, and significantly less educated than the nonpoor (of those age 15 and older).[18] An important caveat is that these estimates assume that the relationship between gross domestic product (GDP) per capita growth and (change in) poverty is distribution neutral in all countries, which implies that a loss in GDP affects all parts of the distribution proportionately. If that were not the case (that is, if the crisis affects some groups more than others) the profile and composition of the poor may be more or less heterogeneous.

Preliminary country-level estimates of COVID-19 poverty impacts reflect these patterns. In Indonesia, the sharpest relative increase in poverty is estimated to be in urban centers, precisely where pre-pandemic poverty rates were lowest (World Bank 2020b, 2020c). Across sectors, a much higher share of the new poor (compared with the pre-COVID-19 poor) are in traditional services (wholesale and retail, transport and warehousing, accommodation and restaurants, and other sectors), and a much smaller share in agriculture. In Armenia and Georgia, the new poor are similarly less likely to be from rural areas, and more than a third of them have tertiary education (compared with 10 percent in Armenia and 14 percent in Georgia, among the poor before COVID-19).

This new composition of the poor matters for policy. Although many countries are experiencing issues with the targeting and coverage of existing safety nets, support to the existing poor who are already covered by such programs can be mobilized relatively quickly. Meanwhile, those in the informal sector affected by job and income losses, along with seasonal migrants and refugees, may not always be covered by the emergency response measures being deployed. Evidence from Indonesia suggests that more than half of those employed in traditional services (and almost 60 percent of the self-employed) would not be covered by the various food assistance and cash transfer programs aiming to mitigate the impact of the pandemic on the poor. In Armenia and Georgia, 27 percent and 49 percent, respectively, of the existing poor are covered by the flagship social assistance programs, compared with only 9 percent and 4 percent among the new poor.

As indicated earlier in this chapter, the deleterious effects of conflict and of climate change on poverty are also likely to be concentrated among those whose incomes are not far above the poverty threshold and are likely to fall back into poverty because of the pandemic. A profile of the population below the US$3.20-a-day threshold provides a better sense of the global poverty profile for households that may fall below the international poverty line because of the COVID-19 pandemic or other negative income shocks. This profile of the core sociodemographic characteristics of the population below the US$3.20-a-day threshold shows that it is also predominantly rural, underaged, underschooled, and with higher exposure to armed conflict. As indicated in previous paragraphs, new evidence shows that the "new poor" are different, but the total profile of global poverty will still contain a large proportion of rural groups, children, and underschooled adults, and a significant share of them will also be affected by armed conflict and climate change–induced shocks. This underscores the double challenge of implementing new and specific policy reactions for the "new poor" without diminishing support to the regularly vulnerable.

Policy implications

The challenges posed by COVID-19 (as with the conflict and climate change risks discussed previously) highlight two important features of the global profile of the poor. First, many of the households that escape extreme poverty as measured by the international poverty line are not necessarily very different from the global poor in their core sociodemographic characteristics, including areas where they reside and their educational attainment. In other words, even if not poor today, they may still be quite vulnerable to external shocks and lack the human, social, and physical capital, or access to services, that would make them resilient to such shocks. Second, these challenges highlight the difficulty of eradicating extreme poverty in Sub-Saharan Africa. Chapter 1 of this report documents both the high incidence of extreme poverty in Sub-Saharan Africa and its stagnation at high levels over the past three decades. This chapter documents the fact that the overlaps between conflict and poverty, and between climate risks and poverty, are also most pronounced in Sub-Saharan Africa, and a number of Sub-Saharan African countries are characterized by the triple burden of high poverty incidence, a history of conflict, and high exposure to climate change risks. Our ability to make progress in eradicating extreme poverty globally, and in Sub-Saharan Africa in particular, will require formulating effective responses to these challenges.

The pandemic may have an expansive effect that increases the share of people from all regions in the world who reside in urban areas, are better-schooled, and work in nonagricultural sectors. Still, children, women, the less schooled, and the rural population constitute the largest share of the poor and those vulnerable to poverty. Moreover, the poor in general are sometimes more exposed to conflict and climate risks, and are generally less able to cope with these risks. Policies to reduce poverty need to be inclusive and pay special attention to these groups. The usual development efforts to enhance sanitation, education, and inclusive growth are needed to lift the poorest and the more vulnerable out of poverty. These antipoverty policies also require attention to the resolution of conflicts, the mitigation and adaptation to climate change, and an effective combat against the pandemic. The prevention of all risks is also crucially needed for a complete antipoverty policy. In addition, COVID-19 and the ensuing economic crisis calls for a focus on groups that fall into poverty because of the crisis, but who are not the usual beneficiaries of antipoverty programs.

Annex 3A

New vintage of the Global Monitoring Database

Chapter 3 uses the most recent data for each economy from the global harmonized household surveys from the April 2020 vintage of the Global Monitoring Database (GMD). In this vintage there are 147 economies with the latest household survey data that include information on monetary welfare measures and household characteristics. More than 90 percent of the data are taken from surveys fielded between 2010 and 2018. Poverty profiles from the GMD are lined up to 2018.

Changes in profiles over time are based on comparisons of the current vintage to the 2018 vintage used for the previous *Poverty and Shared Prosperity* report. The global poverty profile of this and the previous vintage are updates of the global profile of the poor first reported in Castaneda et al. (2018) for 2013. The methodological details of poverty profiling are presented in the original paper (see also appendix A of World Bank [2018a]). The previous exercise covered 91 economies and lined up the survey-based poverty profiles to 2015.

A full list of the economies with new surveys included in this vintage is included in table 3A.1.

TABLE 3A.1 New Surveys in the Global Monitoring Database, April 2020 Vintage

Economy	Survey used	Economy	Survey used	Economy	Survey used
Albania	HBS 2017	Georgia	HIS 2018	North Macedonia	SILC-C 2017
Angola	IDREA 2018	Ghana	GLSS-VII 2016	Norway	EU-SILC 2018
Argentina	EPHC-S2 2018	Greece	EU-SILC 2018	Panama	EH 2018
Armenia	ILCS 2018	Guinea-Bissau	ILAP-II 2010	Paraguay	EPH 2018
Austria	EU-SILC 2018	Honduras	EPHPM 2018	Peru	ENAHO 2018
Belarus	HHS 2018	Hungary	EU-SILC 2018	Poland	EU-SILC 2018
Belgium	EU-SILC 2018	Iceland	EU-SILC 2016	Portugal	EU-SILC 2018
Bhutan	BLSS 2017	Iran, Islamic Rep.	HEIS 2017	Romania	EU-SILC 2018
Bolivia	EH 2018	Ireland	EU-SILC 2017	Rwanda	EICV-V 2016
Bosnia and Herzegovina	HBS 2011	Italy	EU-SILC 2018	São Tomé and Príncipe	IOF 2017
Botswana	BMTHS 2015	Jordan	HEIS 2010	Serbia	HBS 2018
Brazil	PNADC-E1 2018	Kazakhstan	HBS 2017	Seychelles	HBS 2013
Bulgaria	EU-SILC 2018	Kosovo	HBS 2017	Sierra Leone	SLIHS 2018
Burkina Faso	EMC 2014	Kyrgyz Republic	KIHS 2018	Slovak Republic	EU-SILC 2017
Cabo Verde	IDRF 2015	Latvia	EU-SILC 2018	Slovenia	EU-SILC 2018
Chile	CASEN 2017	Lesotho	CMSHBS 2017	Spain	EU-SILC 2018
Colombia	GEIH 2018	Liberia	HIES 2016	Sweden	EU-SILC 2018
Costa Rica	ENAHO 2018	Lithuania	EU-SILC 2018	Switzerland	EU-SILC 2018
Croatia	EU-SILC 2018	Luxembourg	EU-SILC 2018	Tanzania	HBS 2018
Cyprus	EU-SILC 2018	Malawi	IHS-IV 2016	Thailand	SES 2017
Czech Republic	EU-SILC 2018	Malaysia	HIS 2016	Timor-Leste	TLSLS 2014
Denmark	EU-SILC 2018	Maldives	HIES 2016	Tonga	HIES 2015
Djibouti	EDAM 2017	Malta	EU-SILC 2018	Tunisia	NSHBCSL 2015
Dominican Rep.	ECNFT-Q03 2018	Mauritius	HBS 2017	Turkey	HICES 2018
Ecuador	ENEMDU 2018	Mexico	ENIGHNS 2018	Tuvalu	HIES 2010
Egypt, Arab Rep.	HIECS 2017	Moldova	HBS 2018	Ukraine	HLCS 2014
El Salvador	EHPM 2018	Montenegro	SILC-C 2016	United Kingdom	EU-SILC 2017
Estonia	EU-SILC 2018	Morocco	ENCDM 2013	Uruguay	ECH 2018
Eswatini	HIES 2016	Namibia	NHIES 2015	Vanuatu	HIES 2010
Finland	EU-SILC 2018	Nepal	LSS-III 2010	West Bank and Gaza	PECS 2016
France	EU-SILC 2018	Netherlands	EU-SILC 2018		
Gabon	EGEP 2017	Nigeria	HBS 2018		

Sources: Global Monitoring Database, Data for Goals (D4G), World Bank, Washington, DC.
Note: The survey year reported in this table refers to the starting year of survey fieldwork. For economies where EU-SILC is used, the income data is from the year prior to the survey year. For example, the EU-SILC 2018 survey uses income data from 2017.

Annex 3B

Robustness of poverty profiles: Adding and subtracting countries

This profile of the poor is based on harmonized household surveys from 147 economies in the GMD. It updates the previous profile, which was based on the harmonized data for 91 countries for 2015. Table 3B.1 describes how this new database represents the global population and the population in extreme poverty (that is, below the international poverty line of US$1.90 a day) in each region except South Asia. The low coverage among high-income countries is due to lack of data-sharing agreements rather than to a lack of data.

The new profile of the poor comes with an important caveat: it misses a large group of the global poor, those who live in India. Although chapter 1 of this report presents a poverty range estimate for India in 2017, not having detailed micro data from an up-to-date survey makes it impossible to describe profiles of the population living below the international poverty line in India. This is an important omission, given that India accounts for 139 million of the total 689 million people living in poverty in 2017. Do the demographic characteristics of the global poor change dramatically, depending on whether India is included in the global data set? Without new micro data for India, this question cannot be answered directly.[19] However, table 3B.2 presents the results of a counterfactual exercise for the earlier 2015 global poverty profile, estimating it with and without data for India. The key message from this exercise is that excluding India from the global profile does not alter the urban-rural or gender profile of the global poor, but it does increase the relative share of children up to age 14 among the global poor by 2 percentage points. The most notable implication of excluding India from the 2015 global

profile of the poor is that it decreases the share of poor adults (age 15 and older) with no schooling from 42.6 percent to 36.3 percent and increases the share of the poor with primary education from 32.4 percent to 34.6 percent.

In addition to describing the profile of the poor in 2018 on the basis of the most recent available survey data, this chapter also examines whether the 2018 profile differs in notable ways from the profile of the poor in 2015. One notable difference, already mentioned, relates to the expanded set of micro data for 2018 that allows for more complete coverage of the population (and of the global poor). This raises questions about whether any observed changes over time may be due to changes in sample composition. This is explored in table 3B.3, which reproduces the 2018 profile for the full set of economies and for the subset of economies that constitutes a country panel with 2015. The results show that the global profile based on the panel looks virtually identical to the profile based on the full 2018 sample, in part because the increase in the total number of economies with micro data in the 2018 global profile largely reflects the inclusion of high-income economies and countries in the Europe and Central Asia region. Because the incidence of international poverty in these countries is very low on average, their inclusion does not substantially change the core characteristics of the global poor. For consistency, this chapter describes the changes in the profile of the poor over time by comparing the 2015 and 2018 profile for a panel of economies present in both years. But the estimates in table 3B.3 suggest that this does not imply a loss of generality.

TABLE 3B.1 Coverage of the Global Population and of the Poor, by Region, without India

Region	Share of global population (%)	Share of poor (%)
East Asia and Pacific	97.34	97.17
Europe and Central Asia	98.82	98.71
Latin America and the Caribbean	96.45	96.51
Middle East and North Africa	86.14	96.52
Other high income	31.05	21.21
South Asia without India	91.74	89.75
Sub-Saharan Africa	96.83	96.97
Total	**84.47**	**95.64**

Source: World Bank estimates based on Global Monitoring Database data.

TABLE 3B.2 Implications of Removing India from the Global Profile of the Poor

	Share of the global poor (%)		Share of the global population (%)	
	With India	**Without India**	**With India**	**Without India**
Age group				
0–14	44.6	46.6	27.1	26.6
15–24	17.0	17.1	16.6	16.0
25–34	13.2	12.5	16.0	15.8
35–44	10.3	9.9	13.5	13.6
45–54	6.7	6.5	11.7	12.1
55–64	4.4	4.0	8.3	8.6
65–older	3.7	3.5	7.0	7.4
Sector of employment (age 15 and older)				
Agriculture	62.2	65.6	29.2	24.5
Nonagriculture	37.8	34.4	70.8	75.5
Level of education (age 15 and older)				
No education	42.6	36.3	20.4	11.7
Primary (complete or incomplete)	32.4	34.6	32.3	37.0
Secondary (complete or incomplete)	22.3	24.4	32.4	31.4
Tertiary (complete or incomplete)	2.7	4.8	14.8	19.9
Sex				
Female	50.4	50.5	49.3	50.0
Male	49.6	49.5	50.7	50.0
Residence				
Rural	78.6	78.0	53.7	48.3
Urban	21.4	22.0	46.3	51.7

Source: World Bank estimates based on Global Monitoring Database data.
Note: Numbers are based on the 2015 global poverty profile.

TABLE 3B.3 **Comparing the 2018 Poverty Profile (Full Set of Economies) with Those Economies also Present in the 2015 Poverty Profile**

	Share of the global poor (%)		Share of the global population (%)	
	Full sample	Panel	Full sample	Panel
Age group				
0–14	49.3	49.4	25.4	25.4
15–24	16.3	16.2	15.2	15.3
25–34	11.5	11.5	13.6	13.7
35–44	9.4	9.5	13.6	13.8
45–54	6.2	6.3	12.6	12.8
55–64	3.7	3.8	10.3	10.3
65–older	3.4	3.4	9.2	8.6
Sector of employment (age 15 and older)				
Agriculture	68.0	70.1	23.8	25.5
Nonagriculture	32.0	29.9	76.2	74.5
Level of education (age 15 and older)				
No education	36.0	35.8	11.2	11.1
Primary (complete or incomplete)	35.4	35.0	34.4	37.4
Secondary (complete or incomplete)	26.0	26.4	33.1	30.5
Tertiary (complete or incomplete)	2.7	2.8	21.3	21.0
Sex				
Female	51.1	51.1	50.5	50.4
Male	48.9	48.9	49.5	49.6
Type of residence				
Rural	80.6	81.1	47.8	49.1
Urban	19.4	18.9	52.2	50.9

Source: World Bank estimates based on Global Monitoring Database data.

Annex 3C

Construction of the Global Subnational Atlas of Poverty, Second edition

The Global Subnational Atlas of Poverty (GSAP) is produced by the World Bank's Poverty and Equity Global Practice, coordinated by the Data for Goals (D4G) team, and supported by the six regional statistics teams in the Poverty and Equity Global Practice. The second edition of the GSAP includes lineup poverty estimates in 2018 for 166 economies based on the latest available survey data in GMD for each economy, with 95 percent of the data ranging from 2010 to 2018. The most recent household survey is used for each country in GMD, with some Europe and Central Asia region countries using Luxembourg Income Study data. Poverty is shown for more than 1,900 subnational areas based on survey representativeness and availability of matched spatial boundaries. Further technical details about the construction of the subnational poverty maps can be found in Azevedo et al. (2018).

There are some exceptions. For China, because of the lack of microdata, the subnational map is based on the 2018 official estimates of poverty in rural areas, published by the National Bureau of Statistics. For India, the subnational estimates are based on the 2015 lineup estimates because there are no lineup data for India for 2018. Poverty can only be shown at the national level for 23 economies.

Because the household surveys necessary to measure poverty are conducted in different years and at varying frequencies across economies, producing global and regional poverty estimates entails bringing each of the economy-level poverty estimates to a common reference, or "lineup" year. For economies with surveys available in the reference year, the direct estimates of poverty from the surveys are used. For other cases, the poverty estimates are imputed for the reference year using the country's recent household survey data and real growth rates from national accounts data. The procedures for this exercise depend on the survey years available for the country.

When a survey is available only before the reference year, the consumption (or income) vector from the latest survey is extrapolated forward to the reference year using real growth rates of per capita GDP (or household final consumption expenditure) obtained from national accounts. Each observation in the welfare distribution is multiplied by the growth rate in per capita GDP (or household final consumption expenditure) between the reference year and the time of the survey. Poverty measures can then be estimated for the reference year. This procedure assumes distribution-neutral growth—that is, no change in inequality—and that the growth in national accounts is fully transmitted to growth in household consumption or income. If the only available surveys are after the reference year, a similar approach is applied to extrapolate backward. More details can be found in Prydz et al. (2019).

Notes

1. The Global Monitoring Database (GMD) is an ex post harmonization effort based on available multitopic household surveys, including household budget surveys and the Living Standards Measurement Study. The data are stored on secure servers accessible only to subscribed or approved users. A brief description of surveys included is described in annex 3A.

2. In this chapter, India is not included in the numerator and denominator of the World and South Asia population and population in poverty groups and the distribution of these groups by demographic characteristics (see below in the chapter). For details on the composition and comparability of the current version of the GMD, as well as the impact of the lack of survey data on the profiles of the global poor produced in this chapter, see annex 3B.

3. The reader is reminded that these comparisons are based on global data without India. Annex 3B explains that global poverty profiles without India underestimate the proportion of the poor without schooling.

4. See chapter 5 in World Bank (2018a) for a detailed discussion of the difficulties in accounting properly for intrahousehold resource allocation, as would be necessary to estimate poverty separately for each member of a given household.

5. As indicated in notes 2 and 3, and in annex 3b, the lack of India survey data may affect the intertemporal comparison of profiles by education and age. Moreover, different definitions of age groups for children may render different results. For a discussion, see Silwal et al. (forthcoming).

6. For a detailed discussion of the issue of uncounted populations, see Parry (2020).

7. "FY20 List of Fragile and Conflict-Affected Situations," World Bank, Washington, DC, http://pubdocs.worldbank.org/en/1760015944 07411053/FCSList-FY06toFY20.pdf.

8. The six components of the Human Capital Index are (1) probability of survival to age five, (2) fraction of children under five not stunted, (3) adult survival rate, (4) expected years of schooling, (5) harmonized test scores, and (6) learning-adjusted years of school. See HCI (Human Capital Index) (database), World Bank, Washington, DC, https://datacatalog. worldbank.org/dataset/human-capital-index.

9. For details on the construction of the Global Subnational Atlas of Poverty and the construction of poverty estimates for principal subdivisions of subnational territories or administrative divisions, such as provinces or states, see annex 3C.

10. An area is designated conflict affected if it has a debt burden value of 0.19 or higher (see definition of conflict debt in the note to map 3.1). This threshold is chosen because the empirical relationship between poverty and conflict debt of less than 0.19 is not statistically significant. For a single-year conflict episode, this threshold is equivalent to nine consecutive years of peace. For details, see Mueller and Techasunthornwat (2020). Note that the conflict data refer to both current and historic conflict. For instance, for Nepal, the conflict data used to compute the share of poor in areas with a conflict history refer to the period 2002–04.

11. These are unweighted estimates, averaging over the shares of the poor in areas with conflict debt across countries within a given region.

12. These figures are consistent with earlier estimates from the World Bank's *Shock Waves* report, which estimates that, if unaddressed, climate change has the potential to push more than 100 million people into poverty by 2030 (Hallegatte et al. 2016).

13. Winsemius et al. (2015) examine the poverty exposure bias to droughts and floods, or the ratio between the share of poor people exposed to a hazard and the share of the total population exposed minus one, such that a positive value identifies greater exposure of the poor and a negative value a greater degree of exposure of the nonpoor population.

14. The risk categories are based on data in "Think Hazard," Global Facility for Disaster Reduction and Recovery, World Bank, Washington, DC, https://thinkhazard.org/en/.

15. In Nepal, the share of the poor in conflict-affected areas is based on historic conflict debt, as measured in 2010, which is the year for which poverty estimates are available, and conflict data refer back to the period 2002–04.

16. For consistency with the rest of the chapter, this regional distribution does not include India because of lack of survey data with which to engage in detailed demographic profiling. However, on the basis of nowcast data in chapter 1, if India is included, the share within the global poor of South Asia's poor under the US$3.20-a-day poverty line becomes as large as Sub-Saharan Africa's, that is, approximately 40 percent each. See chapter 1, annex 1A.

17. This section relies heavily on Lakner et al. (2020) and World Bank (2020b, 2020c).

18. World Bank estimates as of August 6, 2020 (https://www.worldbank.org/en/topic/poverty/brief/Profiles-of-the-new-poor-due-to-the-COVID-19-pandemic).

19. Other sources of data on India are available, such as the India National Family Health Survey (from the Central Statistics Office), or the Centre for Monitoring Indian Economy survey data, but the World Bank relies on certain official surveys that are specially designed for poverty measurement. The results of India's most recent consumption expenditures survey are not currently available, for reasons explained in chapter 1, box 1.2.

References

Abadie, Alberto, and Javier Gardeazabal. 2003. "The Economic Costs of Conflict: A Case Study of the Basque Country." *American Economic Review* 93 (1): 113–32.

Akresh, Richard, Sonia Bhalotra, Marinella Leone, and Una Okonkwo Osili. 2012. "War and Stature: Growing up during the Nigerian Civil War." *American Economic Review* 102 (3): 273–77.

Akresh, Richard, Philip Verwimp, and Tom Bundervoet. 2011. "Civil War, Crop Failure, and Child Stunting in Rwanda." *Economic Development and Cultural Change* 59 (4): 777–810.

Azevedo, João Pedro, Minh Cong Nguyen, Paul Andres Corral Rodas, Hongxi Zhao, Q. Lu, J. J. Lee, Raul Andres Castaneda Aguilar, et al. 2018. "Global Subnational Poverty: An Illustration of the Global Geodatabase of Household Surveys." World Bank, Washington, DC.

Beegle, Kathleen, and Luc Christiaensen, eds. 2019. *Accelerating Poverty Reduction in Africa*. Washington, DC: World Bank.

Bundervoet, Tom, Philip Verwimp, and Richard Akresh. 2009. "Health and Civil War in Rural Burundi." *Journal of Human Resources* 44 (2): 536–63.

Carr-Hill, Roy. 2013. "Missing Millions and Measuring Development Progress." *World Development* 46 (June): 30–44.

Castañeda, Andrés, Dung Doan, David Newhouse, Minh Cong Nguyen, Hiroki Uematsu, João Pedro Azevedo, and World Bank Data for Goals Group. 2018. "A New Profile of the Global Poor." *World Development* 101 (C): 250–67.

Collier, Paul. 1999. "On the Economic Consequences of Civil War." *Oxford Economic Papers* 51 (1): 168–83.

Corral, Paul, Alexander Irwin, Nandini Krishnan, Daniel Gerszon Mahler, and Tara Vishwanath. 2020. *Fragility and Conflict: On the Front Lines of the Fight against Poverty*. Washington, DC: World Bank.

Dijkstra, Lewis, Ellen Hamilton, Somik Lall, and Sameh Wahba. 2020. "How Do We Define Cities, Towns, and Rural Areas?" *Sustainable Cities* (blog), March 10, 2020. https://blogs.worldbank.org/sustainablecities/how-do-we-define-cities-towns-and-rural-areas.

Ghobarah, Hazem A., Paul Huth, and Bruce Russett. 2003. "Civil Wars Kill and Maim People—Long after the Shooting Stops." *American Political Science Review* 97 (2): 189–202.

Hallegatte, Stéphane, Mook Bangalore, Laura Bonzanigo, Marianne Fay, Tamaro Kane, Ulf Narloch, Julie Rozenberg, David Treguer, and Adrien Vogt-Schilb. 2016. *Shock Waves: Managing the Impacts of Climate Change on Poverty*. Climate Change and Development Series. Washington, DC: World Bank.

Hallegatte, Stéphane, and Jun Erik Maruyama Rentschler. 2015. "Risk Management for Development: Assessing Obstacles and Prioritizing Action." *Risk Analysis* 35 (2): 193–210.

Jafino, Bramka Arga, Brian Walsh, Stéphane Hallegatte, and Julie Rozenberg. 2020. "Outlook of Future Shared Prosperity and Extreme Poverty under Socioeconomic and Climactic Uncertainties." Background paper for this report, World Bank, Washington, DC.

Lakner, Christoph, Daniel Gerszon Mahler, Mario Negre, and Espen Beer Prydz. 2020. "How Much Does Reducing Inequality Matter for Global Poverty?" Global Poverty Monitoring Technical Note 13 (June), World Bank, Washington, DC.

Mueller, Hannes. 2016. "Growth and Violence: Argument for a Per Capita Measure of Civil War." *Economica* 83 (331): 473–97.

Mueller, Hannes, and Chanon Techasunthornwat. 2020. "Conflict and Poverty." Background paper for this report, World Bank, Washington, DC.

Mueller, Hannes, and Julia Tobias. 2016. "The Cost of Violence: Estimating the Economic Impact of Conflict." IGC Growth Brief 007, International Growth Centre, London School of Economics and Political Science, London.

Muñoz-Boudet, Ana María, Antra Bhatt, Ginette Azcona, Jayne Jungsun Yoo, and Kathleen Beegle. 2020. "A Global View of Poverty, Gender, and Household Composition." World Bank, Washington, DC.

Narayan, Ambar, Roy van der Weide, Alexandru Cojocaru, Christoph Lakner, Silvia Redaelli, Daniel Gerszon Mahler, Rakesh Gupta N. Ramasubbaiah, and Stefan Thewissen. 2018. *Fair Progress? Economic Mobility across Generations around the World.* Equity and Development Series. Washington, DC: World Bank.

Parry, Katie. 2020. "Missing Persons." Background paper for this report, World Bank, Washington, DC.

Prydz, Espen Beer, Dean Jolliffe, Christoph Lakner, Daniel Gerszon Mahler, and Prem Sangraula. 2019. "National Accounts Data Used in Global Poverty Measurement." World Bank, Washington, DC.

Rentschler, Jun Erik Maruyama. 2013. "Why Resilience Matters: The Poverty Impact of Disasters." Policy Research Working Paper 6699, World Bank, Washington, DC.

Rentschler, Jun, and Melda Salhab. 2020. "People in Harm's Way: Flood Exposure Analysis for 189 Countries." Background paper, World Bank, Washington, DC.

Silwal, Ani Rudra, Solrun Engilbertsdottir, Jose Cuesta, Enrique Delamónica, David Newhouse, and David Stewart. Forthcoming. "Updated Global Estimates of Children in Monetary Poverty." World Bank, Washington, DC.

Simler, Kenneth. 2016. "Pinpointing Poverty in Europe: New Evidence for Policy Making." Poverty and Equity Global Practice, World Bank, Washington, DC.

Singhal, Saurabh. 2019. "Early Life Shocks and Mental Health: The Long-Term Effect of War in Vietnam." *Journal of Development Economics* 141 (November): 102244.

UNHCR (United Nations High Commissioner for Refugees). 2019. "Global Trends: Forced Displacement in 2018." June 20, UNHCR, Geneva.

UNHCS (United Nations Human Settlement Programme). 2003. *Global Report on Human Settlements 2013: Planning and Design for Sustainable Urban Mobility.* Nairobi, Kenya: UNHCS; New York: Routledge.

Winsemius, Hessel C., Brenden Jongman, Ted I. E. Veldkamp, Stéphane Hallegatte, Mook Bangalore, and Philip J. Ward. 2015. "Disaster Risk, Climate Change, and Poverty: Assessing the Global Exposure of Poor People to Floods and Droughts." Policy Research Working Paper 7480, World Bank, Washington, DC.

World Bank. 2017. *Monitoring Global Poverty: Report of the Commission on Global Poverty.* Washington, DC: World Bank.

World Bank, 2018a. *Poverty and Shared Prosperity 2018: Piecing Together the Poverty Puzzle.* Washington, DC: World Bank.

World Bank. 2018b. "The Human Capital Project." World Bank, Washington, DC.

World Bank. 2020a. *World Bank Group Strategy for Fragility, Conflict, and Violence 2020–2025.* Washington, DC: World Bank.

World Bank. 2020b. "Poverty and Distributional Impact of COVID-19 Shock in Indonesia." Poverty and Equity Global Practice, World Bank, Washington, DC.

World Bank. 2020c. "Profiles of the New Poor Due to the COVID-19 Pandemic." August 6, Poverty and Equity Global Practice, World Bank, Washington, DC.

Navigating Tough Terrain: Sound Principles, Good Maps, and Adaptive Learning

4

The recent slowdown in inclusive growth and global poverty reduction has suddenly intensified into a historic reversal. This turnaround is primarily the result of COVID-19 (coronavirus), which has already precipitated the worst economic crisis in 80 years, but the reversal is being accentuated by violent conflict in some countries and the steadily intensifying effects of climate change the world over. The most urgent challenge is halting the spread of COVID-19 and its impact on lives and livelihoods, even as more familiar development problems remain and are likely to deepen the longer COVID-19 persists. Responding effectively to both COVID-19 and persistent development issues will require devising sound policies, but their successful realization will entail building robust and adaptive implementation systems, while leaders will also need to secure widespread citizen support for response measures that are likely to be contentious and onerous, especially for the poor. Hence, discerning how to ensure the legitimacy of these measures will be vital. The urgency of this moment cannot be overstated: the longer it takes to find and enact effective responses, the harder these challenges will become.

Halting COVID-19 and reversing its economic effects will require a combination of familiar and new approaches. Governments need to act decisively to expand financial support to vulnerable households and small businesses, and to prudently take on the debt needed to pay for this support. The very novelty, complexity, and intensity of this moment, however, mean that much needs to be learned—quickly, effectively, at scale, by everyone. This effort will entail creating space for innovative local responses from communities and firms, widely sharing emerging lessons through communities of practice, and forging a strong sense of collective purpose. Collecting and curating data will be central to tracking the effectiveness of these responses, to allocating scarce resources to where they are needed most, and to equalizing opportunities. The situation underscores the importance of investing in comprehensive prevention, preparedness, and resilience measures to minimize the likelihood that such catastrophic events happen in the first place, and, if they do happen, to ensure that decisive early steps can be taken and that the most vulnerable groups are protected. Global problems ultimately require global solutions, underscoring the need for cooperation and coordination at all levels, and for giving full support to organizations and procedures that are designed to serve precisely this purpose.

Introduction

After nearly a quarter century of steady global declines in extreme poverty to historically unprecedented levels, there has been a sudden reversal. This setback stems overwhelmingly from the effects of a pandemic (COVID-19) and the global economic crisis it has caused. However, in some places the reversal is being accentuated by violent conflict (the effects of which have been accumulating in recent years) and climate change (a slowly accelerating risk that is already driving millions into poverty). In one sense, these challenges are new versions of old calamities. Pandemics—and contagious diseases more generally—have existed since humans began domesticating animals and living in urban settlements, thousands of years ago. Humans have been in violent conflict with each other throughout recorded history and long before. Across the ages, erratic weather, natural disasters, and changing temperatures have led to droughts, famines, floods, plagues, and migrations. Instances of all these challenges are cited in ancient texts, emblematic of the extent to which humans and nature, singularly or in concert, can inflict enormous suffering, especially on those least able to protect themselves.

But the current moment is different. How the world responds to the three major challenges today, especially COVID-19, will have a direct bearing on whether the current reversals in global poverty reduction can be turned around. Effective responses must begin by recognizing what makes these challenges not just different and difficult, but so devastating for the poor. COVID-19 may not be the world's first pandemic, but no previous disease has become a global threat so quickly or been experienced simultaneously in every country in the world; its scale, the uncertainties created, and the pervasive externalities to which it gives rise are without precedent. Never before have the world's poorest people resided so disproportionately in conflict-affected territories and countries, including parts of middle-income economies (Corral et al. 2020). Changes in global weather patterns induced by human activity are also unprecedented, with vastly disproportionate contributions from wealthy countries affecting the entire world, while the poorest countries and peoples suffer the most. Responding effectively to these challenges requires collective action at all levels (Ferguson 2020).

The key messages from the preceding three chapters are that (1) poverty is expected to be much higher over the next decade as a result of COVID-19, hence the highest priority needs to be halting the pandemic and resuming inclusive growth as soon as possible; (2) COVID-19 and its associated economic crisis are likely to have uneven impacts on people and places, so measures to prevent widening inequalities are needed, along with inclusive growth; and (3) those falling back into extreme poverty as a result of COVID-19 (the "new poor") have certain distinctive characteristics (mostly urban, working in services and informal businesses), so targeted policies focused on their specific needs are essential (Nguyen et al. 2020). Previous chapters also stressed, however, that rates of global poverty reduction were declining before COVID-19, that the addition of the "new poor" only partly changes the overall global profile of people living in extreme poverty (who will remain predominantly rural, underaged, and underschooled), and thus that much remains to be done to promote development policies focused on global poverty reduction, inclusive growth, human capital accumulation, and protection against risks.

This moment is also different because COVID-19, conflict, and climate change are the downside effects of processes that make development itself, and thus poverty reduction, possible. The transmission of COVID-19 around the world in a matter of weeks is a product of globalization, which enables rapid, low-cost, high-volume, worldwide exchange of both goods and "bads." The same mechanisms that enable global trade and travel also spread diseases and generate vast amounts of carbon dioxide, while supporting the flow of weapons, illicit funds, and digital threats (World Bank 2020f). Without effective governance and political will, both within and between countries, navigating between opportunities and risks is harder than ever, making it more likely that the negative effects of the risks will occur more frequently (Rodrik 1999, 2011).

The poorest suffer most from COVID-19, conflict, and climate change

All countries and population groups are experiencing the human and economic effects of COVID-19, conflict, and climate change; but the poor and vulnerable suffer the most. In both the baseline and downside scenarios described in this report, more than 80 percent of the more than 100 million people likely to fall back into extreme poverty in 2020 are projected to come from middle income economies, reflecting the vulnerability of those who have ostensibly escaped extreme poverty.[1] Even in wealthy countries, it is likely to be the poorest who face the highest incidence of the virus and the highest death rates (Cajner et al. 2020; Hooper, Nápoles, and Pérez-Stable 2020; Yancy 2020). As documented in chapter 3, the effects of COVID-19—as well as climate change and violent conflict—fall hardest on the poor, less because of their exposure to such risks than because of their high vulnerability. Poor people's vulnerability reflects a lack of access to institutional resilience mechanisms (such as social protection, insurance, and credit), possession of few leveragable assets, and reliance on low-quality public services, among other factors. COVID-19 disproportionately affects the poor because low-income communities around the world have the lowest coverage and quality of medical care, and because choices involved in enacting effective responses are also the most wrenching for poor people (Brown, Ravallion, and van de Walle 2020).

"Stay-at-home" orders, for example, can be devastating for the poor: because most cannot work from home, they may earn far less income and thus struggle to feed their families, especially if food prices rise as a result of disruptions to supply chains. Data from COVID-19 phone surveys in Nigeria suggest that fully 85 percent of households have experienced rising food prices, with half reducing their food consumption as a coping strategy (Siwatu et al. 2020). If sustained, this pattern could have enduring effects on children's cognitive development and on adult health and productivity.[2] The places where the poorest work and live are least likely to

be able to accommodate social distancing, home-based work, and remote learning during sustained school closures (Dingel and Neiman 2020; Van Lancker and Parolin 2020). As of August 2020, more than a billion children—about two-thirds of the world's learners—remained affected by school closures,[3] leaving the task of educating and caring for young children to the family. But poorer families are more constrained in the time, resources, and quiet spaces for learning they can provide. The poorest individuals, especially refugees and migrants, may also lack the formal identification and linguistic capacity needed to secure any available government assistance and to protect their basic human rights (Kluge et al. 2020). Stringent lockdown measures are likely to lead women and children to suffer heightened levels of domestic violence (Galea, Merchant, and Lurie 2020; UN Women 2020).

More broadly, and beyond COVID-19's immediate public health and human capital effects, a deepening recession is predicted to result in a global growth decline of 5.2 percent in 2020, the steepest drop in eight decades. The enduring effects of this recession could leave lasting scars (World Bank 2020a)—on investment levels, remittance flows, the skills and health of the millions rendered unemployed, learning outcomes (from closure of schools), and disrupted supply chains. Unlike other recent global economic crises, which spared some regions or had offsetting factors that reduced their severity (such as high commodity prices or sustained growth in China), the current economic recession is truly global and cross-sectoral. Thus, its effects are likely to be widespread and enduring, and recovery slow (Reinhart and Reinhart 2020). As a result of this global recession, inclusive growth is set to decline in the coming years, as noted in chapter 2 of this report, in all but 13 of the 91 economies for which data projections are available. Lessons from the long-term effects of previous pandemics suggest that the scale of COVID-19 will lead to an increase in economic inequality, a decline in social mobility, and lower resilience to future shocks (Hill and Narayan 2020; International Monetary Fund and World Bank 2020).

Conflict also has especially pernicious effects on the poorest. In its most extreme form, violence can lead to wars that destroy lives, households, assets, and natural resources, leaving a legacy from which a society may take many years to recover. Research conducted for this report shows that widespread violence creates a "conflict debt," measured by the incidence of poverty over time, which can be "repaid" only if stable peace can be achieved. If conflict resumes, initial gains can quickly be lost. Even after a decade of peace, about a quarter of this conflict debt is likely to remain (Mueller and Techasunthornwat 2020). An assessment of the conflict in the Syrian Arab Republic between 2011 and 2016 suggests that the country's gross domestic product declined by US$226 billion (World Bank 2017b) during this period. As noted in chapter 1, the intensity of recent wars in the Middle East and North Africa has resulted in rising poverty at all levels, with regional extreme poverty increasing from 2.3 percent in 2013 to 7.2 percent in 2018 (Corral et al. 2020). Likewise, the effects of violent conflict on physical and mental health can endure long after peace is established (Ghobarah, Huth, and Russett 2003).[4]

For the poorest small countries, climate change is perhaps the most difficult challenge, and the problem is not of their own making. New analysis presented in this report, refining earlier estimates, indicates that an additional 132 million people may fall into poverty by 2030 because of the combined effects of climate change on productivity, food prices, health, and natural disasters. Human-induced increases in global temperatures and sea levels are almost entirely a product of levels of energy use by high-income nations and large, rapidly growing middle-income economies (Hsiang and Kopp 2018). Poor countries can only adapt, but their efforts stand a better chance of success if rich countries do their part by reducing the intensity of the problem in the first place, providing resources and technical support to facilitate adaptation in low-income economies, and accepting more immigrants (Pritchett and Hani 2020). These actions require sustained global cooperation. Climate change also poses a serious problem of time inconsistency for poor people and cash-strapped governments. Their vastly more pressing concern is to meet basic needs now, rather than making costly sacrifices that will enable

potential benefits to others, but only in the distant future. Despite such tensions, these countries are also the places where children constitute the largest share of the population: making efforts now to reduce climate change is an inescapable moral responsibility to their own future generations.

Because the poorest also reside disproportionately in South Asia and Sub-Saharan Africa—and, in the latter, in situations of fragility and conflict—efforts in these regions to save lives, protect livelihoods, and ensure basic security are especially important, both during and after COVID-19. The poorest people in parts of certain Sub-Saharan African countries (for example, Cameroon, Liberia) and Nepal are potentially susceptible to all the major challenges discussed in this report at the same time: a pandemic, a recession, current or old conflicts (with enduring effects), and climate change (notably through flood risks). In such "hot spot" contexts, an array of responses commensurate with the scale and scope of these compounding challenges will be needed to advance inclusive growth and sustain poverty reduction.

Poverty cannot be fully understood in monetary terms alone. As documented in chapter 1, deprivations in other dimensions such as education, health, housing, and infrastructure are also pervasive and often as damaging to poor people. The multidimensional nature of poverty in countries such as Burkina Faso and Niger, where the effects of income poverty are exacerbated by deprivations in access to basic infrastructure and education, highlights the importance of implementing policies that can address the many obstacles blocking people's efforts to escape from poverty. As part of its response to COVID-19, Niger has announced the Learning Improvement for Results in Education project, which seeks to reach children unable to attend school and develop an online platform to enhance teacher training. In a country where, before COVID-19, half of children between ages 7 and 12 were not in school at all, or completed primary schooling but with few basic skills, the Learning Improvement for Results in Education project has the potential to help families manage the COVID-19 crisis while also modernizing Niger's education system.[5]

Familiar development challenges persist

Although addressing COVID-19 and its associated economic crisis must be the priority now, countries should also remain focused on the obstacles that most poor people face most of the time. These more familiar development challenges do not go away during an emergency; indeed, they are only likely to intensify as a result of the stresses imposed by the pandemic itself and the claims it makes on finite fiscal resources and political attention. It is important to recognize that 80 percent of the world's poor reside in rural areas—and that rural poverty will predominate in the post-COVID-19 recovery period. Chapter 3 documents that the poorest are also primarily children and youth, female, and less educated, which makes it essential to continue long-standing efforts to increase agricultural productivity, expand rural infrastructure and employment options, improve public services (especially health and education), and build better systems to anticipate and manage everyday risks. Such investments are the foundation upon which societies can forge the shared resilience, generate the necessary public resources, and acquire the organizational capability to better anticipate and respond to major challenges in the future. Redoubling efforts on such issues is crucial for reversing the slowdown in global poverty reduction that was already underway before COVID-19, and that will need even stronger support once it has passed.

An enduring development challenge for poor people, especially in rural areas, is that they live in poor places (Hausmann et al. 2014). In such settings, economic returns to people's work and skills are low, assets slowly accumulate but can quickly erode, vulnerability to risks is high, social and physical connections to markets are few, discrimination is common, people's ability to influence broader policy decisions is weak, and public services are of low quality.[6] The consequences for human capital accumulation are often severe. Before COVID-19, for example, a child born in Sub-Saharan Africa could expect to achieve only 40 percent of her potential productivity as an adult worker, given shortfalls in health and education in the region,

meaning that an African child would grow up to be just 58 percent as productive as a child raised in Europe and Central Asia (World Bank 2020c). The isolation of poor places may mean that they are initially spared the worst effects of external forces such as pandemics and armed conflict, but, should such forces eventually arrive, recovery from them in poor settings may also be slower, further eroding the community's resilience, especially if young people, service providers, and business leaders depart for better opportunities elsewhere.

Less dramatic but familiar events can precipitate negative changes in the lives of vulnerable communities. Beyond armed conflict, for example, other forms of conflict also routinely ensue from changes in the norms, rules, and incentives governing everyday life that are brought about by development itself (Barron, Diprose, and Woolcock 2011). These more frequent forms of social conflict include domestic violence (Hoeffler and Fearon 2014), contested claims to land and inheritance, and disputes with mining and logging companies (Berman et al. 2017). The provision of basic education can be socially disruptive if it creates an intergenerational literacy divide and alters expectations of career options, gender relations, marital choices, and familial obligations (see Berry [2015] on Rwanda). A major economic crisis can expose and exacerbate these underlying social fault lines, potentially leading to conflict and mass migrations if effective social protection measures are not in place to mitigate the tensions.

These twin imperatives—of responding to both the novel but urgent needs generated by COVID-19 and the more familiar but important development problems—should be regarded as complementary rather than competing challenges. Lessons emerging from each can fruitfully inform the other. The sections that follow briefly explore the mix of familiar and innovative policy responses to COVID-19 that have been deployed in different countries. Only with the passing of time will it be clear which of these efforts have had lasting success: initial gains from certain responses may subsequently prove ephemeral; others with more modest initial impact may gain greater traction over time; certain responses may succeed in some contexts but greatly disappoint in others; successful pilots may not work at scale. There is certainly no presumption that the approaches described are necessarily the "best" way to respond, but despite the inherent uncertainty, decisive action has had to be taken rapidly in every country. The point of sharing selected examples is the sharing itself—to offer snapshots of what is being done, with the hope that it can usefully inform and inspire efforts elsewhere. Precisely because the current moment is without historical precedent, everyone has much to gain from the experiences of others. Over time, such exchanges can help organizations and teams learn, both in real time now and from subsequent evaluations, how best to navigate such complex development challenges. Through such a process, a more detailed and reliable "map" of this unfamiliar terrain begins to take shape.

Responding to COVID-19 presents unique challenges

Responses at the scale required to combat COVID-19 and its associated economic crisis cost money at levels that many countries cannot afford, even though failing to incur such costs will only make matters worse. Sovereign and corporate debt levels were already at historic highs (Kose et al. 2020) before the global pandemic arrived, driving 90 percent of the world's economies into recession. Compared with 2009, fewer emerging market and developing economies, especially those heavily dependent on tourism, remittances, and energy exports, are well placed to respond with aggressive monetary or fiscal strategies. Because stopping the spread of COVID-19 and protecting livelihoods have become each country's highest priorities (even if the available means for doing so vary enormously), countries have had little choice but to reprioritize spending, mobilize additional fiscal resources, and, if these efforts are insufficient or prove unfeasible, take on additional debt to finance the necessary responses.[7] Though significant investments in additional public health and social protection measures are justified in these circumstances, any additional

debt can lead to higher interest rates, a higher likelihood of cascading defaults—and then to a protracted financial crisis. And, precisely because almost all of the world's major economies are now in recession, none can act as an alternative source of positive growth; thus, the importance of cooperation and coordination between countries and multilateral agencies only intensifies.[8] So, too, do the imperatives to extend debt moratoriums, raise domestic revenue to fund additional support for households and firms, and allow banks to draw down capital and liquidity buffers (World Bank 2020a).

Numerous steps are already being taken on these fronts, though policy makers need to keep a careful eye on the future stability of the financial sector so that they can withdraw certain measures once economies stabilize and growth resumes. Indonesia, for example, has taken assertive steps to curb the human and economic costs of COVID-19, initiating four fiscal policy packages since March 2020, each more expansive than the last, with the most recent, in early June 2020, amounting to 4.2 percent of gross domestic product. These packages have been launched as part of a national economic recovery program, and have focused on (1) boosting the health care sector to expand its COVID-19 testing and treatment capability; (2) increasing social protection programs to low-income households in the form of cash transfers, electricity subsidies, and food aid, and expanding unemployment benefits to workers in the informal sector; (3) implementing tax deductions for individuals (with a ceiling) and those who work in the tourism sector; and (4) applying a permanent reduction of the corporate income tax, from 25 percent to 22 percent in 2020–21 and to 20 percent in 2022. Capital has also been provided to shore up state-owned industries, support credit guarantees, and lend restructuring funds to micro, small, and medium enterprises.[9]

In most countries, responses to COVID-19 and the ensuing economic crisis have rightly prioritized saving lives and protecting the most vulnerable citizens (for example, the elderly), while striving to ensure that livelihoods, jobs, and businesses remain viable in the short term and are primed for a quick and sustained rebound once the worst of the pandemic has passed. Delivering on these goals requires sound policies, strong institutions, and secure investments—especially when large sums of money are being quickly mobilized and dispersed, creating opportunities for misappropriation. From the start of the pandemic, countries have focused on tailoring responses to their specific health, economic, and social shocks, with donors creating various "fast-track" mechanisms to ensure that pressing health concerns, in particular, can be addressed in a timely manner. In countries such as Cambodia and Ethiopia, the response to COVID-19 has entailed securing resources to strengthen public health systems in anticipation of rising demand for protective equipment, as well as upgrading treatment centers, enhancing health-screening facilities, and supporting public communications and outreach.

Countries seeking to protect and promote employment during the COVID-19 crisis are generally following a sequenced strategy based on relief, restructuring, and recovery.[10] During the initial relief phase, efforts have focused on saving livelihoods, especially those of women and informal sector workers. In the subsequent restructuring phase, the emphasis will shift to helping enterprises adjust while sustaining business growth; and in the recovery phase the focus will be on promoting skills, reforms, and tools that contribute to sustainable and resilient enterprise development. In at least 33 countries thus far, such actions have been informed by data from COVID-19 Business Pulse Surveys, which use phone and online platforms to assess the real-time impacts of the pandemic on firms; similar efforts use high-frequency monitoring surveys to track the effects on households and workers (see box 2.2 in chapter 2 of this report). Because crises also create opportunities, recovery may encourage the promotion of regulatory reform and the expansion of investments in digital technology. In Ecuador, the Philippines, and Uganda, for example, such reforms have facilitated increased access to finance, enabled greater logistical support to small and medium enterprises, and expanded workers' awareness of employment opportunities.

A major practical challenge for many governments is providing monetary assistance to those most in need, for example, social protection payments to those who have recently become unemployed. Direct payments of transfers from governments to people are obviously made much faster, more accurately, and at lower cost if they can be made electronically; but the sophistication of systems varies widely between countries. COVID-19 has already prompted more than 55 countries to expand their government-to-people cash transfer systems (Rutkowski et al. 2020). These measures are helping meet citizens' needs now without the additional health risk of face-to-face human interactions, while also building platforms that, when linked in the future to digital identification and financial systems, will be useful in many additional ways for years to come. Chile, Peru, Thailand, and other countries have already developed such platforms.

Importantly, building monetary transfer systems capable of operating safely, reliably, at scale, and for all is not just an issue of technology. It requires corresponding regulatory efforts by government to modernize rules for such transactions and to enable innovative public-private partnerships. Efforts are also needed to reassure people who are illiterate or intimidated by digital tools (often including the elderly) that electronic transactions are safe, reliable, and easy. The poorest countries are also the most likely to lack the resources to invest in the necessary technology. In partnership with the Bill & Melinda Gates Foundation, the World Bank recently launched a government-to-person initiative called G2PX to expand and refine these efforts.[11]

Restarting economies once the worst of the pandemic has passed provides an opportunity for policy makers to enact reforms and choices consistent with sustainability principles.[12] Such principles pertain not just to the environment but also to employment, economic activity, and risk—as well as to longer-term considerations such as building human, social, and cultural capital; upgrading technology and infrastructure; and correcting market failures. Given this report's emphasis on providing more support to those least able to address the effects of climate change, the priority should be to develop systems that help both governments and poor people better prepare for and respond to natural disasters, which are becoming more frequent and intense as climate change advances. India recently deployed targeted efforts to help rural communities confronting COVID-19 in the midst of cyclone season. Relatively few lives were lost in these highly vulnerable settings, thanks to effective preparedness, demonstrating the importance of such initiatives and the steady improvements that are being made (Kishore 2020).

How might strategies to reverse reversals be strengthened and sustained?

In the current moment, the highest priorities everywhere must be defeating COVID-19 (saving lives) and then reviving economies (restoring livelihoods). Failure to act comprehensively now will create even bigger challenges in the future, especially for the poorest. Some of the policies and delivery mechanisms needed to achieve these priorities, such as social protection systems, are already in place. For example, efforts are well underway in Brazil and Indonesia to expand existing cash transfer programs. Digital technologies can, in principle, facilitate the implementation of such programs in ways that would not have been possible a decade ago; but these solutions risk further exacerbating a digital divide if the poorest cannot access the delivery systems. This divide has been especially consequential in education, where gaps have become readily apparent in students' access to online learning, including in high-income countries. Extending sovereign debt forgiveness is another policy option that is relatively familiar and is being deployed again to enable low-income countries to borrow additional funds.

However, the essence of a new challenge, especially when its effects are compounded by others occurring simultaneously, is that so much remains unknown: potential solutions need to be found and tested very quickly. For example, some countries may have social protection programs that cannot be extended and thus may need to create alternatives. Others may decide to take drastic, unprecedented steps—such as Bolivia and Kenya canceling an entire school year—that buy a short-term reprieve but that could intensify longer-term

challenges (Dahir 2020). The world cannot afford to fail in the fight against COVID-19 and its associated economic crisis. But, as argued in this report, efforts to find effective responses to the triple challenges of COVID-19, conflict, and climate change can draw upon past experience and broad lessons from recent assessments of highly complex development interventions (see, for example, Andrews 2013; Buntaine, Parks, and Buch 2017; Honig 2018; see also Denizer, Kaufmann, and Kraay 2013).

This report serves primarily to document the scale of the current challenges and to support the efforts of governments, firms, citizens, and development partners who are responding to them. Those on the front lines have sometimes had to act at risk to their own lives. This report offers no simple answers to these challenges because there are none. However, it can point to areas of critical importance for making efforts more effective. The lessons from these experiences apply to urgent responses now, but especially to efforts in the future, when there may be time for broader reflection on the messages from this historic moment, including greater preparedness and prevention.[13]

Successfully designing and implementing responses to these kinds of policy challenges requires paying attention to four key issues: building robust implementation systems, promoting rapid learning and improving data quality, investing in preparedness and prevention, and enhancing coordination and cooperation.

1. Closing the gap between policy aspiration and attainment

Successfully addressing the slowdown and reversal in poverty reduction and economic growth requires sound policies. Too often, however, there is a wide gap between policies as articulated and their attainment in practice, and thus between what citizens rightfully expect and what they experience daily. Implementing sound policies, especially as the challenges intensify in reaching and responding to the poorest communities, requires securing adequate political accountability and financial support, building robust implementation systems (Page and

Pande 2018), and providing complementary support factors (for example, hungry children will struggle to learn even in well-equipped schools, so may need food support) (Bergoeing, Loayza, and Piguillem 2016).

Policy aspirations (including constitutional commitments) can be laudable, but there is likely to be considerable variation in the extent to which selected activities can achieve them and which groups benefit from them (Hickey, Sen, and Bukenya 2015; World Bank 2016). This space is the realm of political economy dynamics, in which those who control the state use their power to serve a spectrum of interests, ranging from the common good to securing their own personal advantage (see, among others, Acemoglu and Robinson 2019; Besley 2020; Fritz, Levy, and Ort 2014). Such concerns are ubiquitous: some combination of politics, political economy, and governance issues has been identified as a salient development concern in all 93 of the Systematic Country Diagnoses conducted by World Bank staff since 2015.[14]

These dynamics play out at multiple levels and in different ways, but in response to COVID-19, with vast sums of money needing to be quickly mobilized and dispersed, political economy issues are likely to be especially important. Similarly, the high-stakes pressure of the moment may embolden authoritarian responses and encourage the skirting of regular accountability mechanisms.[15] A failed response under such pressure may erode a government's credibility and legitimacy, a factor that is especially important for navigating sensitive or contentious issues. Alternatively, steering a country (or subnational area) through the current pandemic and economic crisis may reinvigorate a government's standing and trustworthiness. In India, for example, the state of Kerala enacted a statewide response to COVID-19 proactively, collectively, and at scale even before national guidelines had been issued, tapping into that state's long history of social inclusion (Heller 2020), which it has forged despite wide ethnic and religious diversity (Singh 2011). Similarly, the state of Meghalaya achieved one of India's lowest rates of COVID-19 by focusing on screening returning migrants, having discerned quickly that most of its cases stemmed

from this group (Das 2020). Using available evidence in a crisis to identify where to target finite resources, especially when solutions are initially unclear and potentially contentious, is crucial for governments to resist unwarranted political influence.

Political economy issues are also likely to manifest at the global level, reflected in the extent to which rich and poor nations get access to finite global supplies of medical equipment (such as ventilators and protective equipment) and opportunities to acquire the first supply of effective vaccines. Indeed, more than 70 countries have already imposed restrictions on the export of medical supplies (Nkengasong 2020). In response to such measures, multilateral organizations, including the United Nations and the African Union, have established working groups seeking to ensure that crucial supply chains for medical equipment and testing kits remain available to low-income countries, and to help forge agreements between African nations enabling them to negotiate as a bloc with medical suppliers. Using this approach, countries can ensure a more equitable outcome for their poorest citizens (Garber et al. 2020). Such measures can play a vital (if often underappreciated) role in sustaining inclusive growth.

Sound policies, adequate supplies of equipment and medicines, and robust financial support are necessary but insufficient for vital health services to be provided: all of these still need to be structured into a reliable implementation system that can deliver key services to millions of people every day. Unfortunately, recent research suggests that levels of implementation capability in most low-income economies have been stagnant or declining in recent years (Andrews, Pritchett, and Woolcock 2017; Pritchett 2020). This low capacity has been clearest in the global struggle to enhance learning outcomes (World Bank 2018) but is also readily apparent in health care. When implementation systems are already struggling to accomplish their long-standing tasks, asking them to respond to an existential crisis such as COVID-19 suggests that vastly greater attention needs to be given not just to "getting policies right" but also to building the capabilities of the administrative systems that are tasked with implementing those policies.

Even so, much can already be learned from instances in which, despite the odds, governments, firms, and communities have found ways to achieve initial success in the fight against COVID-19. These examples can be especially important when they involve the "new poor" identified in chapter 3—including adults living in urban areas engaged in informal businesses, domestic work, and tourism, as well as migrants. These populations may be particularly difficult to reach with services because many had not previously received government support. In Mumbai, India, for example, officials faced the daunting task of trying to stem the rapid spread of COVID-19 in Dharavi, one of the city's largest urban settlements. With limited resources and cases rapidly increasing, the decision was made to concentrate efforts on the five specific areas with the highest number of cases, screening as many people as possible for fever or low oxygen levels. Staff at private clinics were enlisted in the effort, with officials asking them to work longer hours in stifling heat in exchange for providing them with additional safety equipment. Hundreds of public latrines in prominent areas were sanitized three times a day. To house quarantine and treatment facilities, officials took over a sports complex and neighboring buildings to set up a makeshift 200-bed hospital with oxygen beds. Over a 10-day period, 47,000 people were screened, 400 symptomatic individuals were tested (80 of whom were positive), and an additional 4,000 people were placed in institutional quarantine. By July, the number of reported cases was just 20 percent of its peak in May. To help poor families during the lockdown, foundations, nongovernmental organizations, and volunteers provided thousands of households with ration kits. As Masih (2020) concludes, Dharavi's unlikely success stems from a combination of "customized solutions, community involvement, and perseverance."[16]

A related implementation issue, exposed under the pressure of COVID-19 but also an aspect of more familiar development challenges, is the priority typically given to the technical aspects of complex problems (for example, for COVID-19, a vaccine, better personal protective equipment, and low-cost technology enabling large-scale testing and contact tracing). Addressing the technical aspects of policy problems is necessary but insufficient. A key lesson from many decades of promoting sanitation in Indonesia, for example, is the complementary importance of addressing nontechnical issues if outcomes are to be realized. Initial efforts to promote sanitation in the country viewed it primarily as an engineering and finance problem: well-designed latrines, affordably priced, would lead to widespread uptake. Instead, the initial result was uptake at a rate so low it fell behind population growth. Only when attention focused on the more laborious work of promoting behavior change—village by village, across provinces, adapting strategies forged in Bangladesh and India—was success at scale finally achieved (Glavey and Haas 2015). During COVID-19, attention to such issues is likely to be especially important when reaching out to uncounted (or undercounted) populations, such as migrants and refugees (see chapter 3), as well as those (including non-native-language speakers and those who are illiterate) who may struggle to understand or respond appropriately to complex policy guidelines. Members of these vulnerable groups may be hard to identify and reach with conventional policies.

2. Enhancing learning and improving data

Much about the novel coronavirus, by definition, remains unknown. The speed and scale with which it has affected the world have overwhelmed response systems in rich and poor countries alike. Faced with unprecedented scientific, organizational, and societal uncertainty, governments and agencies need to learn—quickly, effectively, at scale—how to identify and enact context-specific responses. Innovative responses often come from communities and firms, which may have a better sense of the problems that should be prioritized and may enjoy greater local legitimacy to convey and enforce difficult decisions such as stay-at-home requirements; such cross-sectoral innovation is reflected in the effective response to an initial outbreak of COVID-19 in Mumbai, India, described above (Masih 2020).[17] No matter the source, agencies need to remain open to learning from initial successes and failures and to encouraging experimentation with new ideas. This principle is embodied in the "living paper" initiative developed by hundreds of social protection colleagues in organizations around the world, each contributing real-time insights on how to implement job support programs during COVID-19 (Gentilini et al. 2020). No one has a road map for navigating novel terrain. The map has to be produced, and the faster everyone learns from each other, the more accurate, detailed, and useful it will be. Another example is the Republic of Korea's widely applauded response to COVID-19, which has been attributed in part to efforts to learn from the country's "painful experience" (Lee, Yeo, and Na 2020) when responding to the Middle East Respiratory Syndrome Coronavirus (MERS-CoV) in 2015.[18]

Such navigation is crucially enhanced by investing in comprehensive data collection and curation at multiple levels (World Bank, forthcoming). In responding to the challenges of COVID-19, conflict, and climate change, more extensive use of new technologies can help inform real-time decisions, especially in fragile and conflict-affected situations, where the collection of primary data may put enumerators at great risk.[19] But, for the everyday management of key development issues, retaining a strong long-term commitment to data collection, curation, and use across six core domains—household surveys, enterprise-based surveys, agricultural statistics, price data, administrative data, and national accounts data—is vital.[20] The information provided is essential for ensuring that limited resources are optimally deployed, assessing the quality and reach of public services, providing assistance to groups with particular needs (for example, those with disabilities), and equalizing opportunities for all (for example, across racial, income, and gender lines).

More broadly, comprehensive, high-quality data are the foundation for conducting official and accurate tracking of global poverty and inclusive growth over time and space. Policy in general, and the prevention and mitigation of crises in particular, cannot be effective without evidence derived from carefully interpreted data. The scale and quality of data for assessing progress on global poverty and inclusive growth are steadily improving, but data too often remain unavailable for many reasons—surveys are not produced; surveys are conducted but are of poor quality or low relevance for tracking poverty reduction and inclusive growth among specific groups; surveys are done well but poorly curated over time; or surveys are conducted but not openly shared. As shown in chapters 1, 2, and 3 of this report, these kinds of data problems have hindered more accurate assessment of global poverty levels, trends in shared prosperity, and the changing profile of the global poor. More important, pervasive data problems limit developing countries' own abilities to practice evidence-based policy design and implementation. Accessible, high-quality, and useful data are a public good whose importance only increases during crises.[21]

3. Investing in preparedness and prevention

COVID-19, together with climate change and persistent conflict, is providing an urgent reminder of the importance of maintaining investments in comprehensive preparedness and prevention measures (Osterholm and Olshaker 2020). These challenges are risks, and they should be professionally managed as such (Clarke and Dercon 2016). "Pay now or pay later" may be a cliché, but in the current moment the world is surely learning this lesson again, the hard way. Sustaining administrative measures to anticipate and prepare for crises is hard. Prevention measures often have low political payoff, with little credit given for disasters averted.[22] Preparedness and prevention are areas in which multilateral agencies are already active, for example, the Global Facility for Disaster Reduction and Recovery.[23] The importance of preventing conflict, and not just recovering more quickly from it, is the main message of the report *Pathways to Peace: Inclusive Approaches to Preventing Violent Conflict* (United Nations and World Bank 2018), which reflects broader principles from fields such as nutrition and public health. It is also the main message of all the major reports on climate change (for example, Stern 2007). The common principle, though politically difficult to uphold, is that preventing problems is vastly cheaper than responding to them after the fact.[24]

As an extreme shock, COVID-19 has exposed and exacerbated weaknesses in existing preparedness systems. Some wealthy countries initially ranked as having health care systems that would be "most prepared" for a pandemic have in practice struggled to respond effectively, especially for their most vulnerable citizens (NTI and CHS 2019). Beyond such specific indexes, a key lesson from the current moment is the nature of state-society relations as itself a "preparedness" factor, even if this relationship is hard to quantify as a single metric. When a pandemic strikes, it is vital that political leaders and citizens be willing and able to respond quickly, effectively, and with a shared sense of purpose despite the inherent uncertainty. In this regard, the prompt initial responses to COVID-19 in Vietnam and India's Kerala state (discussed earlier in this chapter) provide important lessons for rich and poor countries alike.

More broadly, an example of successful international cooperation and preparation is the Indian Ocean Tsunami Warning and Mitigation System (IOTWMS). Of the 28 countries around the Indian Ocean rim, most had seismological units that detected the earthquake that initiated the region's devastating December 2004 tsunami, but none was prepared to issue an official warning. Australia, India, Indonesia, Malaysia, and Thailand forged ahead after the earthquake to set up their own warning centers but struggled to agree on who would host the regional alert centers and issue warnings across the area. After years of effort and coordination, but also political jockeying and technical glitches, IOTWMS became fully operational in 2013. Since the 2004 Indian Ocean tsunami, regional warning systems have also been created in the Caribbean and the Mediterranean, which, together with those in the Pacific and Indian Oceans, operate under the guidance of the United Nations Educational, Scientific and Cultural Organization's Intergovernmental Oceanographic Commission. This is just one example of efforts that continue across countries and multilateral agencies to promote cooperation, coordination, and commitment on problems that affect more than one country.

A focus on poverty and shared prosperity also implies investing in preparedness and prevention measures at the household level. Since their inception in the 1500s, social protection programs in the form of cash transfers, basic insurance, and identity registration have been called for on the grounds that they provide assistance to vulnerable populations during good times and bad, thereby enabling them to steadily build assets and have resources at hand when faced with a major calamity. In their most recent guise, such programs—in the form of adaptive social protection (Bowen et al. 2020)—have been expanded and refined to respond to precisely the challenges of this moment, namely, covariant shocks such as a pandemic, an economic crisis, conflict, or a natural disaster. The explicit goal of adaptive social protection is to help vulnerable households prepare for, cope with, and adapt to such shocks—before, during, and after they occur.

Proper preparation and prevention require prediction (Kleinberg et al. 2015), which in turn requires good data, along with sound theory (for interpreting findings) and innovative methods to compensate for a lack of data. Recent methodological and computing advances (for example, machine learning) enable future events to be predicted in ever more sophisticated and defensible ways (Mueller and Rauh 2018). If the question for pandemics, violent conflict, and events related to climate change is not whether they will happen again but when, where, and at what scale—and if the world now possesses the technology enabling such predictions—then on both moral and strategic grounds the corresponding investments in prevention measures need to be undertaken. Indeed, we might hope that, over time, embedding prediction measures into the policy process at the "beginning" will one day have the same stature as evaluation now has at the "end."

4. Expanding cooperation and coordination

Contributing to and maintaining public goods require extensive cooperation and coordination among individuals, groups, regions, and countries. This cooperation is necessary not only for promoting widespread learning and improving the empirical foundations of policy making, but also for forging a sense of shared solidarity in the midst of crises and ensuring that the difficult policy choices made by officials are both trusted and trustworthy. Pervasive negative externalities and information asymmetries associated with COVID-19 can be exploited by opportunistic leaders even as such problems demand greater cooperation and coordination. Here, too, there are additional challenges to be overcome. At a historic moment for development agencies, when international cooperation is needed more than ever to help combat COVID-19, conflict, and climate change, global organizations can play a central role in helping countries confront problems that are large, complex, novel, and rapidly evolving, promoting the sharing of ideas, experience, and evidence needed to inform increasingly effective responses. Cooperation and coordination are crucial tasks for regional agencies as well, such as the Regional Disease Surveillance Systems Enhancement Project (in West and Central Africa) and the East Africa Public Health Laboratory Networking Project (Wetzel 2020)—all the more so if the effects of COVID-19 linger or periodic outbreaks eventuate. Regional cooperation will be essential to reviving economies after the public health crisis has passed.

The consequences of crises and policy decisions are experienced most directly in households and communities, and here too cooperation and commitment are vital.[25] It is at this level that variation becomes apparent in the ways in which countries—and subnational areas and communities within them—have responded to COVID-19, along with corresponding variations in the effectiveness of those responses. Some leaders have enacted decisive policies willingly supported by citizens from the outset; others have essentially ignored or denied the threat until it was too late. This variation can be understood as stemming from key differences in three interacting domains: science, states, and society. By virtue of the virus being novel, much of the underlying science remains unknown or fluid, with the virus itself seemingly able to quickly mutate. But, in an age in which even the consensus views of scientists—for example, concerning the reality of climate change—are often looked upon with deep skepticism, it is harder still to provide citizens with clear, consistent, and compelling guidance on how to protect themselves and others when the subject matter (in this case COVID-19) remains only partially understood.

Vietnam stands out as a country that, despite this inherent uncertainty, provided clear and regular public information from the outset, thereby crowding out space for "fake news," conspiracy theories, and misinformation (Ravallion 2020). Precisely because much of the science remains uncertain, however, the means by which public guidance is provided, by whom, and on what basis matter enormously for ensuring its legitimacy, and thus maximizing the likelihood that unwelcome requirements and recommendations will be adhered to. Even seemingly basic public goals such as "flattening the curve" of COVID-19 infections are likely to have different meanings for different groups, as will the perceived credibility of the proposed steps to ensure that these goals are met. Similarly, upholding the legitimacy of the response process is especially important for negotiating peace agreements, which may well entail asking those who have directly experienced violent trauma to forgive their enemies, or even form a joint government with them (Kleinfeld 2018; Philpott 2015).[26] In such circumstances, high-quality leadership assumes an even more important role (Kerrissey and Edmondson 2020).

Even where professional expertise informs a credible COVID-19 response strategy, and where this strategy is ably conveyed to citizens and adequately supported by public leaders, citizens themselves still need to comply willingly with recommended and legally prescribed actions. These actions may range from the onerous (closing one's business) to those that are merely inconvenient but require daily practice (washing hands, wearing a mask). Success requires everyone to abide by these prescribed actions, over long periods, given that lapses by a few can rapidly lead to the infection of the many. As noted, the costs of these actions fall disproportionately on the poor, and especially poor women. But the fact that *all* social groups are affected is an opportunity for skillful leaders to actively promote a sense of social inclusion and collective resolve, and to publicly recognize those who are suffering the most or making the largest sacrifices to confront the pandemic (for example, frontline health workers). Societies and communities vary in the extent to which they are willing and able to do this. In less cohesive societies, a patchwork of partial, idiosyncratic responses emerges (Yong 2020), undermining attempts to forge a prompt, unified, and effective strategy. However, as the examples above from India, Indonesia, Sub-Saharan Africa, and elsewhere demonstrate (thus far), innovative and effective responses to the current crises are being implemented. In the coming year, countries and their partners will need to find, share, refine, fund, and scale up many more of these initiatives to overcome evolving policy and implementation challenges and restore inclusive growth and poverty reduction.

Conclusion

The global shocks of COVID-19, conflict, and climate change require policies enabling economies to recover from them and prevent their further recurrence—through strengthened health systems, lasting peace, and improved climate change adaptation and mitigation. As important as it is to address these shocks in the present moment, for countries to sustain poverty reduction in the long term, attention must also continue to be focused on the ongoing development agenda of promoting inclusive growth, investing in poor people's acquisition and protection of productive assets, and improving the quality of public services. Given the global nature of the shocks unleashed by COVID-19, conflict, and climate change, countries must adopt policies that elicit the collaboration of multiple groups within the nation as well as coordination with other countries. The more integrated the world becomes, the more necessary it is to take coordinated and cooperative action to maximize integration's benefits and minimize its inherent costs (Nixon 2020; World Bank 2017c).

In these uncertain times, responding to these three global threats and to more familiar development challenges is difficult and sometimes dangerous work. It is likely to be time consuming and expensive, with successes hard to measure, sometimes even to discern. Some of the best responses will likely unfold fitfully over long, idiosyncratic, nonlinear trajectories. Campaigns to promote greater accountability and to end gender-based violence, for example, have followed such paths, with outcomes sometimes initially getting worse before they eventually get better. Accurately assessing such efforts will require making major corresponding investments in diverse evaluation strategies, including novel forms of evidence and methods to collect, curate, interpret, and learn from the data. Crafting and implementing a more economically just, socially inclusive, and politically legitimate development process—as a necessary complement to the adoption of technically sound policies—provides the world its best chance of reversing today's reversals of fortune.

However, reversing even a massive reversal of fortune, such as the world is experiencing with COVID-19, is necessary, desirable, and possible. It has been done many times in the past, in the face of what were regarded at the time as insurmountable challenges—for example, eradicating smallpox, ending World War II, creating national parks, closing the hole in the ozone layer—and it will be done again in the future. This global crisis is also a defining historical moment. To address development challenges, whether large or small, the world needs to commit to cooperation and coordination, both within and between countries. We must commit to working together, and to working better—now especially, but also for the long term.

Notes

1. For now, however, the very poorest African countries appear to have fared better than initially anticipated (Mbow et al. 2020).
2. See also Amare et al. (2020), drawing on panel data evidence. A recent phone survey from Myanmar (World Bank 2020b) reports that a much lower share of households, 7.3 percent, have reduced their food consumption, but

that 75 percent of rice-growing farmers had delayed planting for the monsoon rice season, raising concerns of a potential food crisis in the coming months. In Latin America and the Caribbean, seven countries have reported 40 percent or more of people running out of food during lockdowns (Hill and Narayan 2020). For a broader assessment of the effects of COVID-19 on childhood malnutrition, see Headey et al. (2020).

3. See "World Bank Education and COVID-19," World Bank, Washington, DC, https://www.worldbank.org/en/data/interactive/2020/0 3/24/world-bank-education-and-covid-19.

4. See Akresh, Verwimp, and Bundervoet (2011) and Akresh et al. (2012) on the enduring effects of war on stunting (in Rwanda and Nigeria, respectively); similar effects are reported by Bundervoet, Verwimp, and Akresh (2009) for Burundi. See Singhal (2019) on the long-term effects of the Vietnam War on the mental health of civilians. A broader overview of the micro effects of violent conflict are documented in Justino, Brück, and Verwimp (2013).

5. See "Niger to Receive $140 million to Improve Quality of Education and Learning," Press Release, World Bank, Washington, DC, https:// www.worldbank.org/en/news/press -release/2020/04/06/niger-to-receive-140 -million-to-improve-quality-of-education-and -learning.

6. This may be less true for the poor in urban areas, where there are greater opportunities to access markets and better public services, but, as Pritchett and Hani (2020) show, real wage comparisons of workers with identical observed and unobserved human capital characteristics in poor and rich countries show "massive gaps" in earnings, suggesting the existence of "a 'place premium'—or space-specific wage differentials that are not due to intrinsic worker productivity."

7. See also the range of initial responses outlined in World Bank (2020d); a broader array of current policy initiatives and data sources is available at "Oxford Supertracker," Oxford University, Oxford, UK, https://supertracker .spi.ox.ac.uk/.

8. As World Bank (2020a, 7) puts it, in the current context "global coordination and cooperation—of the measures needed to slow the spread of the pandemic, and of the economic actions needed to alleviate the economic damage, including international support—provide the greatest chance of achieving public health goals and enabling a robust global recovery."

9. Helpful summaries of the macroeconomic and fiscal initiatives undertaken by countries in response to COVID-19 are available at "Policy Responses to COVID-19," International Monetary Fund, Washington, DC, https:// www.imf.org/en/Topics/imf-and-covid19/ Policy-Responses-to-COVID-19#I.

10. The World Bank's Jobs and Economic Transformation (JET) initiative has been particularly active in this area. JET seeks to create more and better jobs by increasing worker productivity by expanding private sector investment, increasing integration with markets and value chains, and improving ties to the digital economy. Further details are available at "Jobs and Economic Transformation," International Development Association, Washington, DC, https://ida.worldbank.org /theme/jobs-and-economic-transformation.

11. See "G2PX: Digitizing Government-to-Person Payments," World Bank, Washington, DC, https://www.worldbank.org/en/programs /g2px.

12. A checklist of such principles, as articulated by the World Bank's Climate Change group, is available at "Proposed Sustainability Checklist for Assessing Economic Recovery Interventions April 2020," World Bank, Washington, DC, http://pubdocs.worldbank. org/en/223671586803837686/Sustainability -Checklist-for-Assessing-Economic-Recovery -Investments-April-2020.pdf.

13. These issues will be explored in more detail in a forthcoming companion volume to this report.

14. More specifically, the concept of "governance" appeared at least 10 times in all but 4 of these 93 Systematic Country Diagnoses (SCDs); on average, it was referred to about 50 times in each report, as was the word "political." "Political economy" concerns were mentioned in 67 of the 93 SCDs. "Governance" or "political" appeared more than 100 times in the SCDs on Brazil, Burundi, Democratic Republic of Congo, Côte d'Ivoire, Guinea, Guinea-Bissau, Iraq, Lebanon, Mauritania, Mongolia, North Macedonia, Papua New Guinea, the Russian Federation, Solomon Islands, and Tunisia.

15. The World Bank's Governance Global Practice has prepared several guidance notes on how

to anticipate and respond to such concerns. These and other contributions are available at "Governance & Institutions COVID-19 Response Resources," World Bank, Washington, DC, https://www.worldbank.org/en/topic/governance/brief/governance-institutions-covid-19-response-resources.

16. This effort has been publicly praised by the World Health Organization (see Masih 2020). For more general examples of such "pockets of effectiveness" in public administration, see Brixi, Lust, and Woolcock (2015) on service delivery in the Middle East and North Africa region and McDonnell (2020) on Ghana.

17. Despite the enormous development challenges Somalia faces, for example, its informal sector has shown remarkable capacity to provide an array of public services in urban areas (see World Bank 2020e).

18. Sachs et al. (2020) rank the Republic of Korea first among Organisation for Economic Co-operation and Development (OECD) nations for its response thus far to COVID-19; more telling, perhaps, is the wide variation in response effectiveness among the 33 relatively wealthy member countries of the OECD. On the details of Korea's response, see also Ladner, Hamaguchi, and Kim (2020).

19. On this issue, see the thoughtful contributions in Hoogeveen and Pape (2019).

20. At the World Bank, advancing efforts in these domains is being overseen by the Data for Policy Initiative; further details are available at "Data for Policy (D4P) Initiative," Poverty and Equity Notes 23, World Bank, Washington, DC, https://openknowledge.worldbank.org/handle/10986/33857. See also a related effort based in the United Kingdom, https://dataforpolicy.org/.

21. These principles are articulated more formally in the World Bank's Open Data Initiative; see "World Bank Open Data: Free and Open Access to Global Development Data," https://data.worldbank.org/.

22. Formally assessing the effectiveness of prevention measures is also a challenge; most evaluation efforts are spent assessing the effectiveness of interventions promoting a desired outcome, not avoiding an undesired one.

23. See "Global Facility for Disaster Reduction and Recovery" website, https://www.gfdrr.org/en.

24. A corresponding literature has long argued for investing in more effective insurance mechanisms for addressing the types of everyday risks that the poor themselves encounter (for example, Dercon 2005). See also *World Development Report 2014: Risk and Opportunity—Managing Risk for Development,* which rightly notes that "[i]n the absence of an effective global risk governance mechanism with an international body that has appropriate accountability and enforcement powers over sovereign nations, the international architecture necessary to provide the global public goods and address global risks has not kept pace with the connectivity that glues the world together and the complexities such connectivity creates" (World Bank 2013, 269). And, as World Bank (2017a) also rightly argues, taking a "development approach" to an issue such as refugees and internally displaced peoples *means* giving full attention to preparedness and prevention measures.

25. See Van Bavel et al. (2020) for an extensive list of practical recommendations grounded in the social and behavioral sciences for promoting empathy, social solidarity, and cooperation during COVID-19.

26. On the broader role of process legitimacy for deliberative democracy and poverty reduction, see Rao (2019).

References

Acemoglu, Daron, and James Robinson. 2019. *The Narrow Corridor: States, Societies, and the Fate of Liberty.* New York: Penguin Press.

Akresh, Richard, Sonia Bhalotra, Marinella Leone, and Una Okonkwo Osili. 2012. "War and Stature: Growing Up during the Nigerian Civil War." *American Economic Review* 102 (3): 273–77.

Akresh, Richard, Philip Verwimp, and Tom Bundervoet. 2011. "Civil War, Crop Failure, and Child Stunting in Rwanda." *Economic Development and Cultural Change* 59 (4): 777–810.

Amare, Mulubrhan, Abay Kibrom, Luca Tiberti, and Jordan Chamberlin. 2020. "Impacts of COVID-19 on Food Security: Panel Data Evidence from Nigeria." IFPRI Discussion Paper 01956, International Food Policy Research Institute, Washington, DC.

Andrews, Matt. 2013. *The Limits of Institutional Reform in Development: Changing Rules for Realistic Solutions.* New York: Cambridge University Press.

Andrews, Matt, Lant Pritchett, and Michael Woolcock. 2017. *Building State Capability: Evidence, Analysis, Action*. New York: Oxford University Press.

Barron, Patrick, Rachael Diprose, and Michael Woolcock. 2011. *Contesting Development: Participatory Projects and Local Conflict Dynamics in Indonesia*. New Haven, CT: Yale University Press.

Bergoeing, Raphael, Norman Loayza, and Facundo Piguillem. 2016. "The Whole Is Greater than the Sum of Its Parts: Complementary Reforms to Address Microeconomic Distortions." *World Bank Economic Review* 30 (2): 268–305.

Berman, Nicolas, Mathieu Couttenier, Dominic Rohner, and Mathias Thoenig. 2017. "This Mine Is Mine! How Minerals Fuel Conflicts in Africa." *American Economic Review* 107 (6): 1564–610.

Berry, Marie E. 2015. "When 'Bright Futures' Fade: Paradoxes of Women's Empowerment in Rwanda." *Signs: Journal of Women in Culture and Society* 41 (1): 1–27.

Besley, Timothy. 2020. "State Capacity, Reciprocity and the Social Contract." *Econometrica* 88 (4): 1307–35.

Bowen, Thomas, Carlo Del Ninno, Colin Andrews, Sarah Coll-Black, Ugo Gentilini, Kelly Johnson, Yasuhiro Kawasoe, Adea Kryeziu, Barry Maher, and Asha Williams. 2020. *Adaptive Social Protection: Building Resilience to Shocks*. Washington, DC: World Bank.

Brixi, Hana, Ellen Lust, and Michael Woolcock. 2015. *Trust, Voice and Incentives: Learning from Local Success Stories in Public Service Delivery in the Middle East and North Africa*. Washington, DC: World Bank.

Brown, Caitlin S., Martin Ravallion, and Dominique van de Walle. 2020. "Can the World's Poor Protect Themselves from the New Coronavirus?" Working Paper 27200 (May), National Bureau of Economic Research, Cambridge, MA.

Bundervoet, Tom, Philip Verwimp, and Richard Akresh. 2009. "Health and Civil War in Rural Burundi." *Journal of Human Resources* 44 (2): 536–63.

Buntaine, Mark T., Bradley C. Parks, and Benjamin P. Buch. 2017. "Aiming at the Wrong Targets: The Domestic Consequences of International Efforts to Build Institutions." *International Studies Quarterly* 61 (2): 471–88.

Cajner, Tomaz, Leland D. Crane, Ryan A. Decker, John Grigsby, Adrian Hamins-Puertolas, Erik Hurst, Christopher Kurz, and Ahu Yildirmaz. 2020. "The US Labor Market during the Beginning of the Pandemic Recession." Working Paper 27159 (August), National Bureau of Economic Research, Cambridge, MA.

Clarke, Daniel J., and Stefan Dercon. 2016. *Dull Disasters? How Planning Ahead Will Make a Difference*. Oxford: Oxford University Press.

Corral, Paul, Alexander Irwin, Nandini Krishnan, Daniel Gerszon Mahler, and Tara Vishwanath. 2020. *Fragility and Violence: On the Front Lines of the Fight against Poverty*. Washington, DC: World Bank.

Dahir, Abdi Latif. 2020. "Kenya's Unusual Solution to the School Problem: Cancel the Year and Start Over." *New York Times*, August 5, 2020. https://www.nytimes.com/2020/08/05/world/africa/Kenya-cancels-school-year-coronavirus.html.

Das, Manosh. 2020. "How Meghalaya Managed to Keep Its Covid Count Low." *Times of India*, June 30, 2020. https://timesofindia.indiatimes.com/city/shillong/how-meghalaya-managed-to-keep-its-covid-count-low/articleshow/76709859.cms.

Denizer, Cevdet, Daniel Kaufmann, and Aart Kraay. 2013. "Good Countries or Good Projects? Macro and Micro Correlates of World Bank Project Performance." *Journal of Development Economics* 105 (November): 288–302.

Dercon, Stefan, ed. 2005. *Insurance against Poverty*. Oxford: Oxford University Press.

Dingel, Jonathan I., and Brent Neiman. 2020. "How Many Jobs Can Be Done at Home?" Working Paper 26948, National Bureau of Economic Research, Cambridge, MA.

Ferguson, William D. 2020. *The Political Economy of Collective Action, Inequality, and Development*. Stanford, CA: Stanford University Press.

Fritz, Verena Maria, Brian David Levy, and Rachel Lemay Ort, eds. 2014. *Problem-Driven Political Economy Analysis: The World Bank's Experience*. Directions in Development: Private Sector Development Series. Washington, DC: World Bank.

Galea, Sandro, Raina M. Merchant, and Nicole Lurie. 2020. "The Mental Health Consequences of COVID-19 and Physical Distancing: The Need for Prevention and Early Intervention." *Journal of the American Medical Association (JAMA): Internal Medicine* 180 (6): 817–18.

Garber, Kent, Mary Margaret Ajiko, Sandra M. Gualtero-Trujillo, Samuel Martinez-

Vernaza, and Alain Chichom-Mefire. 2020. "Structural Inequities in the Global Supply of Personal Protective Equipment." *British Medical Journal* 370:m2727. http://dx.doi.org/10.1136/bmj.m2727.

Gentilini, Ugo, Mohamed Almenfi, Ian Orton, and Pamela Dale. 2020. "Social Protection and Jobs Responses to COVID-19: A Real-Time Review of Country Measures." World Bank, Washington, DC. https://socialprotection.org/discover/publications/social-protection-and-jobs-responses-covid-19-real-time-review-country.

Ghobarah, Hazem A., Paul Huth, and Bruce Russett. 2003. "Civil Wars Kill and Maim People—Long after the Shooting Stops." *American Political Science Review* 97 (2): 189–202.

Glavey, Sarah, and Oliver Haas. 2015. "How to Scale Up Rural Sanitation Service Delivery in Indonesia." GDI Case Study (September), Global Delivery Initiative, Washington, DC.

Hausmann, Ricardo, César A. Hidalgo, Sebastián Bustos, Michele Coscia, and Alexander Simoes. 2014. *The Atlas of Economic Complexity: Mapping Paths to Prosperity.* Cambridge, MA: MIT Press.

Headey, Derek, Rebecca Heidkamp, Saskia Osendarp, Marie Ruel, Nick Scott, Robert Black, Meera Shekar, Howarth Bouis, Augustin Flory, Lawrence Haddad, and Neff Walker. 2020. "Impacts of COVID-19 on Childhood Malnutrition and Nutrition-Related Mortality." *The Lancet* 396 (10250): 519–21.

Heller, Patrick. 2020. "A Virus, Social Democracy, and Dividends for Kerala." *Hindu*, April 18, 2020. https://www.thehindu.com/opinion/lead/a-virus-social-democracy-and-dividends-for-kerala/article31370554.ece.

Hickey, Sam, Kunal Sen, and Badru Bukenya, eds. 2015. *The Politics of Inclusive Development: Interrogating the Evidence.* Oxford: Oxford University Press.

Hill, Ruth Vargasm, and Ambar Narayan. 2020. "How Is COVID-19 Likely to Affect Inequality? A Discussion Note." Unpublished, World Bank, Washington, DC.

Hoeffler, Anke, and James Fearon. 2014. "Benefits and Costs of the Conflict and Violence Targets for the Post-2015 Development Agenda: Post-2015 Consensus." Conflict and Violence Assessment Paper (August 22), Copenhagen Consensus Center, Copenhagen.

Honig, Dan. 2018. *Navigation by Judgment: Why and When Top-Down Management of Foreign Aid Doesn't Work.* New York: Oxford University Press.

Hoogeveen, Johannes, and Utz Pape. 2019. *Data Collection in Fragile States: Innovations from Africa and Beyond.* New York: Palgrave Macmillan.

Hooper, Monica Webb, Anna María Nápoles, and Eliseo J. Pérez-Stable. 2020. "COVID-19 and Racial/Ethnic Disparities." *Journal of the American Medical Association* 323 (24): 2466–67.

Hsiang, Solomon, and Robert E. Kopp. 2018. "An Economist's Guide to Climate Change Science." *Journal of Economic Perspectives* 32 (4): 3–32.

International Monetary Fund and World Bank. 2020. "Enhancing Access to Opportunities." International Monetary Fund and World Bank, Washington, DC. https://www.imf.org/external/np/g20/pdf/2020/061120.pdf.

Justino, Patricia, Tilman Brück, and Philip Verwimp. 2013. "A Micro-Level Perspective on the Dynamics of Conflict, Violence and Development." Oxford: Oxford University Press.

Kerrissey, Michaela J., and Amy C. Edmondson. 2020. "What Good Leadership Looks Like during This Pandemic." *Harvard Business Review,* April 13, 2020. https://hbr.org/2020/04/what-good-leadership-looks-like-during-this-pandemic.

Kishore, Kamal. 2020. "Managing Tropical Storms during COVID-19: Early Lessons Learned and Reflections from India." *World Bank Blogs: Development and a Changing Climate,* July 27, 2020. https://blogs.worldbank.org/climatechange/managing-tropical-storms-during-covid-19-early-lessons-learned-and-reflections-india.

Kleinberg, Jon, Jens Ludwig, Sendhil Mullainathan, and Ziad Obermeyer. 2015. "Prediction Policy Problems." *American Economic Review* 105 (5): 491–95.

Kleinfeld, Rachel. 2018. *A Savage Order: How the World's Deadliest Countries Can Forge a Path to Security.* New York: Pantheon.

Kluge, Hans Henri P., Zsuzsanna Jakab, Jozef Bartovic, Veronika D'Anna, and Santino Severoni. 2020. "Refugee and Migrant Health in the COVID-19 Response." *The Lancet* 395 (10232): 1237–39.

Kose, M. Ayhan, Peter Nagle, Franziska Ohnsorge, and Naotaka Sugawara. 2020. *Global Waves of Debt: Causes and Consequences.* Washington, DC: World Bank.

Ladner, Debra, Katsumasa Hamaguchi, and Kyuri Kim. 2020. "The Republic of Korea's First

70 Days of Responding to the COVID-19 Outbreak." GDI Case Study (April 13), Global Delivery Initiative, Washington, DC.

Lee, Seulki, Jungwon Yeo, and Chongmin Na. 2020. "Learning from the Past: Distributed Cognition and Crisis Management Capabilities for Tackling COVID-19." *American Review of Public Administration* 50. https://doi.org/10.1177/0275074020942412.

Masih, Niha. 2020. "How a Packed Slum in Mumbai Beat Back the Coronavirus, as India's Cases Continue to Soar." *Washington Post*, July 31, 2020. https://www.washingtonpost.com/world/asia_pacific/how-a-packed-slum-in-mumbai-beat-back-the-coronavirus-as-indias-cases-continue-to-soar/2020/07/30/da859532-d039-11ea-826b-cc394d824e35_story.html.

Mbow, Moustapha, Bertrand Lell, Simon P. Jochems, Badara Cisse, Souleymane Mboup, Benjamin G. Dewals, Assan Jaye, Alioune Dieye, and Maria Yazdanbakhsh. 2020. "COVID-19 in Africa: Dampening the Storm?" *Science* 369 (6504): 624–26.

McDonnell, Erin Metz. 2020. *Patchwork Leviathan: Pockets of Bureaucratic Effectiveness in Developing States*. Princeton, NJ: Princeton University Press.

Mueller, Hannes, and Christopher Rauh. 2018. "Reading Between the Lines: Prediction of Political Violence Using Newspaper Text." *American Political Science Review* 112 (2): 358–75.

Mueller, Hannes, and Chanon Techasunthornwat. 2020. "Conflict and Poverty." Background paper, World Bank, Washington, DC.

Nguyen, Minh Cong, Nobuo Yoshida, Haoyu Wu, and Ambar Narayan. 2020. "Profiles of the New Poor Due to the COVID-19 Pandemic." Unpublished, Poverty Global Practice, World Bank, Washington, DC.

Nixon, Stewart. 2020. "Global Integration Is More Important than Ever to Contain the Economic and Health Fallout and Exit the COVID-19 Pandemic Crisis." Research and Policy Brief No. 37, World Bank Malaysia Hub, Kuala Lumpur.

Nkengasong, John. 2020. "Let Africa into the Market for COVID-19 Diagnostics." *Nature* 580 (7805): 565.

NTI (Nuclear Threat Initiative) and CHS (Johns Hopkins Center for Health Security). 2019. *Global Health Security Index: Building Collective Action and Accountability*. October. Washington, DC: NTI; Baltimore: CHS, Johns Hopkins Bloomberg School of Public Health.

Osterholm, Michael T., and Mark Olshaker. 2020. "Chronicle of a Pandemic Foretold: Learning from the COVID-19 Failure – Before the Next Outbreak Arrives." *Foreign Affairs* 99 (4): 10–24.

Page, Lucy, and Rohini Pande. 2018. "Ending Global Poverty: Why Money Isn't Enough." *Journal of Economic Perspectives* 32 (4): 173–200.

Philpott, Daniel. 2015. *Just and Unjust Peace: An Ethic of Political Reconciliation*. New York: Oxford University Press.

Pritchett, Lant. 2020. "Trends in State Capability, 1996–2018: An Update of National Indicators." Background paper, World Bank, Washington, DC.

Pritchett, Lant, and Farah Hani. 2020. "The Economics of International Wage Differentials and Migration." In *Oxford Research Encyclopedia of Economics and Finance*. Oxford: Oxford University Press. doi:10.1093/acrefore/9780190625979.013.353.

Rao, Vijayendra. 2019. "Process-Policy and Outcome-Policy: Rethinking How to Address Poverty and Inequality." *Dædalus* 148 (3): 181–90.

Ravallion, Martin. 2020. "Pandemic Policies in Poor Places." CGD Note (April 24), Center for Global Development, Washington, DC.

Reinhart, Carmen, and Vincent Reinhart. 2020. "The Pandemic Depression: The Global Economy Will Never Be the Same." *Foreign Affairs* 99 (5): 84–95.

Rodrik, Dani. 1999. "Where Did All the Growth Go? External Shocks, Social Conflict, and Growth Collapses." *Journal of Economic Growth* 4 (4): 385–412.

Rodrik, Dani. 2011. *The Globalization Paradox: Democracy and the Future of the World Economy*. New York: W. W. Norton and Co.

Rutkowski, Michal, Alfonso Garcia Mora, Greta L. Bull, Boutheina Guermazi, and Caren Grown. 2020. "Responding to Crisis with Digital Payments for Social Protection: Short-Term Measures with Long-Term Benefits." *World Bank Blogs: Voices*, March 31, 2020. https://blogs.worldbank.org/voices/responding-crisis-digital-payments-social-protection-short-term-measures-long-term-benefits.

Sachs, Jeffrey, Guido Schmidt-Traub, Christian Kroll, Guillaume Lafortune, Grayson Fuller, and Finn Woelm. 2020. *The Sustainable Development Goals and COVID-19. Sustainable Development Report 2020*. Cambridge: Cambridge University Press.

Singh, Prerna. 2011. "We-ness and Welfare: A Longitudinal Analysis of Social Development in Kerala, India." *World Development* 39 (2): 282–93.

Singhal, Saurabh. 2019. "Early Life Shocks and Mental Health: The Long-Term Effect of War in Vietnam." *Journal of Development Economics* 141: 102244.

Siwatu, Gbemisola Oseni, Amparo Palacios-Lopez, Kevin Robert Mcgee, Akuffo Amankwah, Tara Vishwanath, and M. Abul Kalam Azad. 2020. "Impact of COVID-19 on Nigerian Households: Baseline Results." World Bank Group, Washington, DC.

Stern, Nicholas. 2007. *The Economics of Climate Change: The Stern Review*. Cambridge: Cambridge University Press.

United Nations and World Bank. 2018. *Pathways to Peace: Inclusive Approaches to Preventing Violent Conflict*. Washington, DC: World Bank.

UN Women. 2020. "COVID-19 and Ending Violence against Women and Girls." UN Women, New York. https://www.unwomen.org/-/media /headquarters/attachments/sections/library /publications/2020/issue-brief-covid-19-and -ending-violence-against-women-and-girls-en .pdf?la=en&vs=5006.

Van Bavel, Jay J., Katherine Baicker, Paulo S. Boggio, Valeria Caprero, Aleksandra Cichocka, Mina Cikara, Molly J. Crockett, et al. 2020. "Using Social and Behavioural Science to Support COVID-19 Pandemic Response." *Nature: Human Behaviour* 4: 460–71. https://doi .org/10.1038/s41562-020-0884-z.

Van Lancker, Wim, and Zachary Parolin. 2020. "COVID-19, School Closures, and Child Poverty: A Social Crisis in the Making." *The Lancet Public Health* 5 (5): e243–e244.

Wetzel, Deborah. 2020. "Pandemics Know No Borders: In Africa, Regional Cooperation Is Key to Fighting COVID-19." *World Bank Blogs: Africa Can End Poverty*, May 20, 2020. https://blogs .worldbank.org/africacan/pandemics-know -no-borders-africa-regional-collaboration-key -fighting-covid-19.

World Bank. 2013. *World Development Report 2014: Risk and Opportunity—Managing Risk for Development*. Washington, DC: World Bank.

World Bank. 2016. *Making Politics Work for Development: Harnessing Transparency and Citizen Engagement*. Policy Research Report. Washington, DC: World Bank.

World Bank. 2017a. *Forcibly Displaced: Toward a Development Approach Supporting Refugees, the Internally Displaced, and Their Hosts*. Washington, DC: World Bank.

World Bank. 2017b. *The Toll of War: The Economic and Social Consequences of the Conflict in Syria*. Washington, DC: World Bank.

World Bank. 2017c. *World Development Report 2017: Governance and the Law*. Washington, DC: World Bank.

World Bank. 2018. *World Development Report 2018: Learning to Realize Education's Promise*. Washington, DC: World Bank.

World Bank. 2020a. *Global Economic Prospects, June 2020*. Washington, DC: World Bank.

World Bank. 2020b. "Household Level Impact of the COVID-19 on Myanmar." World Bank, Washington, DC. https://www.worldbank.org /en/news/infographic/2020/08/13/household -level-impact-of-the-covid-19-on-myanmar.

World Bank. 2020c. *The Human Capital Index 2020 Update: Human Capital in the Time of COVID-19*. Washington, DC: World Bank.

World Bank. 2020d. *Protecting People and Economies: Integrated Policy Responses to COVID-19*. Washington, DC: World Bank. http://hdl.handle.net/10986/33770.

World Bank. 2020e. "Somalia Urbanization Review." World Bank, Washington, DC.

World Bank. 2020f. *Violence without Borders: The Internationalization of Crime and Conflict*. Washington, DC: World Bank.

World Bank. Forthcoming. *World Development Report 2021: Data for Better Lives*. Washington, DC: World Bank.

Yancy, Clyde W. 2020. "COVID-19 and African Americans." *Journal of the American Medical Association* 323 (19): 1891–92.

Yong, Ed. 2020. "America's Patchwork Pandemic Is Fraying Even Further." *Atlantic*, May 20, 2020. https://www.theatlantic.com/health/archive/2020 /05/patchwork-pandemic-states-reopening -inequalities/611866/.